Decolonizing Qualitative Approaches *for* and *by* the Caribbean

A volume in
Innovations in Qualitative Research
Luca Tateo, *Series Editor*

Decolonizing Qualitative Approaches *for* and *by* the Caribbean

edited by

Saran Stewart
University of the West Indies, Mona

INFORMATION AGE PUBLISHING, INC.
Charlotte, NC • www.infoagepub.com

Library of Congress Cataloging-in-Publication Data

A CIP record for this book is available from the Library of Congress
http://www.loc.gov

ISBN: 978-1-64113-731-7 (Paperback)
978-1-64113-732-4 (Hardcover)
978-1-64113-733-1 (ebook)

Cover Illustration by Patasha Geerings
Cover Design by Tashiya Young

Printed in the United States of America

CONTENTS

PART I

THEORIZING THE FIELD OF DECOLONIZING RESEARCH
IN THE CARIBBEAN

v

PART II

MOVING FROM THEORY TO PRAXIS: APPLICATION OF DECOLONIZING RESEARCH IN THE CARIBBEAN

PART III

LESSONS LEARNED AND BEST PRACTICES FOR FUTURE RESEARCH

FOREWORD

DECOLONIZING WESTERN KNOWLEDGE OF QUALITATIVE RESEARCH

Independence has been one of the most deceptive processes of decolonization in the Caribbean. For many, on paper, independence has been achieved but mentally, the socio-economic and political systems reflect the damaging legacy of colonization; underdeveloped countries on the peripheries of dependency. To this end, a westernized education system has manifested from the period of enslavement to independence and same holds true for academics' approach to qualitative research.

It is through this colonial education system that illiteracy plagues my family, community and my country, Jamaica. Being a first generation graduate, I have first-hand experience of how education and the lack thereof has left many families and communities in an impoverished state; having had to become a vessel for teaching relatives and friends how to read, complete permission slips and pronounce basic words. Fast-forward twenty years later and I am the author of this foreword; a responsibility normally granted to someone eminent who can lend credibility to the book. I am not eminent by western normative academic standards but I am the personification and embodiment of decolonization. I am the descendant of slave quarters and represent the dispossessed communities of indigenous people who for generations in my community of August Town have been treated as disposable.

Decolonizing Qualitative Approaches for and by the Caribbean, pages vii–x
Copyright © 2019 by Information Age Publishing
All rights of reproduction in any form reserved.

I am not the first research assistant to be asked to contribute to a faculty book project but I am one of few from my community that are able to bridge theory and praxis, and understand the importance of my voice and experiences in decolonizing the academy.

Education has been my metaphorical permission slip to access opportunities. My reality is that many of my family members were not afforded an education; a sad reality in the inner cities of Kingston, Jamaica. I was raised on the streets of August Town, Jamaica, a community known for its high gang violence and murder rate. A community that was named (in part) after the month of emancipation, August; one that is located in close proximity to the former Mona and Papine plantations; one that remains in an impoverished state. With unpredictable volatility, education was my escape from my community's high gun violence. The neighborhood children considered me to be a hermit, reclusive and quiet; a little girl that would take her teacher's chalks home to teach the trees while in primary school.

Decolonizing qualitative methods are rooted in those very memories of teaching the trees and deeply embedded in critical theory and grounded in social justice, resistance, change and emancipatory research for and by the *Other* (Said, 1978). To this end, academic researchers, do not often question their methodologies to gather data in the way they were taught and by whom they were taught. As innovators of new knowledge they ask questions and probe where necessary to obtain data to support their studies but have they ever questioned the whole notion of research and its origin? For Caribbean researchers, the issue of decolonizing research is even more sensitive as it comes with the various 'isms' and as such research is heavily influenced by their past 'isms' of colonialism, post-colonialism and imperialism. To this end, there is a need to challenge the paradigm of Western research with indigenous methodologies, so as to obtain a balanced perspective.

We contend that research, as we know it, is based on a Eurocentric worldview and has dominated the way in which academia conducts research. For the readers, this book volume is not trying to compete with the normative worldview but to promote a semblance of inclusion of both indigenous methodologies and participants as part of the research. Annells (1996) shared that one's philosophical beliefs can influence their choice of method for the study. Therefore, this volume is intended to instill a sense of pride in Caribbean researchers to emancipate their minds and expand and deepen their philosophical beliefs that transcends into researchers feeling empowered to use their own emotions, spiritual and cultural being to influence the way in which qualitative research is approached.

The origins of qualitative inquiry in the Caribbean can be traced to political and economic discourses—Marxism, postcolonialism, neocolonialism, capitalism, liberalism, postmodernism—which have challenged ways of knowing and the construction of knowledge. Evans (2009) traced the origins of qualitative inquiry to slave narratives, proprietor's journals, missionaries' reports and travelogues. Common to the Caribbean is an understanding of how colonial legacies of research have ridiculed oral traditions, language, and ways of knowing, often rendering them valueless and inconsequential.

INTERROGATING THE *OTHER* IN CARIBBEAN RESEARCH

Rodney's (1969) legacy of "groundings" provides a Caribbean oriented ethnographic approach to collecting data about people and culture. It is an anti-imperialist method of data collection focused on the socioeconomic and political environment within the (post) colonial context. Similar to Rodney, other critical Caribbean scholars have moved the research discourse to center on the notions of resistance, struggle (Chevannes, 1995; Feraria, 2009) and decolonizing methodologies. This edited volume provides a collective body of scholarship for innovative uses of decolonizing qualitative research.

In order to theorize and conduct decolonizing research, one can argue that the researcher as *self* and as the *Other* needs to be interrogated. This level of interrogation includes frameworks such as Reasonable Humanism in which there is a clear understanding of the role of the researcher and researched from a physiological and psychosocial standpoint. Thereafter, the researcher is better prepared to enter into a discourse about decolonizing methodologies. In this regard, the researcher's background plays a crucial role in his/her worldview. Interrogation being carried out by the scholar is based on the worldview of the researcher which "determines the way the research is conceived and conducted" (Redman-MacLaren & Mills, 2015, p. 3). A focus on the foundations of research as we know it, must examine the axiology, ontology and epistemology of research. A researcher's positionality without the examination of these roots will be skewed towards the Eurocentric view of research and be manifested through the work of Caribbean researchers.

Accordingly, Redman-MacLaren and Mills (2015), define axiology as values critical to the research process. To further address this issue of decolonizing research, the analysis of the *self* in which Caribbean researchers must interrogate their true ethical and moral values that embody who they are as a researcher and in the space that the research is being conducted. In decolonizing research in the Caribbean, both the academic expert and participants must be seen as co-researchers as the participants' perspectives are just as critical as those which the researcher chooses to document.

The quest for decolonizing qualitative research in the Caribbean is deeply rooted in the researchers' experiences and the social constructs that will define their values and research practices. Specifically, researchers must explore their indigenous roots in an effort to challenge the assumptions of traditional qualitative research methodologies. The superstructure of Eurocentrism has to be challenged in order to support Caribbean pedagogy with liberating and authentic approaches for qualitative research. This volume meets those challenges in ten chapters dedicated to the deconstruction of power, oppressions and the colonial gaze. To close, it is only when researchers in academia accept the fact that the gerund decolonizing is a continuous process that reinstitutes indigenous cultural practices and historical perspectives that research will be truly decolonized.

—**Shenhaye Ferguson**

REFERENCES

Annells, M. (1996). Grounded theory method: Philosophical perspectives, paradigm of inquiry, and postmodernism. *Qualitative Health Research, 6*(3), 379–393. Retrieved from http://journals.sagepub.com/doi/pdf/10.1177/104973239600600306

Chevannes, B. (1995). *Rastafari: Roots and ideology*. Mona: UWI Press.

Evans, H. (2009). The origins of qualitative inquiry in the Caribbean. *Journal of Education and Development in the Caribbean, 11*(1), 14–22.

Feraria, P. (2009). Arts-based inquiry in educational research: Making the familiar strange to see differently. *Journal of Education and Development in the Caribbean, 11*(1), 130–146.

Redman-MacLaren, M., & Mills, J.E. (2015). Transformational grounded theory: Theory, voice, and action. *International Journal of Qualitative Methods, 14*(3), 1–12.

Rodney, W. (1969). *The groundings with my brothers*. London, England: Bogle L'Ouverture.

Said, E. (1978). *Orientalism*. New York, NY: Pantheon Books.

DECOLONIZATION OF QUALITATIVE RESEARCH

One of the important lessons of the story of Siddhartha-Buddha is that when one is raised in a condition of privilege, acquired by birth or by over-powering, one can believe to deserve such a condition because of her natural superiority or because of a divine will. Accordingly, the privilege must be maintained and extended to one's offspring. It takes a tremendous effort to question this assumption, and a very open mind, to reverse what one thinks is a natural law. Indeed, only in the 17th century, the philosopher Giambattista Vico introduced in the systematic study of civilizations the idea that any culture perceives itself as the most ancient and noble, creating a narrative of superiority to justify it (Tateo, 2017). Besides, any civilization goes through cycles of development and decay, of flourishing and barbarism, conservativism and sudden changes, rendering untenable the idea of linear progress and of constant cultural development (Tateo, 2017).

The narrative of superiority has been used anytime, in history of mankind, to justify acts of domination and violence by one culture over the other. Yet the narrative of superiority has also its counter-part in the narrative of acquired helplessness: if one is raised into a condition of dominance and helplessness, acquired by birth or domination, one can believe that it is a natural condition. The colonization of imaginaries and of self-consciousness is deceitful (Nederveen Pieterse & Parekh, 1995).

No linear progress of civilization, though. The last decade has clearly showed how the narrative of superiority has changed its theme but not its function. It looks like the justification by birth or blood (the concept of "race"), has been replaced by the concept of "way of life." This is adamant in the public discourse about migration flows and about refugees' crisis in Europe and North America. The migrant population is treated with either repulsion or piety: two feelings both related to a sense of superiority. "They" (the migrants) must accept our "way of life" (a mix of economic privilege and self-destructive behaviors that threaten the environment and the mankind's survival). The other version is that "they" (often identified with the Muslim terrorists) want to destroy our "way of life." A third version says that "they" (in this case the refugees) must be grateful if we accept them (despite our very same countries are often the direct cause of turmoil, conflicts and exploitation of the refugees' countries), but they must accept our "way of life."

So, "way of life" is the "new black" of the narrative of superiority based on capitalistic economic and political order. The naturalization of the "way of life" implies a certain "gaze," a way of building causal explanations, a way of understanding normative processes at both personal and collective level. These are all challenges for social sciences and humanities. This is the urging question for a number of scholars, who are developing the decolonization project. The third volume of the series *Innovations in Qualitative Research* focuses on a theoretical innovation that has to do with decolonizing the eye of the social researcher. If social sciences constitute the way a culture looks at itself critically, then it is important that scholars develop reflective projects based on an ideographic and local perspective, voicing the identities rather than be silenced or ventriloqued by a Western ethnocentric perspective. The decolonization project aims at multiplying the gazes and the mirrors, in order to be able to look at oneself from any direction, including from your back. One can learn to look at the other in relation to oneself, one can deconstruct and unmask the processes through which the other is narrated in relation to oneself, their power dynamics and traps. The deconstruction of Western ethnocentrism must not become the justification for just a different form of ethnocentrism.

This volume is topical, in a historical moment in which a political conjuncture of Western authoritarian democracies, that seem to jeopardize the existence a number of populations (e.g., Kurds, Palestinians, Guarani, Rohingya, etc.), and at the same time to question a number of human rights, that seemed to be acquired once for all. The message sent from the Caribbean with this volume says that decolonizing social research today means also to unveil the hypocrisy of those using the rhetoric of progress and the naturalization of authoritarian and neocolonialist capitalism to perpetuate unacceptable violence and injustice on the planet's face.

—**Luca Tateo**

REFERENCES

Nederveen Pieterse, J., & Parekh, B. (Eds) (1995). The Decolonization of Imagination. Culture, Knowledge and Power. London & New Jersey: Zed Books.

Tateo, L. (ed) (2017). Giambattista Vico and the New Psychological Science. Transaction Publishers.

ACKNOWLEDGMENT

There is a certain grace in recognizing those who continue to keep you accountable, motivated and in the pursuit of education as the practice of freedom. Thank you to the authors who worked tirelessly and meticulously on their chapters, and shared pieces of themselves in being and becoming a decolonizing researcher. Thank you to my family who continue to provide their unwavering support, love, time and energy in protecting and sustaining me throughout projects like these. I salute the sacrifices of those who have paved the road to decoloniality and made it possible for emerging scholars such as myself to follow suit.

PART I

THEORIZING THE FIELD OF DECOLONIZING RESEARCH
IN THE CARIBBEAN

CHAPTER 1

FROM SLAVE NARRATIVES TO "GROUNDINGS"

Moving from the Peripheries to the Centre of Knowledge

Saran Stewart

find me a woman who will break into shouts,
who will let loose a river of lament,
find the howl of the spirit,
teach us the tongues of the angry so that our blood,
my pulse—our hearts flow
with the warm healing of anger.

Kwame Dawes, *Talk* (excerpt)

By layering excerpts of Caribbean poetry, I layer in epigraphs of myself as a decolonizing researcher. Throughout the chapter, I pair selected stanzas with each section to illustrate the heuristic process of becoming decolonized or the constant process of resisting the colonizer's gaze (Yancy, 2008). I selected an excerpt from "Talk" by Kwame Dawes as it specifically called upon women to not be silent but reveal their deepest grief and sorrow in hopes of healing and finding agency. It precedes the edited excerpt below

Decolonizing Qualitative Approaches for and by the Caribbean, pages 3–22

from my doctoral dissertation (Stewart, 2013) where I re-tell the narratives of some of the hidden female figures of slavery in Jamaica.

It was 1829; Massa "called old Charles to pick the largest bundle of bamboo switches he could find" (Jamaica, 1831, p. 4). Rev. Mr. Bridges, Rector of St. Ann, commanded old Charles to cut all the flesh off Kitty Hilton, a female quadroon slave.

> She was then stripped of every article of dress, tied up by the hands, her toes barely touching the ground, and flogged until the back part of her, from the shoulders down to the calves of her legs, was one mass of lacerated flesh. (Jamaica, 1831, p. 4)

Kitty Hilton escaped and ran to the nearest magistrate, only to be turned away and sent back to her Massa (Jamaica, 1831). She ran again and found a magistrate that could "see" her—her hanging flesh and beaten-in eye socket. Kitty Hilton did not receive justice in the formal sense, because the House of Magistrates ruled 14 to 4 that Mr. Bridges should not be prosecuted (Jamaica, 1831). However, her narrative was written in the form of abolitionist letters that objected to the ruling and called for an end to slavery. I remembered vividly the day I came across these letters, combing through hundreds of archives and the heavy burden of ethical responsibility to document her story so that it no longer laid dormant under the mounds of House of Commons papers. I questioned why I had never read her name prior to my doctoral dissertation, why wasn't her story printed in the Jamaican history books I had read as a student. That day, I searched somewhat frantically for her name on the internet and found nothing but then I searched for her massa's name, Rev. Mr. Bridges, Rector of St. Ann and found multiple sites and archives on him. A feeling of disappointment swept over me, as I felt the proverbial colonial noose tighten around my memory of home, my own educational journey, realizing that research in Jamaica was only as emancipated as far as the colonizers gaze would allow. The colonizer's gaze as Yancy (2008) explains, "is that broadly construed epistemic perspective, a process of seeing without being seen, that constructs the Black body into its own colonial imaginary" (p. 6). For the most part, research in the Caribbean is a mirrored image of colonial epistemology and "in its broadest sense as an organized scholarly activity that is deeply connected to power" (Smith, 2005, p. 87). It is within a need to dismantle that power that decolonizing research becomes important. As such, "decolonizing research, then is not simply about challenging or making refinements to qualitative research" (p. 88). Decolonizing research,

> involves the unmasking and deconstruction of imperialism, and its aspect of colonialism, in its old and new formations alongside a search for sovereignty; for reclamation of knowledge, language, and culture; and for the social

transformation of the colonial relations between the native and the settler. (pp. 88–89)

There have been Caribbean scholars who have contributed significantly to decolonizing research, such as Maureen Warner-Lewis, Walter Rodney, Sir Hilary Beckles, Rupert Lewis, and Carolyn Cooper to name a few, where they have an intentional agenda to disrupt and transform the institution of research. In doing this, they are mindful of the communities they serve and respect of participant-researchers in their studies. They center from the margins and legitimize forms of knowledge such as Beckles' (1999) book, *Centering Woman: Gender Discourses in Caribbean Slave Society Work*, where he acknowledges the prowess and sacrifices of enslaved women such as the infamous Phibbah, the creole housekeeper in a Jamaican sugar plantation who later became the wife of the sadistic slave owner Thomas Thistlewood. Beckles could have defamed Phibbah and other enslaved women who navigated the sociosexual relations of their time to earn their freedom and manumit their kin. Instead, he honoured her name and legacy and essentially provided a strengths-based counter narrative for enslaved women. Renowned scholars such as Carolyn Cooper in her many books, but namely *Noises in the Blood: Orality, Gender and the "Vulgar" Body of Jamaican Popular Culture*, uses her writing as forms of resistance and decolonizing cultural studies. She offers up her work "from an insider, transmitting a 'bottoms-up' history of working-class resistance in Jamaica" (1995, p. x). Scholars such as Rupert Lewis provided a comparative political understanding of the iconic Walter Rodney, in his book, *Walter Rodney's Intellectual and Political Thought* (1998). Lewis (1998) illustrated how Rodney's life and death brought about a "political upsurge in radical politics" (p. 247), drawing on comparative global protests in 1968 such as the Civil Rights movement in the USA and the shift to the political right in the 1980s with the election of Ronald Reagan in the USA, Edward Seaga in Jamaica and the murder of Maurice Bishop in Grenada. Lewis provided a form of radical honesty in his writing and more so, he paid homage to the life of a Caribbean 20th century martyr. Lewis also explained how Walter Rodney engaged in forms of decolonizing qualitative methodologies such as "groundings" where Rodney would meet anywhere and to anyone (often times left wing individuals) about African and Caribbean history. More so, groundings "acted as catalysts to the growth in social and political consciousness" (p. 95) and was considered a grassroots mobilization to collectively co-create knowledge with the masses. Arguably, it is a style of conducting focus group interviews that is authentic to the Caribbean context, to reason and derive consciousness from collective wisdom where the lines of power are blurred between the researcher/researched. Female Caribbean scholars such as Camille Nakhid, Margaret Nakhid-Chatoor, Shakeisha Wilson and Anabel Santana are enhancing the Caribbean methodology landscape by introducing Liming and Ole Talk as a culturally relevant methodology for and by the Caribbean (see Nakhid-Chatoor, Nakhid, Wilson, & Santana, 2018). These examples of critical scholars conducting decolonizing research *for* and *by* the Caribbean offer a blue print for scholars to follow.

WRITING OUR PURPOSE INTO EXISTENCE

> Now I write my poetry to rewrite history
> Burn illusions and fantasy
> Shape and create my own destiny
> And create my own reality

Yasus Afari, *Poetry Caan Nyam* (excerpt)

The selected lines above foreshadow what I attempt to do in this chapter by illustrating the origins of this chapter and the creation of my fate in this edited volume. Seventy-five years after Kitty Hilton dragged her bloody body to the nearest magistrate, another Hilton woman would be born by the name of Ethel Hilton of Lucea (some 146 km from St. Ann). I came to know her as my great-grandmother, who at the age of 16 took a boat to the other side of the island and sailed to Kingston to start a new life. She was born betwixt the period of post-emancipation and independence, a period of uncertainty and strict British rule. She raised five daughters (one of which would be my grandmother) on her own and was definitively known as the matriarch of the family. Before my grandmother passed, I had the opportunity to learn about her educational biography and life as a child in colonial Jamaica as a part of a grade-school project. From her, I understood the importance of oral history, one that was passed down from her mother to her and then to me. She spoke about her tenacious attitude and fighting resilient spirit, how she helped her mother every day in the restaurant to feed all the customers. The colourful tales of colonial Jamaica between the 1920s, to 50s, lined with the influx of Chinese migrants, in which her father was one. Little did I know I was engaging in much more than my grandmother's educational biography but the initial drafts of what I have now termed, Afro-Caribbean Feminist Autoethnography (see Stewart, 2019), a decolonizing qualitative methodology. Essentially, her interview formed a blue print to document feminist epistemologies within colonial Jamaica. More so, her interview "pointed to the symptoms of the colonial legacy at the psychological level and the way in which black middle class social mobility and privilege perpetuated values of servility and self-deprecation within the black majority" (Lewis, 1998, p. 93). Then, I was too young to predict my current role in this book project and my emergent identity as a decolonizing researcher. I didn't understand the indelible impact of my great grandmother's history rearing five young girls in colonial, downtown Kingston alone. How her towering stature of 5 feet would command hungry men to wait in line for hours for her delectable corned pork and freshly made, crackling, cornmeal festivals. As an inquisitive, young girl, I had vivid memories of Ma'Tel (Mama Ethel, my great grandmother) "picking" the rice (i.e., the process of cleaning white rice) and saw the reverence that was bestowed upon her by her children, grandchildren and great-grand-children. I compared her prowess as our matriarch to that of Kitty Hilton and *re*/imagined the mirrored similarities of grit, resilience and #BlackGirl-Magic within the physical embodiment of these two women generations apart. This chapter is borne out of those ancestral *re*/imaginings and my need to trace the historical underpinning of decolonizing research *for* and *by* the Caribbean. Interwoven throughout this chapter is an Afro-Caribbean feminist storytelling of Caribbean qualitative researchers who navigate what it means to be a decolonizing researcher. Lastly, this chapter introduces the context and organization of the volume while presenting a critical anaysis of the authors within the book.

TRACING OUR ROOTS

My friend from Guyana
was asked in Philadelphia
if she was from "Iguana."

Iguana, which crawls and then
stills, which flicks its tongue at the sun . . .

Guyana (in the language of Arawaks,
Wai Ana, "Land of Many Waters")
is iguana, veins running through land,
grooves between green scales.
My grandmother from Moruga
(southern-most in Trinidad)
knew the names of things.
She rubbed iguana with bird pepper,
she cooked its sweet meat.

Christian Campbell, *Iguana for A.T.* (excerpt)

The colonial roots of the Caribbean provide an intricate web in which to understand how research was conducted and valued. Whether through the use of indigenous language in poetic form from the lines presented in Christian Campbell's "Iguana for A.T.," or chronologically tracing the colonial roots of qualitative research in the Caribbean, it is important to acknowledge the plurality of the Caribbean region and the Caribbean researcher. More so, "one has to pay careful attention to the social location, status and perspective of the researcher, and the informant and the context in which the study was done" (Evans, 2009, p. 15) given the legacy of colonialism in research. Evans (2009) went on to explain that historically, there were five main categories of qualitative approaches in the Caribbean: (a) slave narratives; (b) diaries and journals; (c) travelogues, observations and missionary reports; (d) formal research reports; and (e) ethnographies. It is critical to illustrate the categories, as slave narratives for example illustrate much more than a qualitative data source but a mode of reifying humanism; a way of knowing and understanding the life experiences of enslaved persons especially Caribbean women as human experiences. Collectively, more than two centuries of qualitative research exist in the Caribbean, however it wasn't until the late 20th century that there was a rise in Afro-Caribbean authored, qualitative accounts (see, Beckles, 1999, 2016; Chevannes, 1994; Warner-Lewis, 2003).

The roots of the Caribbean were planted predominantly by the Arawaks and Caribs, long before colonization (Wilson, 1992). However, there is a rich complexity in understanding the prehistory, oversimplification and misinterpretation of other diverse inhabitants of the Caribbean that made up the mosaic of indigenous people (Wilson, 1992). For the better half of the 20th century, new evidence concerning Caribbean prehistory was collected and "the conclusions reached by early European conquerors concerning the cultural geography of the Caribbean are being challenged" (p. 59). The process of challenging what was once constituted as normative is a practice of decolonization. I first engaged in the practice of decolonizing research in my dissertation. In an attempt to contribute to the cannon of qualitative research *for* and *by* the Caribbean, a section of my dissertation focused on the *re*/construction of social history of education in Jamaica (see Stewart, 2013). This section of my dissertation led me to go beyond the gray literature of parliamentary papers and critically examine court minutes, manuscripts, letters by former slaves, archived newspapers, and reconstituted images of the past. To best contextualize education in slavery, I presented the psychosocial manifestations of slavery that provided context for the lack of presence of an education system for the masses during this era.

My positionality as an Afro-Jamaican woman was present in the documentation of enslaved and freed women's treatment within and on the peripheries of education during colonial times. Toward this end, in a manner similar to colonial discourse analysis, I analyzed the archives, House of Commons Parliamentary Papers, Jamaican Ministry of Education original reports, letters, photographs, CSEC curriculum, performance rates, and memos of British imperialism in Jamaica to examine the legacies of missionaries and the prevailing design of a religious and moral system of education. Coupled with the colonial discourse analysis, I used an anti-colonial discursive framework to (a) incorporate local languages, "Indigenous cognitive categories and cultural logic to create social understandings" (Dei, 2000, p. 117); (b) utilize and combine indigenous literature with socioeconomic understandings of society; (c) recognize and contribute to the importance of research done by "minoritized, indigenous and local scholars in reintegrating local and native languages in the education of the young" (Dei. 2004, p. 260); and (d) celebrate and value the use of oral, visual (i.e., photographs), and traditional materials of resistance and re-historization (Dei, 2000). Thereby, this approach centered the voices of the masses through the lens of the researcher in re-telling the social history, using emotions, narrative, and dialogue as intellectual guides (Stewart, 2013). When collecting data, I respected the language of the participants and reported verbatim the use of Jamaican Creole throughout my data reporting. More so, when I entered the research space, I was aware of my outsider positionality and as such brokered my skills to the institutions and students I engaged with by often teaching classes or providing workshops on demand. There was a conscious and purposeful effort to decolonize the Western dissertation process as much as I could so as to authentically *re/*present the history and knowledge of the people I came from.

Smith (1999) argued that "history is important for understanding the present and that reclaiming history is a critical and essential aspect of decolonization" (p. 30). In this respect, historians such as Hillary Beckles, Jenny Jemmot, and Michael Smith, to name a few have been engaging with decolonizing research for years in their *re*construction of Caribbean history. History in this sense is not the traditional Western construct of history but the testimony to and restoration of a spirit lost, "to bring back into existence a world fragmented and dying" (Smith, 1999, p. 28).

TOWARD AN UNDERSTANDING OF THE DECOLONIZING CARIBBEAN RESEARCHER

To understand what it means to be a decolonizing Caribbean researcher, it was important to invite the authors of the volume to share this space both as researcher and participant. I wanted each author to be reflexive in sharing what it means to be a decolonizing Caribbean researcher across the Humanities, Social Sciences and Education. I asked each author from the volume to respond to the below questions using any medium of decolonizing data sources, such as oral storytelling, poetry, photographs, indigenous artwork, videos, and journaling, to name a few (a combination of all or individual). I reminded them that this process was not meant to be intrusive and that they could opt out. I asked each author to read the below questions, and answer some or all in any language of their choice and to keep in mind the following quote:

> Decolonizing research "involves the unmasking and deconstruction of imperialism, and its aspect of colonialism, in its old and new formations alongside a search for sovereignty; for reclamation of knowledge, language, and culture; and for the social transformation of the colonial relations between the native and the settler" (Smith, 2005, pp. 88–89).

Lastly, I encouraged each author to engage in self-introspection using the following questions as guides and hone in on their respective diasporic and in country/ countries context within the Caribbean:

- What does it mean to be a Caribbean researcher?
- What is decolonizing research in the Caribbean?
- What is culturally appropriate ethics in the Caribbean?
- In your view, what elements of Caribbean research are critical to the development of the region?
- How does the researcher and researched participants benefit mutually from the study?
- How is language in each Caribbean country honoured in decolonizing research?

Some authors responded using podcast, some used diagrammatic representations (see Figure 1.1), some provided an oral *re*/storying of moments in their childhood when they first understood their Caribbean identity, while others journaled. In my own attempt to be accountable and transparent in this process, I answered the questions using epigraphs throughout this chapter by Caribbean poets, while layering an Afro-Caribbean feminist ontology being mindful of citing and referencing Caribbean authors, poets and researchers. Below provides a composite understanding of a Caribbean decolonizing qualitative researcher from the authors' perspectives and a narrative way to introduce the authors in the volume. Essentially, the narrative reflects two overlapping statements that a Caribbean decolonizing qualitative researcher is *Lickle but Tallawah* and in pursuit of disrupting the colonial gaze. Being Lickle but Tallawah symbolizes the resilience of those engaged in decolonizing research in the Caribbean as well as the continuous struggle to validate their research. The pursuit of disrupting the colonial gaze speaks to the continuous journey of those engaged in this work to continue to do the critical-self work needed to resist Eurocentric, normative

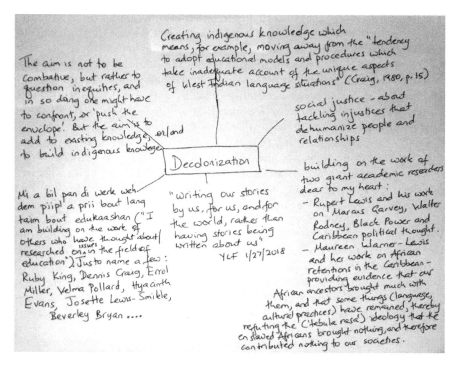

Figure 1.1 Diagramatic framework of decolonizing qualitative methodologies in the Caribbean by Yewande Lewis-Fokum

forms of research *only* and to develop, value and generate decolonizing research *for* and *by* the Caribbean.

Wi Lickle but Wi Tallawah (We are Small but Mighty)

The familiar Jamaican adage, *wi lickle but wi tallah*, is common amongst Jamaicans and those living within the diaspora. It is symbolic in its text as well as in its meaning, that even though we as a nation are small, we are strong and mighty. The authors negotiated their many responses of what it meant to be a Caribbean researcher. For some being a Caribbean researcher meant being ethically responsible for contributing to the cannon of Caribbean knowledge; a sense of strength, pride and resilience given the limited resources and number of persons globally focused on Caribbean research. For others, the identity created a space of community and belonging, and for some it represented a space of tension, statelessness and feeling of uncertainty.

Caribbean researchers have struggled with identity issues due to the impact of our colonial past. Arneaud and Albada (2013) state that "identity issues like acculturation (Brathwaite, 2005) and pluralism (Smith, 1974) . . . issues of race and ethnicity are integrally tied to regional identity scholarship, as these social groupings have stratified Caribbean societies since their colonial beginnings (Barrow & Reddock, 2001)" (p. 340). It is within this context that Caribbean researchers have had to question their identity and what it means to be a Caribbean researcher. For example, Therese Ferguson, even though born in Guyana was unsure of how to initially respond to the question whether or not she was in fact a Caribbean researcher since her formative years were spent in the United States. In grappling with her identity as to whether or not she identifies as a Caribbean researcher, her final response was "maybe the focus needs to be moved from the researcher to the focus of the research [or] maybe the essence of being a Caribbean researcher is not in the identity of the researcher" (Therese Ferguson, Journal Entry, 2018). She further questioned that "maybe it lies in the identities of the Caribbean peoples who are at the centre of the research, and the contexts in which these are developed, experienced, and lived [or] perhaps this is the crux of being a Caribbean researcher" (Therese Ferguson, Journal Entry, 2018). Her entries spoke to the expansive and complex nature of the Caribbean identity as well as Caribbean research.

My identity as a Caribbean researcher resonates with Goodison's poem, "Praise to the Mother of Jamaican Art" and in particular the lines stated below that illustrates the sacrifices mothers bare for their children.

> was the nameless woman who created
> images of her children sold away from her.
> She suspended her wood babies from a rope
> round her neck, before she ate she fed them.
> Lorna Goodison, *Praise to the Mother of Jamaican Art* (excerpt)

My identity as a mother permeates within and throughout my scholarship and the constant struggle to seek equity for Caribbean women, and strike a balance between the demands of the academy and the demands of the home, while othermothering[1] in the classroom. As a Caribbean researcher, I am conscious of my role in the knowledge development of future generations and my constant need to deconstruct the oppressor within (see Stewart, 2016).

Other authors such as Yewande Lewis-Fokum wrote,

> "Mi a bil pan di werk weh dem piipl a prii bout lang taim bout edukaashan"
> [I am building on the work of others who have thought about/researched on issues in the field of education]
>
> —Yewande Lewis-Fokum

Lewis-Fokum, in expressing what it means to be a Caribbean researcher defined this meaning by using Jamaican Creole which is a part of her history and culture as a Jamaican. In her response to the questions, she chose to answer them through her diagrammatic framing of decolonization (see Figure 1.1). She reminds us that the responsibility of the Caribbean researcher is to build on those academic giants, the elders of critical research, paying homage and respect to those who laboured for this work before us. She wrote about two particular academic giants dear to her heart, Rupert Lewis and Maureen Warner-Lewis. As mentioned above, I drew on similar conclusions of Rupert Lewis but I believe what she wrote about Maureen Warner-Lewis hones the epistemological underpinnings of the "Lickle but Tawallawah" adage. She wrote about the colossal contribution of Warner-Lewis' work to Caribbean and African-Diaspora research, and more so the reclamation of critical linkages between African retentions in the Caribbean. Lewis-Fokum wrote,

> Maureen Warner-Lewis and her work on African retentions in the Caribbean—providing evidence that our African ancestors brought much with them, and that somethings (language, cultural practices) have remained, thereby refuting the ('tabula rasa') ideology that the enslaved Africans brought nothing, and therefore contributed nothing to our societies. [see Figure 1.1]

This refutation is deliberated, supported and explained in length in Warner-Lewis' (2003) book, *Central Africa in the Caribbean: Transcending Time, Transforming Cultures*. What's important to remark on is that she has added to the canon of decolonizing research that continues to reject and dispute false claims from early European conquerors.

Interestingly, Ginwright (2008) concludes that "emancipatory research will also require us to move beyond our universities and professional associations to build new infrastructure that can facilitate the free exchange of ideas, tools, and people needed for the greater democratization of knowledge" (p. 21 as cited in Zavala, 2013, p. 67). Therefore as Caribbean researchers, although highly influenced by European culture and educational system, we must aspire to conduct our research grounded in our Caribbean heritage. Likewise for Anne Pajard being a Caribbean researcher means having "the central point of the research emerging from Caribbean grounds." She further states that "the Caribbean research is . . . positioned as a social actor of the contemporary Caribbean" (Anne Pajard, Journal Entry, 2018).

Amanda Thomas shares through an image on her bedroom wall and an accompanying narrative that her Afro-Caribbean, racial and ethnic identity is informed by a deconstruction of colonialism, metaphysical spirituality and forms of knowing that gives her a sense of connectivity and continuity with her African and Caribbean ancestors. She describes a collage of pictures, posters, quotes, artworks and drawings from

> the Kalinago war bird, to the framed picture of ancestral peoples story-ing around an open fire, from the eulogy of the late Dr. Dennis A. V. Brown to student post cards depicting Junkanoo in Bahamas or Keti Koti in Suriname, from LeRoy Clarke's "El Tucuche" virtuosity to my first international conference in New Orleans to speak about community decline in LaBrea, Trinidad.

She credits her communal sense of space and place to her social background of being raised in a rural agricultural village in Trinidad and Tobago where she connects with livelihoods sustained by the natural environment, community mentorship and collective solidarity. Thomas states that "these are the elements that inform her identity as a transformative scholar and methodologist." One that is actively seeking to deconstruct knowledge and research encoded in deficit thinking and forms of domination and silencing perpetuated as an outcome of colonialism in the Caribbean and elsewhere. Similarly, Gordon stated in her written response, "I am a researcher located in the Caribbean region where I am from, and because of that history, my epistemological and methodological perspectives are shaped by cultural and intellectual currents in this region" (Doreen Gordon, personal communication, 2018). Lois George answered her questions in a podcast and described her desire to contribute to her island-state of Dominica. She meticulously reminisced on her dissertation research process and the call to contribute to knowledge development in math education in her country. Her sense of patriarchy and innate need to contribute to the development of the youth undergirded her podcast response. In this light, her understanding of what it means to be a Caribbean researcher was tied to her work as a math educator and co-creator of knowledge.

For others being a Caribbean researcher "is an ongoing battle between the self that is framed by experiences and thought processes rooted in authentic Caribbean sociocultural epistemologies and practices...... [that] grants value to theorizations and practices...because they emerge from a Eurocentric system" (Aisha Spencer, Journal Entry, 2018). Spencer on her self-introspection journey brought to light the fact that the struggle is not only with being a Caribbean researcher but the fact that as a female Caribbean researcher, there are more challenges in navigating Caribbean research because of the systems of knowledge that are deeply rooted in patriarchal constructs throughout all aspects of societies. For example, Bissessar (2014) in her political study articulated that "although women continue to outnumber men in terms of educational achievement, this advancement has translated into a greater involvement for women in the corridors of political power" (p. 32).

For those who reside in the diaspora, like Frank Tuitt, born of Guyanese and Montserratian parentage, they are often in "an emancipatory move refuting not the connection with one's place of origin but rather one's unequal status vis-a-vis homelanders and hostlanders" (Laguerre, 2017, p. 22). This dual status often leaves him stateless with a feeling of not completely belonging to either the United States or the Caribbean. As such he shared in his interview that his identity as a Black man in the United States permeates his understanding of what it means to be a decolonising researcher; one that aims to dismantle the heteronormative power structures that leave systems of oppression intact. He reminisces on his childhood being born in Great Britain but raised in the United States and recalls the instances of racism that signalled his positionality within society.

Emancipation in the Wings: Disrupting the Colonial Gaze

> Wat a joyful news, miss Mattie,
> I feel like me heart gwine burs
> Jamaica people colonizin
> Englan in Reverse . . .
>
> Wat a devilment a Englan!
> Dem face war an brave de worse,
> But me wonderin how dem gwine stan
> Colonizin in reverse
>
> Louise Bennett, *Colonization in Reverse* (excerpt)

When Louise Bennett wrote "Colonization in Reverse" in Jamaican creole and discussed the migration movement of Jamaicans to England, she posited the idea about reverse colonization. The poem in its entirety is symbolic of decolonization given the use of Jamaican Creole instead of Standardized English. In this respect it is reminiscent of disrupting the colonial gaze. I selected this poem as a symbolic representation of how Bennet, herself embodies resistance in her writing and my aspiration to follow in her legacy to disrupt the colonial gaze.

Douillet (2010) in his work *The Quest for Caribbean Identities*, uses Derek Walcott's poems "A Latin Primer" and "The Light of the World" to explore the realities of colonialism on the Caribbean which both directly and indirectly forged the Caribbean's contemporary identities. According to Douillet (2010) in analysing Walcott's poems it was evident that there is an intricate relationship between the colonized and the colonizer. He further states that the Caribbean self-embraces this identity where there is also division between the different places. This identity crisis is reflected in

Walcott's writing where there is a split between the colonizers and the colonized. In light of this, to decolonize research in the Caribbean, researchers and other contemporary authors of the Caribbean must write from a place of authenticity where their Caribbean identity comes alive in their writing more so than that of their Eurocentric ideologies and philosophies.

Ferguson in her journal entry stated that, "decolonizing Caribbean research means that persons, all aspects of their identity, are emancipated through the full and authentic expression and representation of themselves" (Therese Ferguson, Journal Entry, 2018). She further believes that it "involves sharing the research process in a collaborative manner and ensuring that the process and its results are emancipatory and that ... knowledge becomes something that is co-created and discovered jointly" (Therese Ferguson, Journal Entry, 2018). Douillet (2010) alluded to the fact that for Walcott "past colonial and racial divisions constitute the crux of Caribbean identity and the question of the divided nature of the post-colonial self is central to his intellectual quest" (p. 1).

Language being a conduit for power and oppression remains a symbolic element of decolonizing research. Ferguson believes that "the language of decolonised research is not technical, specialised, or jargonised but easily written and read, accessible to participants." Our language is intrinsic to our Caribbean identity and as such it needs to be retained "to ensure authentic representation." Her belief was not one that was expressed with the language of the colonizers but of her ancestors and those who have laid the foundation for Caribbean researchers, for example, Ruby King, Dennis Craig, Errol Miller, Velma Pollard, Hyacinth Evans, Josette Lewis-Smilele and Beverly Bryan, to name a few.

Although Walcott writes Caribbean poetry, he shares the same identity struggles like all Caribbean researchers and writers as Douillet (2010) agrees that Caribbean writers are influenced by two traditions, one which is the African culture and the other is that of the Europeans. Similarly, those who are from the African Diaspora like Chayla Haynes-Davison share that similar double-conscious identity.

Chayla Haynes-Davison not being from or of Caribbean descent, shared this space as a Black decolonizing researcher and grounded theorist who centers her work on the purposeful dismemberment of power and oppression in the academy. When asked about her identity as a decolonizing researcher, her response was,

> My understanding of decolonizing research or how I position myself as a critical qualitative researcher is really rooted in the understanding of a decolonized mind and my positionality as both researcher and pedagogue as informed by bell hooks.

She further asserts herself as a critical qualitative researcher who explores issues of power and powerlessness through the scholarship of teaching. To that end, her scholarly contributions promote innovation in college teaching, the advancement of educational equity among racially minoritized college students, and the application of critical race theory to postsecondary contexts and problems.

Lewis-Fokum in her journal entry shared similar sentiments about the importance of the African traditions. For example, Lewis-Fokum stated the importance of language and culture to our identity. She shares that African ancestors brought much with them and that some elements such as language and cultural practises have remained. She further states that the ideology that enslaved Africans brought nothing and therefore contributed nothing to our societies is flawed, as the Caribbean's rich heritage is deeply connected with the enslaved Africans.

For Anne Pajard decolonizing research in the Caribbean involves a pathway for reaching freedom, a movement that searches how the colonial past still impacts Caribbean societies. Zavala (2013) argues that for researchers, we must create "spaces of recovery and healing that become fertile soil for seeds on inquiry and research that are inherently political, ethical and accountable to the communities that make research possible" (p. 68). Additionally, those who have been impacted directly or indirectly by imperialism and colonialism "begin to claim our research by first decolonizing the spaces that makes research possible, our identities are also transformed" (Zavala, 2013, p. 68).

Lewis-Fokum in Figure 1.1 reminds us that decolonizing research means "Writing our stories by us, for us, and for the world rather than having stories being written about us." With faculty being pressured to 'publish or perish', Ferguson aligns with Lewis-Fokum by questioning whether or not the priority of researchers should be focused on academic publications or to engage in a process that ultimately benefits the participants of the communities that are researched. Doreen Gordon in responding to the questions described her experiences as a Jamaican anthropologist in Brazil and South Africa. Her analysis of decolonizing research is layered with the socio-cultural understanding of African descent populations. She states,

Decolonizing research involves searching for and experimenting with appropriate methodologies that are culturally relevant and useful in the context that one is carrying out research ... This is particularly relevant among the African descendant populations that I have carried out research on in Brazil, South Africa, and to a lesser extent in Jamaica. This is because cultural practices and beliefs in the black diasporic community are often passed down from generation to generation in oral form, such as story-telling, riddles, jokes, and sayings. In addition, the theatre tradition is strong in Jamaica where entertainment for many young people begins in the church, in a setting where children are expected to perform for audiences (musical recitals, singing, drama skits, and so on). This means devising culturally appropriate methods that make use of these traditions and skills, thereby opening spaces in our largely western-informed epistemologies and methods to give centre stage to the voices of the people we are trying to represent in our writing. (Gordon, personal communication, 2018)

In understanding their roles, decolonizing identities and positionalities, researchers such as Gordon are better able to navigate the black diasporic community and engage meaningfully with her participants' lived experiences. The approaches that the authors in this book offer underscore the importance of interrogating systemic oppression and reshaping practices within research that perpetuate colonial practices. Each of these authors provide unique perspectives on the experiences conducting research in the Caribbean, South America and South Africa, as emergent decolonizing researchers. Each of the authors are advancing research pertaining to decolonization that is valuable and important with opportunities to create calls for crafting systemic change in how qualitative research is conducted. Given the context of the volume and the perspectives of the authors, what follows is a brief introduction of the sections of the volume to better contextualise the purpose and aims of the book.

EXPECT THE UNEXPECTED: OVERVIEW OF THE VOLUME

This edited volume acknowledges the significance of decolonizing approaches to qualitative research in the Caribbean and the wider Caribbean diaspora. It includes an audience of scholars, teacher/researchers and students primarily in and across the humanities, social sciences and educational studies. Additionally, this volume allows readers to think of new imaginings of research design that deconstruct power and privilege to benefit knowledge, communities and participants. It sparks ideas, new understanding, directions and frameworks for deeper discussions and interrogations to disrupt normative, westernized and hegemonic approaches to qualitative research. Lastly, the volume welcomes empirical studies of application of decolonizing methodologies and theoretical studies that frame critical discourse.

The volume is organized in three sections: (a) Part I: Theorizing the Field of Decolonizing Research in the Caribbean; (b) Part II: Moving from Theory to Praxis: Application of Decolonizing Research in the Caribbean; and (c) Part III: Lessons Learned and Best Practices for Future Research.

Part I: Theorizing the Field of Decolonizing Research in the Caribbean

Chapters in this section provide insight into theoretical and conceptual understandings of Caribbean research. It explores frameworks, critical discourse and theoretical papers that investigate key underpinnings of decolonizing qualitative research in the Caribbean. Chayla Haynes-Davison and Saran Stewart in Chapter 2 provide researchers and readers with a detailed description of how to use grounded theory methods *for* and *by* the Caribbean populace, while at the same time, encouraging researchers to maintain the authenticity of their research by connecting with the participants and ensuring that their perspectives are also documented without being highly influenced by the colonial way of conducting grounded research. This section closes with Chapter 3 where Aisha Spencer's infusion of decolonizing research in the Caribbean is articulated through the lens of poetry. Spencer takes readers on a journey of how to use participatory observation as a decolonizing tool to critically analyse the way in which English Literature is taught from a Eurocentric lens as well as how to use this tool to restructure how poetry is approached in the Caribbean.

Part II: Moving from Theory to Praxis: Application of Decolonizing Research in the Caribbean

Chapters in this section include empirical studies that use innovative forms of qualitative data collection and analysis from a decolonizing approach in the Caribbean from the perspectives of junior scholars, senior scholars and doctoral students. Thomas opens this section with a review of qualitative research in the English Speaking Caribbean by using the inductive meta-synthesis technique to integrate and interpret the findings from Caribbean qualitative research that spans 1990–2016. Thomas proposes that one's critical consciousness needs to be tapped into through the use of critical and inclusive pedagogy which should be used to challenge the dominant colonial ideologies in Caribbean education and research. In Chapter 5, Lewis-Fokum explores the use of critical discourse analysis as a decolonising approach in Caribbean research and education. Lewis-Fokum addresses how emancipatory action research can result in resolving social justice issues, equalizing power in society and reinforcing ones identity. Thereafter, George highlights the teaching of Mathematics in Chapter 6, and recommends the adoption of the microgenetic method of investigating how students learn mathematical concepts. George also theorizes the use of decolonizing methods such as placing more emphasis on the learners of Mathematics, and how decolonizing methods connects with these learners rather than imposing a curriculum that does not align with students' Caribbean experience. Section II concludes with a reflective Chapter 7 by Ferguson where she compares traditional research approaches to participatory action research. Ferguson outlines concerns about conventional research where academics are seen as the experts and participants as the subjects, therefore perpetuating the issue of power between researchers and participants/co-researchers. She further examines the fact that although participatory action research has been critiqued for its Western origins, it has been proven to be successful in educational based research with a view of more inclusion of participants and their voices.

Part III: Lessons Learned and Best Practices for Future Research

These chapters shape the direction for best practices when conducting decolonizing research. They also look at the future design to benefit knowledge, participants and communities across the humanities and social sciences. For example, in Chapter 8, Gordon examines from a Jamaican, researching-in-Brazil perspective how to decolonize research in the social sciences. She argues that going forward, decolonizing research is less about the challenge of what methods to use and more about creating spaces that would make the decolonizing approach possible by other means such as through dialogue and social action. Similarly, Pajard in Chapter 9 highlights that future research should embrace decolonizing Caribbean heritage and the ingenuity of the people by developing their level of consciousness. By focusing on best practices, the section ends when Tuitt's chapter draws on the wisdom and knowledge of the authors in this volume and attempts to crystalize how researchers interested in engaging in qualitative research in the Caribbean can activate their imagination, and design research that deconstructs power and privilege to benefit knowledge, communities, and participants.

CONCLUDING THOUGHTS

The purposeful use of the gerund "ing" in decoloniz*ing* is to illustrate the ongoing process of this work and that none of the authors nor myself are fully decolonized because we were all trained by the massa's hand within eye-shot of the colonizer's gaze. The overarching frames that reflect the authors' decolonizing positionalities: wi lickle but wi tallawah and disrupting the colonial gaze represent the work still needed to complicate the reward systems in which oppressive methodologies are valued across the academy. As Yancy (2008) pointed out, the premise behind the colonial gaze "is to get the colonized to accept the colonialists point of reference as the only point of reference" (p. 6). In doing this, few would dare contest the validity of the reference or history by colonizers. This chapter purposefully illustrates rather than tells researchers how to conduct decolonizing qualitative research, including key takeaways such as: (a) reading and citing Caribbean authors and researchers; (b) understanding and interrogating the self as a Caribbean researcher, which may conflict with or advance decolonizing research; (c) ethically respecting and empowering participants as co-researchers; and (d) understanding how to constantly disrupt the colonial gaze in the complete research process. Advancing these key takeaways will be critical in the pursuit of decolonizing research in the Caribbean. Caribbean people have been re-writing history and restoring indigenous understanding of knowledge for years. These are not popular movements in the academy as the old dominion of plantation politics still runs deep throughout the halls of higher education institutions throughout the Caribbean. However, the work of decolonizing research and disrupting the colonial gaze has started.

NOTE

1. *Othermothering*, refers to a "relationship [that] goes far beyond that of providing students with either technical skills or a network of academic and professional contacts" (Collins, 2000, p. 191).

REFERENCES

Afari, Y. "Poetry can nyam." Jah Lyrics. Retrieved from http://www.jah-lyrics.com/song/yasus-afari-poetry-caan-nyam

Arneaud, M. J., & Albada, N. A. (2013). Identity development in the Caribbean: Measuring socio-historic structures with psychological variables. *Interamerican Journal of Psychology, 47*(2), 339–346.

Beckles, H. (1999). *Centering woman: Gender discourses in Caribbean slavery*. Kingston, Jamaica: Ian Randle.

Beckles, H. (2016). *The first black slave society: Britain's "barbarity time" in Barbados, 1636–1876*. Kingston, Jamaica: The University of the West Indies Press.

Bennett, L. (n.d.). "Colonization in reverse." Retrieved from http://louisebennett.com/colonization-in-reverse/

Bissessar, A. (2014). Challenges to women's leadership in ex-colonial societies. *International Journal of Gender & Women's Studies, 2*, 13–35. Retrieved from https://www.researchgate.net/publication/272378839_Challenges_to_Women%27s_Leadership_in_Ex-Colonial_Societies

Campbell, C. (n.d.). "Iguana." Peepal Tree Press. Retrieved from http://www.peepaltreepress.com/single_book_display.asp?isbn=9781845231552&au_id=207

Chevannes, B. (1994). *Rastafari: Roots and ideology*. Syracuse, NY: Syracuse University Press.

Cooper, C. (1995). *Noises in the blood: Orality, gender and the "vulgar" body of Jamaican popular culture*. Durham, NC: Duke University Press.

Dawes, K. (n.d). "Talk." Poem Hunter. Retrieved from http://www.poemhunter.com/poem/talk-31/

Dei, G. (2000). Rethinking the role of indigenous knowledges in the academy. *Journal of Inclusive Education, 4*(2), 111–132.

Dei, G. (2004). *Schooling and education in Africa: The case of Ghana.* Trenton, NJ: Africa World Press.

Douillet, C. (2010). The quest for Caribbean identities: Postcolonial conflicts and cross-cultural fertilization in Derek Walcott's poetry. *AmeriQuests, 7*(1). doi:10.15695/amqst.v7i1.169

Evans, H. (2009). The origins of qualitative inquiry in the Caribbean. *Journal of Education and Development in the Caribbean, 11*(1), 14–22.

Goodison, L. "Praise to the mother of Jamaican art." *Bomb* Magazine. Retrieved from http://bombmagazine.org/article/2533/four-poems

Jamaica. (1831). *Papers relating to the treatment of a female slave in Jamaica.* Colonial Department, Downing Street. Archives of the House of Commons Papers, Great Brtitain.

Laguerre, M. S. (2017). *The postdiaspora condition: Crossborder social protection, transnational schooling, and extraterritorial human security.* Europe in Transition: The NYU European Studies Series: Palgrave Macmillan. doi10.1007/978-3-319-52261-6

Lewis, R. C. (1998). *Walter Rodneys' intellectual and political thought.* Barbados: University of the West Indies Press.

Nakhid-Chatoor, M., Nakhid, C., Wilson, S., & Santana, A. F. (2018). Exploring liming and ole talk as a culturally relevant methodology for researching with Caribbean people. *International Journal of Qualitative Methods.* https://doi.org/10.1177/1609406918813772

Smith, L. (1999). *Decolonizing methodologies: Research and indigenous peoples.* New York, NY: Zed Books.

Smith, L. T. (2005). On tricky ground: Researching the native in the age of uncertainty pages. In N. K. Denzin & Y. S. Lincoln (Eds.), *The SAGE handbook of qualitative research* (3rd ed. pp. 85–108). Thousand Oaks, CA: SAGE.

Stewart, S. (2013). *Everything in di dark muss come to light: A postcolonial investigation of the practice of extra lessons at the secondary level in Jamaica's education system* (Doctoral Dissertation).University of Denver, Colorado.

Stewart, S. (2016). Advancing a critical and inclusive praxis: Pedagogical and curriculum innovations for social change in the Caribbean. In F. Tuitt, C. Haynes, & S. Stewart (Eds.), *Race, equity and the learning environment: The global relevance of critical and inclusive pedagogies in higher education.* Sterling, VA: Stylus.

Stewart, S. (2019). Navigating the academy in the post-diaspora: #Afro-Caribbean-Feminism and the intellectual and emotional labour needed to transgress. *Caribbean Review of Gender Studies, 13.*

Warner-Lewis, M. (2003). *Central Africa in the Caribbean: Transcending time, transforming cultures.* Kingston: University of the West Indies Press.

Wilson, S. (1992). The cultural mosaic of the indigenous Caribbean. *The British Academy, 81,* 37–66. Retrieved from https://www.britac.ac.uk/pubs/proc/files/81p037.pdf

Yancy, G. (2008). Colonial gazing: The production of the black body as "Other." *The Western Journal of Black Studies, 32*(1), 1–15.

Zavala, M. (2013). What do we mean by decolonizing research strategies? Lessons from decolonizing, Indigenous research in New Zealand and Latin America. *Decolonization: Indigeneity, Education & Society, 2*(1), 555–571.

CHAPTER 2

FRAMING THE CARIBBEAN LANDSCAPE

Approaching Grounded Theory From a Decolonizing Perspective

Chayla Haynes
Saran Stewart

BACKGROUND ON GROUNDED THEORY: AIMS AND EVOLUTION OF GROUNDED THEORY

Grounded theory is an approach of qualitative research by which the researcher generates a general explanation (a theory) of a process, action, or set of interactions shaped by the view of a large number of participants (Strauss & Corbin, 1990). Likewise, grounded theory is also correctly and commonly referred to as the intended outcome of this complex research process (Bryant & Charmaz, 2007a; Charmaz, 2003). Grounded theorists, and qualitative researchers alike, refer to the methodology by many names, including but not limited to: grounded theory (GT), the grounded theory method (GTM), and the grounded theory approach (GTA).

Emerging in the 1960s from the works of Barney Glaser and Anselm Strauss (1965, 1967, 1968), GT was developed to demonstrate that

Decolonizing Qualitative Approaches for and by the Caribbean, pages 23–41
Copyright © 2019 by Information Age Publishing
All rights of reproduction in any form reserved.

qualitative research was not only rigorous but also able to produce the type of significant findings readily associated with quantitative research (Bryant & Charmaz, 2007a). Bryant and Charmaz (2007a) concluded that in the creation of GT, Glaser and Strauss challenged positivist-oriented concerns about qualitative research when they offered researchers a methodology with a solid core of data analysis and theory construction.

Fast-forward to the 21st century, the use of grounded theory from a method to methodology has increased in recognition and value, and positioned strongly for social justice research (Charmaz, 2005). Within the discourse, a debate has emerged that declares there are two distinct paradigms in grounded theory research. The works of Glaser (1978), though positivist, and Corbin and Strauss (1990), though post-positivist, are characterized within the debate on grounded theory research as objectivist. Seemingly then, the post-modernist work of Charmaz (2000), is characterized as constructivist. Where *objectivist grounded theory* assumes that the research process reveals a single reality that an impartial observer discovers through value-free inquiry, *constructivist grounded theory* assumes that the data collection and analysis process are social constructions that illustrate the researcher's experiences within the research process (Charmaz, 2006).

Importantly, what sets the constructivist approach apart is that the researcher is capable and willing to identify the extent to which the phenomenon under study is "embedded in larger and often, hidden positions, networks, situations, and relationships (Charmaz, 2006, p. 130). Quite different than that of objectivist grounded theory, the aim in constructivist grounded theory then becomes exposing and addressing the hierarchies of power among and between people that maintain and perpetuate differing experiences (Bryant, 2002; Charmaz, 2006).

Although different, social justice research shares similar characteristics to decolonizing research such as the purposeful recognition of participants as the subjects of research rather than objects. It is also characterized by a change-driven agenda for and by those who have been traditionally marginalized in research. In this regard, envisioning a decolonizing grounded theory approach for the Caribbean is possible given some of the current mobilization around decolonizing methodologies (Smith, 1999), such as storytelling, testimonies, discovering, creating, protecting, reframing, claiming, celebrating survival and returning.

FRAMING GROUNDED THEORY WITHIN THE CARIBBEAN LANDSCAPE

Grounded theory (GT) being developed by American sociologists, Glaser and Strauss, has always been a Western standard of conducting research using this approach. According to Bishop (2005) and Smith (2005) indigenous scholars have always had the desire "to decolonize Western epistemologies to open up the academy to non-Western forms of... knowledge" (as cited in Denzin, 2007, p. 456). The same is true for Caribbean researchers who have had to conduct studies through the lens of Western colonizers, the founders of the various types of research methods and methodologies. In the words of Smith (1999), "They came, They saw, They named, They Claimed" (p. 80 as cited in Denzin, 2007, p. 456). The "they" for example would refer to the European colonizers in the Caribbean (Shepherd, 2005). Therefore, the knowledge produced by Western grounded theorists has to be localized to be applicable to the socio-historical, geographical and political context of the Caribbean. Furthermore, there is a need to decolonize grounded theory as a methodological approach to develop theories *for* and *by* the people they will impact the most. In this respect, Caribbean researchers seeking to use this approach must operationalize their studies within a decolonizing frame in order to develop critical theories within the region. We use the term "decolonizing" in this chapter to challenge traditional forms of developing theory and valuing more culturally responsive and indigenous ways of knowing.

In decolonizing grounded theory, we would argue that it is imperative that Caribbean researchers be "guided by grounded critical theory" (Smith, 2000 as cited in Denzin, 2007, p. 465). Here, Smith challenges indigenous scholars to consider key questions such as who is the research for, who are the owners of the research, who will benefit from it and who will carry it out. These are critical questions in research that Caribbean researchers can use to move away from the norm of being "pressed to produce technical knowledge that conforms to Western standards of truth and validity" (Denzin, 2007, p. 457). As such, the decolonizing approach involves moving away from this foreign identity that is affiliated with the grounded theory research method.

An extant review of the literature indicates that GT is currently the most widely utilized method to qualitative research across a range of academic disciplines (Timmermans & Tavory, 2007). But despite that, little is written about its use in Caribbean research (in particular as a methodology). Through an analysis of the literature, this chapter explores GT's viability in decolonizing Caribbean research.

Decolonizing Grounded Theory: Utilizing an Ethical Approach for the Caribbean Lens

In evaluating the Caribbean landscape for GT, it was challenging to find other scholarly methods to the Western concepts of grounded theory. A review of Caribbean education literature revealed that very few researchers have used grounded theory as a methodology, while others use the approach as a method. For example, Blackman's (2012) research looked at the roles of principals in managing assessments in schools in Barbados and she used grounded theory as part of the data collection method for the study. Grounded theory as method was used to analyze the data which included transcripts and developing a coding outline. Blackman (2012) also used grounded theory to "extract themes which characterized principals" practices at four schools" (p. 72). Barrow and De Lisle's (2009) study utilized grounded theory as a method for their study in terms of generating analytical codes from the focus group discussions gathered in the study. Notably, other examples include, Newman (2005), who in her Caribbean research on social justice and school leadership adopted the constructivist grounded theory approach. She used GT as a method to code the data collected.

As a methodology, Bailey and Johnson (2014) in their study used GT to collect data on the perspectives of participants on the use of internet-based technology. Notably, Bailey and Johnson (2014) highlighted the fact that for their research GT was unique in developing theories that were grounded in the experiences of the participants of the study. This certainly adds to the non-Western academy of knowledge using the GT approach, where it is not the researchers who are the focus but the participants. Also within this context, the raw data came from the participants themselves. Ibrahim-Ali (2015) also used GT as a method in her study which looked at practices within the English Foreign Language classrooms. She used GTM "to inform grammar teaching and testing" and design an operational theoretical framework specific to the Caribbean context (p. 99).

Similar to Ibrahim-Ali's (2015) need to design more culturally relevant theoretical frameworks for the teaching of second language learners, other Caribbean researchers should engage in theory-based development within the social sciences, humanities and educational research. The need to develop and engage with theoretical frameworks better suited for the Caribbean context is an ongoing debate and one that requires more purposeful interrogation of the identity of the Caribbean researcher. In engaging in the work of GTM, the Caribbean researcher should first familiarize themselves with the practices of the Caribbean people and understand the indigenous way of life. It is through capturing the true cultural traditions, customs and practices of the people or participants that new knowledge deviating from Western standards of conducting research will be created. Smith (2005) argued that the process of decolonization entails "the unmasking and deconstruction of imperialism, and its aspects of colonialism, in its old and new formations... for reclamation of knowledge... and culture; and for the social transformation of the colonial relations between the native and the settler" (p. 88).

In the Caribbean, it becomes important to foreground indigenous epistemologies through native language and dialects as a mode of decolonizing GTM. In this respect, creole, whether in Jamaica, Antigua, or Barbados or Papiamento spoken in Aruba, Bonaire and Curaçao is a welcomed mode of data collection, analysis and reporting. The following section provides a procedural mapping of GT's attributes such as key features and role of literature and attempts to juxtapose the original Western conceptualization of GT with a Caribbean-decolonizing approach to GT. Important to note is that the following attributes distinguishes how researchers approach GT as methods versus GT as methodology. More specifically, if researchers engage critically with the key features detailed below, then they are likely engaging with GT as methodology, if not then the researcher is employing GT as an approach to data analysis.

WHAT SETS GT APART

Knowing the overarching context of GT aids in understanding what separates it from other qualitative approaches and more so how it can be applied in the Caribbean from a decolonizing approach. But to truly comprehend its significance, a more nuanced discussion of its attributes also needs to take place. Moreover, it is through a discussion of GT's attributes (i.e., generating theory, role of the literature, and its key features) that it's viability for Caribbean research, and beyond, can be fully understood (*see* Appendix for an overview of procedures for GT).

Role of the Researcher

Consistent with the perimeters of Constructivist Grounded Theory (CGT), researchers (as well as the members of the research team) should be prepared to assume a reflexive stance in the research process, requiring that they work in conjunction with the research participants to construct interpretations to explain the phenomenon under study. This also necessitates that researchers identify any presuppositions that they have and evaluate how they might affect the research process (Charmaz & Mitchell, 1996). To sufficiently identify these presuppositions, researchers should first acknowledge their positionality within this space of inquiry. Here, the worldview point of the researcher along with their identity as a decolonizing researcher becomes essential to make public, especially as it pertains to how researchers navigate their power and privilege as being researchers.

An exploration of the presuppositions also warrants an examination of how the researcher intends to moderate their effects. Ahern (1999) posited that bracketing is one way that qualitative researchers demonstrate validity of the data in their data collection and analysis process. Moreover, validation procedures are representative of qualitative approaches for establishing credibility, like trustworthiness and authenticity. CGT purports that it is unrealistic to believe that a researcher can enter the field completely free of past experiences, assumptions, or exposure to literature (Charmaz, 2006; Heath & Cowley, 2004). Notably, researchers can employ procedures related to what Ahern (1999) referred to as "reflexive bracketing," which would help them to understand the effects instead of pursuing futile attempts at eliminating them. The abovementioned presuppositions and statement of positionality, according to the pretext of reflexive bracketing, can also help the researchers to (a) understand what facets of the research process they took for granted, (b) locate the power hierarchy within the research, and (c) situate themselves within it. Listed below are additional steps in the process of reflexive bracketing that can be incorporated throughout the research process:

- *Is anything new or surprising in the data collection or analysis?* Ahern (1999) suggested that the researcher should consider whether or not this would be cause for concern before assuming that the code categories have reached saturation. A data collection process that yields no new or surprising data could be an indication that the researcher is "bored, blocked, or desensitized" (p. 409).
- *Even when the researcher has completed the analysis, he/she should reflect on how they will write up the account. For example, will the researcher be quoting more from one respondent than another? If yes, they should ask themselves why.* Ahern (1999) argued that the researcher must evaluate how sensitivity toward participants is being influenced by how much simpler their perspectives were to grasp. She urged that researchers, instead, not solely rely on participants who make their analytic task easier. If necessary, she urged that the researcher must do what is necessary to make inferences from each participant's account or incident.
- *A significant aspect of resolving bias is the acknowledgment of its outcomes.* Ahern (1999) stated,

> If you experience a flash of insight that indicates areas of bias might be affecting your data collection or analysis, congratulate yourself. You have become a reflexive researcher. This means that [you are] emotionally and intellectually ready to acknowledge a lack of neutrality and to make corrections. (p. 410)

Researchers who exercise reflexivity must also understand that preconceptions are not easy to abandon.

Role of the Literature

Seen as a *context of discovery* (Glaser & Strauss, 1967), GTM is built on the pretext that the researcher ought to enter the field with an open mind, free from pre-existing conceptions of ideas (Glaser & Strauss, 1967). Accordingly, Holton (2007) posited

> Remaining open to discovering of what is really going on in the field of inquiry is often blocked...by what Glaser (1998) refers to as the forcing of preconceived notions resident within the researcher's worldview, an initial professional problem, on an entrant theory and framework; all of which preempt the researcher's ability to suspend preconception, and allow for what will merge conceptually by constant comparative analysis. (p. 269)

This criterion was and remains a point of contention among grounded theorists (Heath & Cowley, 2004; Holton, 2007; Lempert, 2007), especially when evaluating the role and influence of a literature review.

So, what impact does a review of the literature have on a researcher's ability to effectively execute GTM? There are two rules of thumb where this is concerned. If the researcher has little to no familiarity with the phenomenon under study, then there is just cause to review relevant literature to inform oneself of the best approach to observe the phenomenon (Cutcliffe, 2000). Heath and Cowley (2004) pointed out that this most certainly could be the case if the researcher is pursuing a topic outside of his/her field of study. On the other hand, if a researcher intends to further explore concepts where relevance or significance remains underdetermined in hopes to build an emergent theory, this also could justify his/her need to review the literature prior to entering the field (Cutcliffe, 2000).

Heath and Cowley (2004) indicated that this is a violation of the fundamentals of GTM, which presume that "theory cannot be simultaneously emergent and built on concepts selected from the literature" (p. 143). But, evolutions in thought have revealed divergent arguments among grounded theory's (GT) founders where this is concerned (Heath & Cowley, 2004). Glaser (1998) argued that an early review of the literature could inadvertently alter the direction of an emergent theory from its intended destination. However, Strauss and Corbin (Strauss, 1987; Strauss & Corbin, 1990) found that, as with the past experiences of the researcher, an early review of the literature by the researcher is useful in developing a theoretical sensitivity (Glaser, 1978) and a research hypothesis. These findings are consistent with Gibson's (2007) work on critical theory within grounded theory research, which also asserts that some familiarity with the literature is required for the researcher to develop a theoretical sensitivity. Aside from concerns about forcing data to fit into pre-existing categories resulting in premature completion of the data collection and analysis process (Glaser

& Strauss, 1967), an early review of the literature arguably has much larger positive implications than once thought. Given the two rules of thumb, a decolonizing lens would question not only what literature is being reviewed but who was cited in the literature review. It is critical for all researchers to practice "a conscientious engagement with the politics of citation as a geographical practice that is mindful of how citational practices can be a tool for either the reification of, or resistance to, unethical hierarchies of knowledge production" (Mott & Cockayne, 2017, abstract).

Features of GT

Studies that employ the grounded theory method (GTM) of qualitative research share similar characteristics, as well as differences. Consistent with the majority of qualitative studies, GTM values and utilizes various forms of data collection, including but not limited to participant interviews, field observations, and document analysis (e.g., dairies, newspaper clippings, historical documents, and media materials). But, what sets GTM apart from other forms of qualitative research is its emphasis on theory development through inductive and systematic research measures (Bryant & Charmaz, 2007a; Glaser & Strauss, 1967; Strauss & Corbin, 1990, 1994). A grounded theorist aims to make explicit his/her understanding and subsequent theorizing of the phenomenon under study through repeated interaction with and interrogation of the data, thereby allowing the analysis process to be informed by the rich data collected (Charmaz, 2006; Strauss & Corbin, 1994). Strauss and Corbin (1994) argued that GTM results in the development of a theory of "great conceptual density" (p. 274), rooted in the researcher's intimate understanding and rigorous evaluation of the rich data collected (Charmaz, 2006). Specifically, GTM has four features (i.e., constant comparative method, theoretical sampling, theoretical saturation, and theoretical sorting) that: (a) enables theoretical explanations explicitly derived from data to be constructed (Lewis & Ritchie, 2003) and (b) ensures that the research process is well documented, capable of replication (Bryant & Charmaz, 2007b). These are issues of particular importance to the empirical research process, but especially in dissertation research amidst concerns surrounding the need to establish validity of research findings (Haynes, 2013).

In decolonizing the features of grounded theory for the Caribbean landscape, researchers must ensure that the "research agenda is determined by, or at least agreed to by, indigenous research participants" (Smith, 2012, as cited in Redman-MacLaren & Mills, 2015, p. 2). Therefore, it is important to reposition the power not only in the hands of researchers but in that of the participants as equal co-researchers.

Constant Comparative Method

The constant comparative method (CCM) is embedded within the data collection and analysis process of GTM as a means of enabling the researcher to derive meaning from the data (Coffey & Atkinson, 1996; Lewis & Ritchie, 2003). It is from this purview that a grounded theorist begins to understand the significance of memo writing, coding, and theoretical saturation. CCM has been characterized in the literature several ways, all of which allude to its significance in the application of GTM. Boeije (2002) posited that the method of comparing or contrasting is necessary through all stages of the data analysis process and should influence how categories are formed and bound, and content is organized. Tesch (1990) further underscored this notion when she posited, "The main intellectual tool [used in GTM] is comparison. The goal is to discern conceptual similarities, to refine the discriminative power of categories, and to discover patterns" (p. 96).

Theoretical Sampling

Theoretical sampling is instrumental to a researcher's ability to construct a formal theory from grounded theory research. Grounded theorists, through constant comparative methods, formulate categories as a means of isolating theoretical constructs that undergird their resulting formal theory (Charmaz, 2000; Glaser, 1965; Strauss & Corbin, 1994). When there are unexplained or underdeveloped (e.g., lack of saturation) properties within a category, the researcher engages in theoretical sampling to help fill the gaps (Charmaz, 2000, 2006). "Thus, the aim of this sampling is to refine ideas, not to increase the size of the original sample" (Charmaz, 2000, p. 519). Moreover, where initial sampling is the starting point and used within GTM to determine sampling criteria before entering the field, theoretical sampling informs the direction of the researcher's investigation. Charmaz (2000) posited that the theory-generating process can lead the researcher to conducting theoretical (re)sampling of not only people but also scenes, settings, and documents as a means of gathering more information. This further suggests that a complex and thoroughly constructed grounded theory can only be produced through CCM, instead of a superficial, one-dimensional method of data collection and analysis.

Opposing viewpoints are discussed in the literature regarding when theoretical sampling should take place, with Strauss advocating for its early implementation (Charmaz, 2000). Charmaz (2000, 2006) posited that a researcher ought to consider theoretical sampling in later aspects of the research process, citing that it prevents forced analytic interpretations, redundancy in categories, and premature closure of the data analysis process. Nevertheless, grounded theory's reliance on CCM does not imply that variations will not materialize throughout the data collection process. Variations are certainly likely and often emerge throughout the theoretical sampling process. Charmaz (2006) argued that variations in the data present themselves when researchers are discerning about the data they seek and where they seek it. The focus for the researcher in this process is to understand how, when, and why theoretical categories vary through an exploration of experiences or events, as opposed to placing all the emphasis on the individual (Charmaz, 2006).

A reflection on her own approach to GTM led Charmaz (2006) to ponder how to "account for this phenomenon [as she was constructing her] immersion in illness" (p. 109) category in her own research. She began to realize that the major properties within this category were consistent in terms of the activities involved, but that not every participant's perspective of time changed (e.g., slowed or sped up) (Charmaz, 2006). Theoretical sampling helped her focus her continued data collection, which resulted in additional interviews with participants whose description and effects of time varied, resulting in the formulation of a new category to account for the different experiences participants had with immersion in illness (Charmaz, 2006). This more refined approach to data collection and analysis produces more analytic and insightful memo writing.

Theoretical Saturation

Theoretical sampling can also aid the researcher in achieving *theoretical saturation* (Charmaz, 2000). As referenced in the previous section, theoretical saturation of a theoretical construct implies that no new data (i.e., properties) fit into an already formed category (Charmaz, 2000; Glaser, 1965; Strauss & Corbin, 1994). A researcher has no need to continue theoretical sampling once theoretical saturation (i.e., conceptual density) of a particular category has been achieved. Charmaz (2006) encouraged that researchers must ask themselves the following questions when determining whether their categories have reached theoretical saturation:

1. Which comparison do you make between data within and between categories?
2. What sense do you make of these comparisons?
3. Where do they lead you?
4. How do your comparisons illuminate your theoretical categories? (p. 113)

The literature also addresses concerns with how grounded theorists approach theoretical saturation. Despite being the aim and the standard, theoretical saturation is not consistently employed across all grounded theory research. Some grounded theorists simply claim saturation when their "mundane research questions produce saturated but common or trivial categories" (Charmaz, 2006, p. 114). Methodologists who believe that GTM produces categories through partial, not exhaustive, coding of data further critique grounded theory's attempts at saturation. For instance, Dey (1999) argued that categories in grounded theory are suggested by the data and thereby *theoretically sufficient*, instead of theoretically saturated.

To avoid the pitfalls of saturation that Dey (1999) described, Charmaz (2006) has urged grounded theorists to interact with all that takes place in the field and procedurally allow the guidelines to aid in their management of the data, instead of being bounded by them. In short, grounded theory as methodology enrich research by ensuring that data from the field influenced the analysis process and shaped the final results (Dover, 2016, p. 39).

Done successfully, theoretical saturation of categories enables the researcher to complete theoretical sorting and/or diagramming as a means to integrate the emerging theory.

Theoretical Sorting

Charmaz (2006) asserted that grounded theorists, in particular, employ *theoretical sorting* (and integrating) of memos and diagramming as means of theoretical development of their data analysis. As illuminated in previous sections, analytic memos prove essential in constructing a formal theory. The theoretical sorting of analytic memos and their subsequent integration should reflect the researcher's empirical experience (Charmaz, 2006). It may also aid the researcher to diagram his/her findings to visually see and critique his/her understanding of the relationship between theoretical constructs.

Charmaz (2006), in her description of the process, encouraged the sorting process to be more organic, stating,

> Be willing to experiment with different arrangement of your memos. Treat these arrangements as tentative and play with them. Lay out your memos in several different ways. Draw a few diagrams to connect them. When you create a sorting that looks promising, jot it down, and diagram it. (p. 117)

When researchers diagram their findings, they are also exposing and describing the relationship in terms of power, scope, and the direction that exists between theoretical constructs (Charmaz, 2006). Moreover, the theoretical sorting of analytic memos allows the researcher to integrate theoretical codes that provide contextual conditions and interpretive understanding of the theory's operation (Charmaz, 2006).

Diagrams can take several forms. Two of the most common within grounded theory include conceptual maps and the conditional/consequential matrix. *Conceptual maps*, readily used by Clarke (2003, 2005) to illustrate situational analysis, extend beyond grounded theory's early emphasis on basic social processes and make visible inherently invisible structural relationships. Strauss and Corbin (1990, 1994) promoted the researcher's use of the *conditional/consequential matrix* to inform theoretical sampling decisions and when illuminating the context and pathway in which the phenomenon occurs. "In particular, Corbin and Strauss (1990, 1998) offer this matrix as an analytic device for thinking about macro and micro relationships that might shape the situation the researcher studies" (Charmaz, 2006, p. 118). Regardless of the type of diagram chosen, theoretical sorting combined with the integration of analytic memos provides the researcher with the means of explaining the phenomenon under study through the construction of a conceptually dense grounded theory.

CONCLUSION

The grounded theory method (GTM) has been utilized in qualitative research since it emerged in the 1960s. But despite its many contributions to behavioral and social science research, viability of the methodology for the Caribbean has yet to be adequately demonstrated. Findings from this investigation of the literature suggest that GT's attributes (i.e., ability to generating theory, the role of the literature, and its key features) address concerns about the method's viability in Caribbean research, while also illustrating its level of rigor.

Grounded theory has its advantages and disadvantages; however, for the Caribbean this methodology can be used to decolonize research. Hussein, Hirst, Salyers and Osuji (2014), stated that "for many pragmatic researchers, GT is very useful in answering their questions, enlightening their thinking and for providing them with reassurance when hesitations arise during the research process" (p. 3). Here the authors state that an advantage of grounded theory is that it "provides for intuitive appeal" (p. 3). Another advantage of GT that Caribbean researchers can adopt is the room for creativity. For example, "GT encourages the researcher to move through a process of discovery whereby themes and interpretations naturally emerge from the data" (Hussein et. al., 2016, p. 3). Thereby, unearthing authentic inferences to guide Caribbean research as well as developing new theories that are not influenced by colonial and neocolonial approaches to constructing knowledge. Notably, limitations such as GT being a long and tedious process with a potential for methodological errors, does not negate the fact that it is an applicable and viable decolonizing methodological approach to the Caribbean.

The generation of theory is the intended outcome of GTM, setting it apart from other qualitative research approaches. Further, resulting theories could be either substantive (SGT) or formal (FGT). For those who conduct grounded theory studies, it is inevitable that their future research will generate a FGT from their prior SGT research (Glaser, 2007). The rigorous procedures of GTM equip scholars, in particular, to achieve the goals of Caribbean research and engage in increasing more sophisticated levels of independent research.

Ethical Review Boards, Internal Review Boards (IRB), dissertation requirements, and funding agencies alike, require researchers demonstrate that their research problem is well constructed and original through an investigation of the literature. It would be easy to presume then that GTM would not be a suitable option, as theory cannot be simultaneously emergent and informed by literature, or so it seems. But, grounded theorists contend that an early review of the literature is useful and—at times—necessary. In cases where a researcher has limited familiarity with the phenomenon, a review of the literature can inform the circumstances by which to observe the phenomenon. Additionally, it is also believed that a review of the literature maybe necessary, as it aids in the development of theoretical sensitivity (Haynes, 2017). Theoretical sensitivity allows the researcher to know which data are significant in the construction of a theoretical explanation; which without could potentially pose greater threats to the fundamentals of the method.

Lastly, GTM has four key features: the constant comparative method, theoretical sampling, theoretical saturation, and theoretical sorting. These complex procedures inform how the data collection and analysis procedures are conducted. The constant comparative method has several stages, but together, they enable the data collection and analysis process to be fluid, continually informing one another; keeping the researcher close to the data. For example, Dover's (2016) study on the LGBTQ community struggle of equality in the Caribbean, utilized grounded theory methodology. Like Charmaz, Dover's analysis of the data started while interviews were being conducted. Dover (2016) stated that this allowed her to "direct future interviews towards more pertinent topics of the research and ask questions that only transpired during the interview process" (p. 38).

Through the constant comparative method, the researcher identifies theoretical constructs that seemingly undergird the emerging theoretical explanation. Theoretical sampling is imposed to fill in the gaps. Thus, theoretical sampling involves the direction of the research and is not limited to people, as it intended to refine ideas. A researcher has no need to continue theoretical sampling once theoretical saturation (i.e., conceptual density) has been achieved. Theoretical saturation of a theoretical construct implies that no new data fit into an already formed category. This leaves theoretical sorting. Theoretical sorting is a process of integration involving some form of diagramming that reflects the researcher's empirical experience illustrating the resulting theory's operation, making the inherently invisible visible.

Taken together, the key features of GTM: the constant comparative method, theoretical sampling, theoretical saturation, and theoretical sorting, allow the research process to be well documented, transparent, and replicable; also alleviate any issues with validity of findings that may (or tend to) emerge in the research process, dissertation or otherwise. The grounded theory method (GTM) has earned its place in the context of empirical research literature and practice, most would agree. But the time is also for the scholarly community to also acknowledge that GTM is potentially viable for decolonizing Caribbean research because of its rigorous orientation. Scholars that engage in grounded theory research are desired in our academic disciplines because, they reflect Caribbean-borne epistemologies, theories, and frameworks designed and developed for and by the Caribbean.

Further, Smith (1999) posited that the process of decolonization tackles imperialism and colonialism at various levels. Notably, a decolonizing approach can be useful to not just Caribbean scholars but to all scholars conducting research in postcolonial and neocolonial countries. However, while GTM is suitable for decolonizing research, Caribbean researchers, must tackle the issues raised, one such being, "having a more critical understanding of the underlying assumptions, motivations and values which inform research practices" (Smith, 1999, p. 20). This will create new non-Western knowledge that is not confined to one viewpoint or methodology but that which add to the authenticity of the research being conducted.

APPENDIX

Corbin and Strauss (1990) identified the following tenets which are applicable to both Western and non-Western researchers, while urging researchers to employ these procedures with care because they give a study its necessary rigor:

1. *Data collection and analysis are interrelated processes.* In GTM, analysis begins with data collection and informs the direction of subsequent visits to the field. This approach to data collection and analysis ensures that the research process is influenced by all relevant information regarding the phenomenon as soon as the researcher perceives it. Concepts that the researcher discovers and believes are related to the phenomenon under study must be considered "provisional" until they repeatedly present themselves in the data.
   Corbin and Strauss explained,

   > Requiring that a concept's relevance to an evolving theory (as a condition, action/interaction, or consequence) be demonstrated is one way that grounded theory helps to guard against researcher bias. (p. 7)

2. *Concepts are the basic units of analysis.* Grounded theorists work with conceptualization of the data, not necessarily the "raw data" or the actual incident that was observed or recounted by the participant. This means that the researcher interprets and analyzes his/her observations or participants' accounts as potential indicators of the phenomenon under study. "In the grounded theory approach such concepts become more numerous and more abstract as the analysis continues" (p. 7). In framing this element within the Caribbean landscape, it is critical that researchers utilize the raw data shared by the people of the community and not what they deem necessary. Wilson (2001) in her review of Smith's (1999) stated that acknowledging the shared experiences between indigenous and colonized people is important, however, one must also acknowledge the difference between the two. Therefore, while Grounded theorists work with conceptualization of the data, a Caribbean doctoral dissertation would need to consider all forms of data, as the history of the particular phenomena is grounded in the raw data.

3. *Categories must be developed and created.* Through a process of constant comparative analysis, concepts that describe the same phenomenon eventually become properties that can be grouped together to form categories. Moreover, categories provide the means by which the theory can be integrated.

4. *Sampling in grounded theory proceeds on theoretical grounds.* Theoretical sampling, discussed further in subsequent sections, involves the

researcher's revisiting the field to pursue data that further informs his/her understanding of the phenomenon. "The aim is ultimately to build a theoretical explanation by specifying through action/ interaction, the consequences that result from them, and variations of these qualifiers" (p. 9).

5. *Analysis makes use of constant comparisons.* Embedded within GT, constant comparison analysis, discussed further in subsequent sections, enables the researcher to achieve greater precision and consistency throughout the data collection and analysis process. Incidents noticed by the researcher are to be compared against other incidents for similarities and differences and then labeled appropriately over time.

6. *Patterns and variations must be accounted for.* "The data must be examined for regularity and for an understanding of where that regularity is not apparent" (p. 10). Discussed further in subsequent sections, accounting for variations aids the researcher in ordering and integrating the data.

7. *Process must be built into the theory.* In GTM, process describes not only how the theoretical constructs identified perform but also how the phenomenon responds to the subsequent prevailing conditions. Each must be accounted for in the presentation of the resulting theory.

8. *Writing theoretical memos is an integral part of doing grounded theory.* Theoretical or analytical memos, which they are often labeled, are an essential component of the data collection and analysis process. As discussed in subsequent sections, theoretical memos are eventually integrated into the theory's construction to help ground and contextualize the theoretical explanation of the phenomenon under study. "Writing memos should begin with the first coding session and continues to the end of the research [process]" (p. 10).

9. *Hypotheses about relationships among categories should be developed and verified as much as possible during the research process.* Despite being a subject of debate among grounded theorists, the idea of verification does have its place within the method (Heath & Cowley, 2004). Discussed further in subsequent sections, verification in GTM is seen as a process, requiring the constant revising of your hypothesis until it is supported and/or grounded in the data.

10. *A grounded theorist need not work alone.* GTM, like most approaches to qualitative research, is one that may be facilitated in a research team. A researcher who shares his/her research with others is less prone to the effects of researcher bias and increases his/her own theoretical sensitivity.

11. *Broader structural conditions must be analyzed, however microscopic the research.* According to Corbin and Strauss, "The analysis of a setting must not be restricted to the conditions that bear immediately on the phenomenon of central interest" (p. 11).

REFERENCES

Ahern, K. (1999). Ten tips for reflexive bracketing. *Qualitative Health Research, 9*(3), 407–411.

Bailey, K. R., & Johnson, E. J. (2014). Internet-based technologies in social work education: Experiences, perspectives and use. *Caribbean Teaching Scholar, 4*(1), 23–37.

Barrow, D., & De Lisle J. (2009). A qualitative evaluation of the lower secondary SEMP science curriculum of Trinidad and Tobago. *Caribbean Curriculum, 16*(2), 73–97.

Bishop, R. (2005). Freeing ourselves from neo-colonial domination in research: A Kaupapa Māori approach to creating knowledge. In N. K. Denzin & Y. S. Lincoln (Eds.), *Handbook of qualitative research* (3rd ed., pp. 109–135). Thousand Oaks, CA: SAGE.

Blackman, S. (2012). Principal's roles in managing assessment curriculum and instruction in mainstream and special education in Barbados. *Journal of Education and Development in the Caribbean, 14*(2), 72–96.

Boeije, H. (2002). A purposeful approach to the constant comparative method in the analysis of qualitative interviews. *Quality and Quantity, 36,* 391–409.

Bryant, A., & Charmaz, K. (2007a). Grounded theory in historical perspective: An epistemological account. In A. Bryant & K. Charmaz (Eds.), *The SAGE handbook of grounded theory* (pp. 31–57). Los Angeles, CA: SAGE.

Bryant, A., & Charmaz. K. (2007b). Grounded theory research: Methods and practices. In A. Bryant & K. Charmaz (Eds.), *The SAGE handbook of grounded theory* (pp. 1–28). Los Angeles, CA: SAGE.

Charmaz, K. (2000). Constructivist and objectivist grounded theory. In N. K. Denzin & Y. S. Lincoln (Eds.), *Handbook of qualitative research* (2nd ed., pp. 509–535). Thousand Oakes, CA: SAGE.

Charmaz, K. (2003). Grounded theory. In J. A. Smith (Ed.), *Qualitative psychology: A practical guide to research methods* (pp. 81–110). London, England: SAGE.

Charmaz, K. (2005). Grounded theory in 21st century: Applications for advancing social justice studies. In N. K. Denzin & Y. S. Lincoln (Eds.), *Handbook of qualitative research* (3rd ed., pp. 507–536). Thousand Oakes, CA: SAGE.

Charmaz, K. (2006). *Constructing grounded theory: A practical guide through qualitative analysis.* Thousand Oaks, CA: SAGE.

Charmaz, K., & Mitchell, R. (1996). The myth of silent authorship: Self, substance, and style in ethnographic writing. *Symbolic Interaction, 19*(4), 285–302.

Clarke, A. E. (2003). Situational analyses: Grounded theory mapping after the postmodern turn. *Symbolic Interaction, 26*(4), 553–576.

Clarke, A. E. (Ed.). (2005). *Situational analysis: Grounded theory after the postmodern turn.* Thousand Oaks, CA: SAGE.

Coffey, A., & Atkinson, P. (1996). *Making sense of qualitative data: Complementary strategies.* London, England: SAGE.

Corbin, J. M., & Strauss, A. (1990). Grounded theory research: Procedures, canons, and evaluative criteria. *Qualitative Sociology, 13*(1), 3–21.

Corbin, J. M., & Strauss, A. (1998). *Basics of qualitative research.* London, England: SAGE.

Cutcliffe, J. R. (2000). Methodological issues in grounded theory. *Journal of Advanced Nursing, 31*(6), 1476–1484.

Denzin, N. K. (2007). Grounded theory and the politics of interpretation. In A. Bryant & K. Charmaz (Eds.), *The SAGE handbook of grounded theory* (pp. 454–471). Los Angeles, CA: SAGE.

Dey, I. (1999). *Grounded theory: Guidelines for qualitative inquiry.* London, England: Academic Press.

Dover, C. (2016). *The influence of Caribbean historical institutions on the struggle for LGBTQ equality.* Unpublished Master's Thesis. Retrieved from https://ruor .uottawa.ca/bitstream/10393/34651/1/Dover_Cailey_2016_thesis.pdf

Gibson, B. (2007). Accommodating critical theory. In A. Bryant & K. Charmaz (Eds.), *The SAGE handbook of grounded theory* (pp. 436–453). Los Angeles, CA: SAGE.

Glaser, B. G. (1965). The constant comparative method of qualitative analysis. *Social Problems, 12,* 436–445.

Glaser, B. G. (1978). *Theoretical sensitivity: Advances in the methodology of grounded theory.* Mill Valley, CA: Sociology Press.

Glaser, B. G. (1998). *Doing grounded theory: Issues and discussions.* Mill Valley, CA: Sociology Press.

Glaser, B. G. (2007). Doing formal theory. In A. Bryant & K. Charmaz (Eds.), *The SAGE handbook of grounded theory* (pp. 97–113). Los Angeles, CA: SAGE.

Glaser, B. G., & Strauss, A. L. (1965). *Awareness of death and dying.* Chicago, IL: Aldine.

Glaser, B. G., & Strauss, A. L. (1967). *The discovery of grounded theory.* Chicago, IL: Aldine.

Glaser, B. G., & Strauss, A. L. (1968). *Time for dying.* Chicago, IL: Aldine.

Haynes, C., (2013). *Restrictive and expansive views of equality: A grounded theory study that explores the influence of racial consciousness on the behaviors of White faculty in the classroom* (Unpublished doctoral dissertation). University of Denver, Denver, CO.

Haynes, C. (2017). Dismantling the white supremacy embedded in our classrooms: White faculty in pursuit of more equitable educational outcomes. *International Journal of Teaching and Learning in Higher Education,* 29(1), 87–107.

Heath, H., & Cowley, S. (2004). Developing a grounded theory approach: a comparison of Glaser and Strauss. *International Journal of Nursing Studies, 41*(2), 141–150. https://doi.org/10.1016/S0020-7489(03)00113-5

Holton, J. (2007). The coding process and its challenges. In A. Bryant & K. Charmaz (Eds.), *The SAGE handbook of grounded theory* (pp. 265–289). Los Angeles, CA: SAGE.

Hussein, M. E., Hirst, S., Salyers, V., & Osuji, J. (2014). Using grounded theory as a method of inquiry: Advantages and disadvantages. *The Qualitative Report, 19*(27), 1–15. Retrieved from https://nsuworks.nova.edu/tqr/vol19/iss27/3

Ibrahim-Ali, A. (2015). Defying established practice in the EFL classroom: The development of a theoretical framework for teaching and testing periphrastic verbs. *Caribbean Teaching Scholar, 5*(2), 95–109.

Lempert, L. B. (2007). Asking questions of the data: Memo writing in the grounded theory tradition. In A. Bryant & K. Charmaz (Eds.), *The SAGE handbook of grounded theory* (pp. 245–264). Los Angeles, CA: SAGE.

Lewis, J., & Ritchie, J. (2003). Generalizing from qualitative research. In J. Ritchie & J. Lewis (Eds.), *Qualitative research practice: A guide for social science students and researchers* (pp. 263–286). Los Angeles, CA: SAGE.

Mott, C., & Cockayne, D. (2017). Citation matters: Mobilizing the politics of citation toward a practice of "conscientious engagement." *Gender, Place & Culture, 24*(7), 954–973. https://doi.org/10.1080/0966369X.2017.1339022

Newman, M. (2005). School leadership and social justice: Four Jamaican high school principals. *Caribbean Journal of Education, 27*(1), 3–21.

Redman-MacLaren, M., & Mills, J. (2015). Transformational grounded theory: Theory, voice, and action. *International Journal of Qualitative Methods, 14*(3), 1–12.

Shepherd, V. (2005). Belonging and unbelonging: The impact of Migration on discourses of identity in Jamaican history. *The Journal of Caribbean History, 39*(1), 1–18.

Smith, L. T. (1999). *Decolonizing methodologies: Research and indigenous peoples.* London, England: Zed Books.

Smith, L. T. (2005). On tricky ground: Researching native in the age of uncertainty. In N. K. Denzin & Y. S. Lincoln (3rd ed.). *The SAGE handbook of qualitative research* (pp. 81–108). Thousand Oaks, CA: SAGE.

Strauss, A., & Corbin, J. (1990). *Basics of qualitative research: Grounded theory procedures and techniques.* Newbury Park, CA: SAGE.

Strauss, A., & Corbin, J. (1994). Grounded theory methodology: An overview. In N. K. Denzin & Y. S. Lincoln (Eds.), *Handbook of qualitative research* (pp. 273–285). Thousand Oaks, CA: SAGE.

Tesch, R. (1990). *Qualitative research: Analysis types and software.* London, England: Falmer Press.

Timmermans, S., & Tavory, I. (2007). Advancing ethnographic research through grounded theory practice. In A. Bryant & K. Charmaz (Eds.), *The SAGE handbook of grounded theory* (pp. 493–512). Los Angeles, CA: SAGE.

Wilson, C. (2001). Review of the book decolonizing methodologies: Research and indigenous peoples. *Social Policy Journal of New Zealand, 17,* 214–217. Retrieved from https://www.msd.govt.nz/documents/about-msd-and-our-work/publications-resources/journals-and-magazines/social-policy-journal/spj17/17_pages214_217.pdf

CHAPTER 3

"REMOVING THE STRANGLEHOLD"

Reshaping Encounters with Poetry Through Participatory Observation in Action Research

Aisha T. Spencer

'Eng. Lit., my sister,
Was more than a cruel joke –
It was the heart
Of alien conquest.'

Felix Mnthali, The Stranglehold of English Lit.
(Moore, G., & Beier,1998, p. 172)

As a Caribbean English Literature Educator, I have often felt that I have had to function in a paradoxical role when participating in the process of training secondary school teachers of English or working with secondary school students in the English classroom. On the one hand, there is the thrill of being able to contribute to a significant act of what Ngugi (1986) described

Decolonizing Qualitative Approaches for and by the Caribbean, pages 43–61
Copyright © 2019 by Information Age Publishing
All rights of reproduction in any form reserved.

as "decolonising the mind" (p. 384), where I attempt to take Caribbean literary thought, merged with critical pedagogy, into the various Literature classroom spaces into which I am invited. On the other hand, there is the struggle to ensure that what I am providing for teachers and students at all levels is realistic, relevant, contextual and transformative. Significantly too, is the need to ensure that what I offer conceptually and practically to these teachers and students is uniquely connected to their own identities and experiences (personally, academically and professionally). At no point do I desire to be viewed as the outsider looking in nor do I desire to be a mere symbolic representative of an elitist group of educators from an establishment that might very well be viewed as oppressive and perhaps discriminatory.

In a country that is still so deeply entrenched in colonial beliefs and practices, as Jamaican educators, we need to begin to construct both pedagogy and research practices which give credence to our own ways of being and demonstrate what works well and what is no longer suited to our realities. Since I often utilize the above platforms to conduct research, I constantly assume an interrogative posture pertaining to the processes of preparation and participation as both facilitator and researcher. Who will benefit from my involvement and research? How will the engagement and research conducted enable sustained transformation of the classroom spaces in my nation? How will my work help to promote a sense of identity that is tied to who my participants are as Caribbean people? How can I ensure that through my role I do not end up reinforcing a traditionally existing notion that foreign identities and experiences are somehow superior to national identities and experiences? As I started seeking answers to these questions, I began to examine one of my most common and meaningful roles—that of participant observer. I started to explore ways through which I could create the capacity for me to learn more about the way the literary space functioned in a Jamaican context and to examine at the same time how I could operate as an agent of decolonization through participatory observation.

This chapter will therefore demonstrate how participatory observation can be used in a Caribbean context as a decolonising tool to deconstruct and dissemble perceptions and strategies rooted in Eurocentric modus operandi governing both the teaching of Literature and traditional classroom practices in a Caribbean context. It will also show how as a decolonising method, participatory observation can play an essential part in the creation and construction of new ways of seeing, understanding and participating in the processes of education in our nation.

UNDERSTANDING THE PLACE OF ENGLISH LITERATURE
IN THE JAMAICAN ENGLISH CLASSROOM

The role of an English educator in the Caribbean is a complex one. The concept of an English syllabus in a Jamaican classroom automatically evokes images and feelings of a colonizer-colonized relationship. Craig (2006) reminds us that "English has traditionally been and continues to be the language of [Caribbean] education systems..." (p. 18). The seeming imposition of a standardized and necessary subject area which originated with a colonial education system prior to Jamaica's independence in 1962, and whose very name bears witness to the presence of the *mother country*, is an automatic signifier of tension. The situation of motivating students to learn the English Language is conflated with challenges because of the language's association with elitism, corporate and political spaces of access to wealth and symbolic associations with 'whiteness'. Bryan (2010) outlines the sociohistorical roots of the English Language and how it came to define and characterize achievement for both individuals and institutions. In her discussion about the history of English in the Caribbean islands, Bryan (2010) informs us that "success in English carried high material rewards for the school" (p. 25). Additionally, she points out that English was likely to have been accepted as "the language to learn, the language of status" (p. 25) because of its connection with literacy and the advancement it would enable for children in the post-emancipation period.

The situation of English Literature is even further complicated because of the marginal space it is given in various English classrooms across the island and the minimal attention it receives both from the Ministry of Education and (perhaps subsequently) from school administrators and teachers in various schools. There seems to be a lack of appreciation for its value as a subject on the secondary school curriculum. This has been caused by two main realities. Firstly, the presence of print is still strongly tied to Eurocentric cultures. Orality is a much more common feature of Caribbean culture. Students overhear stories daily through verbal interactions with adults and other children, they go to see the national pantomime through school trips, they listen to numerous stories told through the reggae dancehall, calypso and hip hop songs accessible through the radio or internet and some are used to hearing various forms of stories and drama pieces on the radio. Bryan (2010) posits that in Jamaica, students are more accustomed to hearing a language than to reading it in print. The processes of reading and writing about what has been read are strongly connected with the idea of being intelligent. Intelligence is still in many ways tied to European ideals governing the acquisition of knowledge and is closely connected to formal schooling and the ability to read and write proficiently. These abilities are also deeply associated with an individual's social class and background. The higher up the child is on the social ladder, the more he or she is expected to showcase these abilities. Those schools which do not make it on the list of high performing schools are therefore believed to have students that are not as intelligent as the traditional secondary schools which often appear on this list.

Secondly, culturally, students are not taught the value of English Literature and so cannot see its importance or relevance to them, apart from the constant reminder that to write well, they need to be avid readers. Teachers themselves are unaware of the value of the literature outside of it being used to build analytical skills in learners. Additionally, text selection is a major problem. The texts selected are often relevant based on their category as being texts written for children or adolescents but not much scrutiny occurs regarding their relevance and direct levels of connectivity to students from the various Caribbean regions. Connection occurs not simply through the events of a child's life that can be found in the literary text, but also through the type of emotional and mental journeys of characters which might stimulate the adolescent reader. These two challenges are part of what positions the literary text as a foreign, abstract object to both teachers and students; and because the pedagogy surrounding this text is usually more focused on reading the text to extract knowledge about it, rather than to enable engagement with it, many students often remain disconnected from the learning process in the Literature classroom. English Literature therefore becomes an abstract subject matter that only those who are somehow able to function on a deeply symbolic level as thinkers are believed to access. Such false ideas are also rooted in Eurocentric formalist thinking on the literary text (Barry, 2002) and the process of interpretation, which placed the literary text on a pedestal for its linguistic and literary qualities and promoted the view of the reader as knowledgeable only based on his or her ability to speak to the technicality of these qualities in the presentation of the text's meanings.

Whereas there are education officers for Literacy in The Ministry of Education in Jamaica, there is no educational officer for the area of English Literature and very often the subject is seen merely as another title for the term 'books for reading'. Through workshops I have conducted with teachers across the island and through my own interactions with teachers in the classroom, usually, only a certain set of secondary school students is chosen by English teachers to study English Literature. Those allowed to study Literature at the CXC level are those who have been stereotypically labelled as being *bright* and are therefore selected because they read and write satisfactorily well. English Literature therefore becomes seen as a difficult or challenging subject that requires deep thinking and such traits are often believed by many teachers and students to only belong to students of a certain social background and academic profile. This reality has tended to stir up reactions of fear and avoidance in both teachers and students. Poor performance in CXC examinations will automatically affect the ranking a school will attain. The selection process therefore is merely used to help administrators to monitor performance for subjects being taken at the CXC level, by ensuring that those who granted permission to sit the subject are those who are believed to have the brain power and literacy skills to do so.

Despite both local and regional progress in education, therefore, we are still operating, even at the start of the twenty-first century, out of a colonial mind set and set of practices guiding pedagogy. These alienating beliefs and practices continue to label many impoverished students from lower class or inner-city communities as being *not bright enough, not good enough, too slow,* or *not the kind of student* to function effectively in the English Literature classroom. Many of these students are not permitted to select this subject as an option for the sitting of their external Caribbean Examinations Council (CXC) examinations at the end of their secondary school life, because they are not able to acquire the learned status described at the start of this chapter, due to their language deficiencies.

POETRY IN THE CARIBBEAN ENGLISH CLASSROOM

The genre of poetry functions in a doubly marginal manner than English Literature itself. Poetry typifies a sense of 'Englishness' and is heavily associated with the British culture. This of course is due to Jamaica's colonial past and the ways in which poetry was developed within that past. The poetry taught in Jamaican schools, prior to independence, was British poetry. Our Caribbean poets therefore started off attempting to style their poems through the model of the British poems they were taught until the 1930s and 1940s when as Donnell (2006) details, "the idea of a West Indian or Caribbean aesthetic . . . gained its currency on a wider scale . . ." (p. 13). British models of poetry therefore lay the foundation for not only our own creative writing models (Breiner, 1998) but also for the ways in which we perceived and attempted to understand and interpret poetry. Even in the 21st century Eurocentric (and American) views on literary texts dominate the theoretical and pedagogical frames used by our teachers in the English classroom through traditional classical thoughts on various classical texts or through popular books on practical criticism published by various British publishing houses. Even with the development and influence of a Caribbean aesthetic over the last 50 years, the postcolonial and decolonising theoretical positions provided by Caribbean literary criticism has not been formally used to create and utilize literary pedagogies to guide the teaching of Literature in Caribbean classrooms.

Poetry is often elevated and placed on a pedestal in ways that cause the genre to seem inaccessible and impenetrable. Writing poetry is considered a high order activity, which only very few can do and do well. It also appears to be such a fundamentally mental activity, that it is assumed to be only comprehensible by those who are seen as being intelligent enough to access that mental zone. Reading, interpreting and responding to this kind of writing is consequently seen as being far-fetched if you are not seen as being particularly gifted or perceived to be highly intelligent. Poetry then becomes an avenue many teachers and students avoid at all costs. As Bryan and Styles (2014) point out in their representation of teachers' voices in classrooms in the Caribbean and across the United Kingdom, "the CXC [Caribbean Examination Council] has indicated some dissatisfaction with the delivery of poetry" (p. 96). The reports themselves demonstrate significant fluctuation in students' performance in the poetry section of the examination paper, with minimal increase in performance levels between 2009 and 2014 (www.cxc.org).

As more teachers become introduced to notions of critical thinking and different kinds of literary theory, however, the disparity between what *could* happen and what *actually* happens, in the English classroom, becomes more apparent. Teachers are aware of theories of postcolonialism, Marxism, feminism, deconstructionism and ecocriticism as they read and prepare lessons based on the literary texts they teach. The challenge is however, that even with these ways of reading, processes of teaching and learning continue to occur within and through a colonial, formalist framework, traditionalizing and oppressing even the slightest opportunity to envision alternative ways of knowing and being through the literary text and in the Jamaican English Literature classroom. Through both my role as a practicum supervisor and my role as a participant observer, I have observed that much of the knowledge teachers acquire on these literary texts and many of the activities placed in their lesson plans continue to be constructed through Western frames of reference guiding the study of the text. There is a way in which a more intentional and practical coupling of Caribbean poetics and Caribbean literary pedagogy needs to take place to move teachers from merely *knowing* ways to read the poem to making poems accessible to students through what students are given *to do* as they engage with poetry in the English classroom.

Although the situation of teaching poetry is far removed from what it was decades ago, the Caribbean Literature classroom still exists as a site of conflict because of these colonial and traditional perspectives and practices. The genre of poetry in the classroom therefore pre-empts hesitant, disinterested responses at times and producing questions surrounding its relevance in today's fast-paced globalized world. The situation becomes even further problematized with the teaching of poetry, because of its difference in use of language, form and, according to Andrews (1991), because "it is seen as the most distant from 'everyday life . . . [and is believed to inhabit] . . . an enclosed, self-referential world to which only an elite gain access" (as cited in Lambirth, 2013, p. 35). Teaching poetry in the Caribbean classroom therefore poses on the one hand, challenges which are universal, such as put forward by Andrews, and on the other hand, challenges which are culturally specific.

There are three main characteristics of poetry students encounter in the Jamaican secondary classroom space which tend to pose challenges: (a) the dominant use of the Standard English Language, (b) the presence of sociocultural realities and experiences in the poem that are not associated with or common to the Caribbean, and (c) the heavy (and often overly excessive) isolated focus on formal elements of the poem. Additionally, there are two main poetry classroom experiences which prompt resistance in students in the Jamaican literature classroom, which are highly connected to the role of the teacher. These are: (a) the Eurocentric, traditional 'lecture' style and sometimes excessively abstruse method of teaching poetry and (b) the 'authoritarian teacher-student interaction' described by Darder, Baltodano and Torres, (2009) as one of the factors which block critical pedagogy (p. 23). As Milner and Milner (2008) illustrate in *Bridging English*, within the traditional English classroom space in first world countries, "[t]he literature read were texts that were considered classics of the western world, and the language taught was traditional rules of grammar" (p. 4). This practice was merely replicated in Caribbean educational institutions.

Cultural realities therefore affect the way we perceive English as a subject. Since culture plays such a huge role in framing the experiences of teaching and learning, it becomes increasingly significant that as educators participating in the process of teacher training, we begin to ground our principles of teaching and research in the kind of education that will be informed by our own Caribbean frames. A practical way of achieving this can occur through participatory observation, particularly as it occurs within an action research design. This qualitative research strategy enables us as educators to participate purposefully in understanding the unique dynamics and complexities affecting the processes of teaching and learning for both the teachers and students in the Caribbean classroom (and for Caribbean students in international classroom spaces) and simultaneously, it allows us the opportunity to empower those with whom we interact, through our own involvement in the process.

PARTICIPATORY OBSERVATION IN ACTION RESEARCH AS A DECOLONIZING TOOL AND FRAME OF ANALYSIS

Qualitative research becomes well-suited as a decolonizing approach to the teaching of poetry because, according to Denzin and Lincoln (2000), it focuses on "the socially constructed nature of reality, the intimate relationship between the researcher and what is studied and the situation constraints that shape inquiry" (p. 8). In seeking to offer "answers to questions that stress how social experience is created and given meaning" (Denzin & Lincoln, 2000, p. 8), it would enable observation, reflexivity and the provision of new approaches that would promote a more self-conscious theorizing and practical demonstration of how to promote new and more positive kinds of engagement teachers and students might have with poetry. This is essential for analysing the situation of poetry pedagogy in the Caribbean Literature classroom. Furthermore, this type of approach will capture the traditional, colonial principles at work in the classroom which are based on European constructs of knowledge, and at the same time foster an opportunity to change this modus operandi to one which instead utilizes the philosophical premise that "[t]he education of any people should begin with the people themselves" (Woodson, 1993 as cited in Darder et al., 2000, p. 1). If both teachers and students are going to be stimulated and engaged in the poetry classroom, then they will need to see the value and relevance of the study and use of poetry to their everyday lives, and for this to happen, each moment of poetry they encounter in the classroom will have to be meaningfully connected to who they are and how they need to function in the wider society.

As a type of design which falls within the terrain of qualitative research is an action research design with focus on the participatory observation method. This design and this method enable a space for critiquing existing traditional pedagogies, while at the same time creating paradigm shifts in the way poetry can be taught in a culturally-relevant way and utilizing literary pedagogy constructed through an awareness of our own Caribbean sensibilities and experiences. Action research, argues Zuber-Skerritt (2011), "is *emancipatory* when it aims not only at technical and practical improvement and the participants' better understanding,... but also at changing the system itself or those conditions which impede desired improvement in the system/organization..." (p. 350). This form of research would therefore enable the decolonization of both theories and practices surrounding poetry pedagogy which have prevented both our teachers and students from meaningfully accessing and engaging with poetry in the Jamaican classroom for decades. It is not that all negative experiences with poetry in the classroom are bound up in problems connected to colonial ideologies and precepts, but rather that the entire experience of teaching and learning continues to be intricately connected to traditional ways of thinking and performing which need to be understood through a decolonizing lens.

The function of the participant observer is an integral part of an action research design. Whereas most cases in international research present the participant observer as an outsider entering an *inside* space, participatory observation in educational institutions in various Caribbean countries now occurs in many instances with *our own people*. These participant observers are educators and are usually also trained professionals in the same subject area characterising the classroom space being observed. It is an excellent way to forge relationships across various institutions and entities in the society and to demonstrate the value of democracy in the process of education.

The participant observer who has come out of the same society as the teacher and students in the class, will possess both the experience of having been taught the traditional, colonial-type principles governing responding to and teaching poetry and the exposure, through his or her own professional experience, to alternative, critical pedagogical orientations and practices in the teaching and learning of Literature. Through the balance these perspectives allow, the participant observer is able to engage in a process of questioning and reflection which will deepen his or her participation in and observation of the participants (both teacher and students) in their context and also promote through his or her participation critical thinking on the part of both the participant teacher and the participating students with regard to their attitudes towards and interaction with poetry.

Participatory observation is recognized as one of the common research strategies used by qualitative researchers in a variety of fields. The beauty of participatory observation ties in neatly with one of the qualities of participatory research, where, as stated by Cohen et al. (2011), each "breaks with conventional ways of constructing research, as it concerns doing research *with* people and communities rather than doing research *to* or *for* people and communities" (p. 37). Its dialectal nature promotes an emancipatory and unconventional approach to understanding, exploring and responding to a problem. This is so because it provides room for observing the culturally shifting patterns and trends characterizing the processes of both teaching and learning and concurrently provides the context within which to observe and understand teacher/student responses. Additionally, interpretation of the data collection becomes much more aligned to the context surrounding the data collection process, as the participant observer can utilize the wealth of observation notes surrounding both the simple and complex occurrences within the research environment. As Dewalt and Dewalt (2011) point out, participant observation "puts you where the action is . . . " (p. 2) and thus enables a powerful avenue through which to collect data that will not merely help the researcher and others to identify and comprehend a problem, but also to solve it to the degree that the solution leads to several modes of transformation, for both the participant observer, the research participants and the society at large.

HOW DOES IT ALL WORK?

The Participant Observer and the Students

The way a participant observer engages in the process of research will determine the authenticity and level of revelation possible. Participatory observation is therefore used as both a decolonizing tool and frame of analysis based on the researcher's awareness of the sociohistorical realities shaping the present moment and the cultural perceptions and customs which might be influencing both teacher and student interaction with poetry in the English classroom. Participating in teaching and assisting, whilst, in the same research period, functioning as an observer within the classroom, enables me as both a facilitator and researcher to record and meet specific needs in a short period of time.

As a participant observer, I function as a part of the classroom in a special way. Students see me as a teacher, but they also see me as someone in whom they can confide. This occurs because of the posture I assume once I am introduced by the lead teacher. While the teachers with whom I work are teaching, I will sit with the students at times or observe from afar at other times. I learn about their social interests, the things that stimulate them, the way they view schooling, and what their family experiences are like through directly asking them questions as we work together. When I observe from afar, my focus is on what I can learn indirectly. I explore behavioural patterns, inconsistencies or consistencies in learning patterns or the nature of their responses, how they react to the tasks they are given, what their conversations are about as they participate in the activities being given by their teacher, and very importantly, how they arrive at their interpretations. As time goes on, my notes help me to formulate a checklist from which to begin to observe even more closely how students are learning based on how they are being taught.

The researcher, utilizing the participatory observation method, can, for example, sit down with the students and the teacher to ascertain how to "read" their speech and action based on the instructions they receive or the tasks they are being asked to perform in the class. A table can then be created with categories such as: "Students' immediate responses to poem," "Teacher's instruction," "Students' verbal responses to instruction," and "Students' kinesthetic response to instruction." These are important to understanding the ways in which the teacher's instruction is being received and understood by students. What types of questions or instructions cause the student to shut down? What points of focus by the teacher seem to stimulate students? Much of this will come from observation, but the observation will not merely be based on the subjectivity of the participant observer. Some of the data analysis might reveal universal patterns related to teaching and learning poetry, and this is fine, but there will also be some culturally-specific information. For example, students might compare the style of a poet being studied (Caribbean or otherwise) to the style of a Jamaican artiste. Instead of seeing a comment about this comparison as being non-intellectual or irrelevant, this comment can be later used by both researcher and teacher to compare the poetic styles of songs by Jamaican artistes to poems utilizing the same set of themes. There are teachers I have worked with that have done this and eventually, we are able to see the student approaching very technical features of the poetry they read with confidence simply because the veil of abstraction associated with the Eurocentric approach to practical criticism of a poem has been removed and replaced with a cultural comparison using an artefact the student already knows and finds interesting.

Additionally, the researcher might overhear the use of current slang, such as the word "sick" (a frequently used word amongst Jamaican youth in 2018) to describe the awesomeness of a poetic technique utilized by a poet, that might be missed by the teacher, but should it be caught by the participant observer, the information could be used to create a new strategy for initiating student responses to poetry. Through conferencing between the teacher and the researcher, the teacher might want to later request adjectives from students based on current mass culture terminology and have the students use these adjectives to begin responding to the poetry to which they are introduced. The descriptors used by the researcher would not simply be based on his/her own set of adjectives and perceptions, but will be based on what the researcher has been taught by the research participants to be verbal and physical signifiers expressing interest, displeasure, boredom, excitement and so on. The more this kind of data collection method is utilized as connected with the observation notes of the participant observer, is the more consistent, authentic and relevant the data will be over time. The teacher also becomes more aware through the process of sharing which occurs between him or herself and the researcher.

Another major benefit of using participatory observation as a decolonizing method in the English classroom is that a Jamaican researcher would usually be competent in both the use of Creole language of the people and the institutionalized English language. A major challenge for the average student in the Jamaican society (particularly those in under-resourced high schools) is the fact that the language of the poem and the stylistic ways in which this language is often used tends to be confusing because Jamaican Creole is more widely used and understood by these students, than is Standard English. Even those who are competent in the use of both languages struggle with particular ways the language is presented in the poem. More significantly however, is the reality that many students will also avoid responding aloud to the questions they are asked because they are unable to use the Standard English language fluently. Pollard (2003), Craig (2006) and Bryan (2010) all speak of the struggles faced by the Caribbean student who is unable to effectively communicate using the target language. Through participatory observation this language barrier begins to fall, because the student does not feel obliged to only express themselves in English because of the relationship they have developed with the participant observer. As Bryan (2010) argues, "[i]n the Caribbean situation, children need to be able to use those higher order skills in their first language, as much as they need to develop the communicative understanding of English "(p. 54). Students showcase very deep levels of reasoning when given the chance to use the language with which they are most comfortable. Participatory observation calls for collaboration and working with the research participants to assess their beliefs and perceptions about themselves and the poems they read. Through it, students critically engage their minds in thought-provoking ways that help to nurture and deepen their skills in the interpretation of poetry.

The value of allowing students to articulate their interpretation of a poem through their own voice is very often overlooked in the English classroom where the use of Creole is often seen as bad English. This stems from the historical situation surrounding the use of Creole and English. Since the onset of slavery, Creole has been stereotypically associated with Western notions of blackness as connected to individuals who are uncivilized and uneducated and English as being the language of superiority, associated with whiteness and wealth. Despite the enlightened views promoting Creole as an authentic language to be proudly owned by its people (Bryan, 2010; Craig 2006; Devonish, 2007), the stereotypical views of it being inferior and subsequently placing its speaker in an inferior category are sadly still existent in Jamaican society today and the English classroom is one of the spaces reflecting these views.

A focus which is solely based on studying poetic form is another colonial-related challenge encountered by the student in the Literature classroom. Such a focus invokes the position of Western thought as central to the understanding or interpretation of the poetic and negates other perspectives and ways of seeing. It privileges Western models and concepts governing the poetic and establishes a traditional pedagogical view of the poem as a kind of master piece that only 'masters' can attempt to understand through a specific European-centred formulaic understanding of the poem's formal features. Such a framework insists for example, on a superficial, dominant focus on form and structure over poetic content, or more preferably over a balance of seeing both working together in order to produce meaning. Such formalist ways of focusing on the poem are highly Eurocentric and have in fact even been denounced by literary critics (Milner and Milner, 2008; Rosenblatt, 1995; Showalter, 2003) from across Europe and America, particularly at the start of the 1960s. Formal elements are important, but students will not only engage with British or American poetry, and so they will need to be taught to appreciate the poetic through various perspectives on form (including African, Indian, Chinese and Caribbean stylistic uses of forms).

Students ought to know the formal elements of a poem but how they learn these elements is crucial and will make the difference between the continued perpetuation of a colonial, elitist way of teaching poetry and a pedagogical construct regarding the teaching of poetry that meaningfully connects the individual with the situation/events, persona and characters, emotions, mood, context and so on in the poem first before attempting to dissect the poem to underline, identify or state the location of the metaphor, simile or use of alliteration. The real experience of poetry is not found merely in discussions regarding the formal aspects of a poem, where students swat literary terminology and robotically participate in acts of defining and identifying literary devices and types of poems. Instead, students need to access different perspectives and different worlds. As Paulo Friere (1973) stated, "... creativity does not develop within an empty formalism, but within the praxis of human beings with each other in the world and with the world" (p. 151). Literature automatically lends itself to deconstructive and decolonizing processes of teaching and learning because of the open-ended nature encouraged through the processes of meaning-making encouraged through the reader's interaction with the text. To subject children in the Literature classroom to an experience as spoken of by Olive Senior in her poem 'Colonial Girls School' that causes them to feel "nothing about [them]selves" (Senior as cited in McWatt & Simmons-McDonald, 2005, p. 20), is to compromise all our forefathers and mothers fought for in securing our freedom and independence.

The challenge of helping students to develop critical awareness and empathy for cultures other than their own can also be addressed through participatory observation. Students will not be able to critically respond to poems from other cultures if they are never given the opportunity to engage with the sociohistorical realities shaping those cultures. It is through an observational moment while seated in a class of twenty-five students from a non-traditional high school that I suddenly realised that the current generation of students are not able to fully grasp the experiences of African-Americans despite the similarities of a historical past rooted in slavery, because of their limited knowledge of their own history and the histories of other countries across the globe. absolutely no knowledge of the history of black America. This severely impedes their ability to connect with and understand the varying levels of meaning present within any given poem from any culture. The advancement of technological systems and the age of globalization have thrown students into an automatic relationship with people and cultures across the globe, but this relationship has been informed chiefly by Western systems which promote one set of perspectives and meanings regarding world patterns and trends. Students need to learn to deconstruct and interrogate what they see by understanding that they can determine for themselves how they see and read everything around them, including the poems to which they will be introduced.

As participant observer, it became my responsibility to help to fill this gap. Through the dialogue I had with both teachers and students, the teacher and I were able to have a deeper understanding of where knowledge gaps were for the students concerning African-American history and its connection with our own Caribbean histories. The teacher constructed a series of lessons utilizing poems that connected with various sociocultural contexts and realities tied to both the African-American and Caribbean experience of slavery and post-emancipation. This was done through YouTube videos, historical site visits, and eventually through the students' own poetic recordings (whether orally or in writing) of their imagined experiences of some of the historical realities experienced in the poems with which they engaged. Two poems that were very popular with the students during these sessions, were Michael G. Smith's 'Mi Cyaan Believe It' and Langston Hughes, 'Dreaming Black Boy'. The "mutual creation of knowledge" (Charmaz, 2000, p. 510) enabled through participatory observation gives room for teacher, students and researcher to critically question and discuss the way particular cultures are represented in the poems they read, through vocabulary, sentence structure, sound devices which might convey an accent or a particular rhythm and of course the situation present in the poem. It is not that teachers lack the ability to do this. The idea is of course that the teacher becomes empowered and stimulated through his/her working relationship with the researcher.

Simultaneously, students need to develop their own responses to both facts and opinions regarding sociocultural and historical realities connected to these cultures. This will develop in students the ability to understand the way many cultures have been shaped by a dominant Western tradition that has oppressed and dismantled many indigenous aspects of different cultures globally. Students are empowered through the act of hearing their own voices as they detail their challenges; they are also stimulated through the dialogue they are having with the participant observer, as such opportunities allow them to arrive at their own conclusions and gradually reveal to them that shaping their responses to a poem is part of a process involving thinking-questioning-listening to others' opinions-reading and rereading-thinking again-reflecting-responding, and so forth, and this is not a one-off event. Through conversations with the participant observer, students are also given the chance to dive further into the poem than when they started interacting with it, because they have heard the opinions of the research-er, the teacher and the other students around them. When it is my turn to teach, the lead teacher assists various individuals or groups of students based on their levels of need or in accordance with their requests. They see me as having more roles than the lead teacher and as time goes on they gradually accept the multiple roles I end up playing in the classroom. I sit with the students, walk around and look in their books, talk with them about their ideas and have the opportunity at the same time to do much of the same with the teacher who offers the instruction and determines how students will engage with the poetry in the lesson.

The Participant Observer and the Teacher

I also spend time with the teacher, discussing what has happened during the lesson and how we might move forward. The teacher is usually comfortable and at ease and speaks with me as he or she would another colleague. Although we exist as colleagues, however, as we move on, the teacher expects me to offer guidance and new methodologies to address some of the gaps he or she might have seen in the lesson. When I teach, the lead teacher is freely encouraged to critique and evaluate the method-ologies I utilize and whether they seem to work. By carefully observing how aspects of poetry are taught and learnt, the teacher and I work together to apply a balanced knowledge of both poetry and poetry pedagogy to the processes of planning and delivering lessons which cater to the individual and collective needs of students. Although this might be criticized by Eu-rocentric standards for its supposed lack of scientific rigor, based on its de-pendence in many ways on the presentation of multiple perspectives which are pulled together by the researcher and framed through the researcher's own structuring of what has been noted, the process is highly systematic because it moves away from a linearity that does not characterize the es-sence of Caribbean culture.

The participatory observation method helps to establish "self-critical communities" (Cohen et al., 2011, p. 348). This stands in contrast to the Eurocentric, authoritative patterns that often frame our classroom spaces based on our colonial past. These communities can be defined as groups that over time, through the nature of their engagement with the research and the levels of participation with both the researcher and the other members of the group, begin to demonstrate higher levels of cognitive processing, where nothing is taken at face-value. Critical questioning occurs consistently and is used to help participants to arrive at decisions regarding whether they can locate specific evidence from the poems they read to support their stance, how they might interpret various sections of the poem based on their levels of investigation on the poet, the word choice, or the situation in the poem. This kind of critical engagement promotes self-confidence, empowers students to express themselves, regardless of their positions, and helps them to see the important role they play in the process of learning. It moves the student away from playing a passive, subservient type of role or on the hand an outlandish rebellious role based on how threatened he or she feels based on the control being wielded around by the teacher. The teacher in turn learns to gradually relinquish his or her control or seat of power and to understand the difference between dictating and guiding. Each of these realities stem from a kind of plantation mentality and experience that is unfortunately often noticeable in many Jamaican classrooms. Participatory observation builds an awareness of the significance of our historical realities and the way they shape what we do as practitioners.

Authentic participation is another key characteristic of participatory research (Cohen et al., 2011). For this process to work effectively, a systematic plan must be put in place and both teacher and participant observer will constantly interact and work together to ensure common understanding and to enable the application of decolonizing frames of pedagogy in the classroom. The interaction between the teacher and the students in the Jamaican English classroom needs to lose the common symbolic feel of *the powerful and the powerless* or of *the figure of authority and the subjected*, if the atmosphere in the Literature classroom is going to represent a space for raising the levels of consciousness of all its participants. The teacher is not to feel as though s/he has lost his/her hold on the process of instruction, rather both the researcher and the teacher (as a participant of the research process) are to work together to develop authentic ways of teaching and authentic ways of participating as the teacher. Through reflexivity and planning sessions, the participant observer collaborates with the teacher participant to ensure that certain pedagogical principles are guiding the teaching and learning experience for both the teacher and the students.

Epistemologies and praxis ought to be meaningfully established to break the tradition of the 'lecture style' stance of the teacher in the Caribbean Literature classroom. It must be pointed out, that a 'lecture style' way of teaching can also occur even with the presence of activities. The focus here is on the dominant style of the teacher and the posture of the students in the classroom. For how long is the teacher speaking? Is the teacher making statements or asking questions? If questions are asked, are they closed-ended or open-ended questions? And to use Fisher's (2005) term, does the style of the teacher "encourage student initiative" (p. 22)? Is the teacher always telling the student about the poem or showing the student how literary devices in the poem work? The answers to these questions will greatly determine whether the teacher is utilizing a 'lecture style' manner of teaching. This way of teaching emerged from the Eurocentric, traditional posture assumed by poetry professors as they sought to find the scientific formulae framing and embedded within the poem. The teaching of English – language and literature- has for over a century occurred in a space in which, Milner and Milner (2008) argue, "[t]eachers passed on to the students their superior understanding of literature or language through lectures, whole-class discussions, drills, written exercises, quizzes, and occasional writing assignments" (p. 4).

Participatory observation as a decolonizing tool helps to demystify poetry and provides the opportunity for real life engagement with poetry in a way that helps students unpack meanings in the poem themselves, to question what is there and to work through words, lines and stanzas overflowing with varied levels of meaning. This can only happen when the teacher begins to break ties with the traditional, colonial image of the teacher as the authoritarian figure who is present to deposit information into empty brains. It is far easier for the teacher to detect his or her teaching habits when someone is observing his or her speech and behavioural patterns during a lesson. There are things we do constantly that we may not even recall or realise that we have done. By working closely and developing a relationship of trust with the participant observer, the teacher becomes much more self-aware and both teacher and researcher become more conscious of the realities impacting the teaching and learning of poetry in the English classroom.

CONCLUSION

The method of participatory observation awakens and refreshes, providing support and strength for both the teacher and the students in the classroom. By the time the participant observer is ready to exit the space, the teacher and students have already moved to a place where they can envision for themselves how they desire to participate in the process of teaching and learning in a way that will be beneficial to them and those in the outside world that they will encounter. Participatory observation moments are therefore to be used as an opportunity to work with the teacher participant and the students, rather than be created for the teacher. It is a research process that bears the mark of everyone involved. It is a co-creative process and thus is owned by and shared with all. It is not singular nor linear; it is multiple and multifaceted.

Participatory observation can be used within qualitative research, through designs such as action research, as part of a larger political act which moves beyond merely identifying and discussing problems for the provision of knowledge to governments and educators in the field, to enabling positive growth and transformation in both the researcher and the participants. It seems at times to be a simple, insignificant method enabling the collection of data, but it is an immensely complex and powerful method that can enable sustainable and extensive transformation in the Jamaican nation, when used effectively. When this occurs, the process of qualitative research exists not to serve 'some interests' but to "move participants towards emancipation and freedom" (Cohen, et al., 2011, p. 244), and ultimately provide them with the opportunities to see themselves and those around them in alternate ways.

REFERENCES

Andrews, R. (1991). *The problem with poetry.* London, England: Open University Press.

Barry, P. (2002). *Beginning theory: An introduction to literary and cultural theory.* Manchester, England: Manchester University Press.

Bryan, B. (2010). *Between two grammars: Research and practice for language learning and teaching in a Creole-speaking environment.* Kingston: Ian Randle.

Bryan, B., & Styles, M. (2014). *Teaching Caribbean poetry.* Oxon, England: Routledge.

Breiner, L. (1998). *An introduction to West Indian poetry.* Cambridge, England: Cambridge University Press.

Charmaz, K. (2000). Grounded theory: Objectivist and constructivist methods. In N. Denzin, & Y. Lincoln, (Eds.), *Handbook of qualitative research* (2nd ed., pp. 509–535). London, England: SAGE.

Cohen, L., Manion, L., & Morrison, K. (Eds). (2011). *Research methods in education.* Oxon, England: Routledge.

Craig, D. (2006). *Teaching language and literacy to Caribbean students: From vernacular to Standard English.* Kingston, Jamaica: Ian Randle.

Darder, A., Baltodano, M., & Torres, R. (Eds). (2009). Introduction to part one. *The critical pedagogy reader* (2nd ed., pp. 1–20). London, England: Routledge.

Dewalt, K., & Dewalt, B. (2011). *Participant observation: A guide for fieldworkers.* Lanham, MA: AttaMira Press.

Donnell, A. (2006). *Twentieth-century Caribbean literature: Critical moments in Anglophone literary history.* London, England: Routledge.

Fisher, R. (2005). *Teaching children to learn.* Cheltenham, England: Nelson Thornes.

Friere, P. (1973). *Education for critical consciousness.* London, England: Continuum.

Lambirth, A. (2014). Case study II: "Not puppets on a string"—Learning to love teaching poetry. In S. Dymoke, M. Barrs, A. Lambirth, & A. Wilson, A., (Eds.). *Making poetry happen: Transforming the poetry classroom* (4th ed., pp. 37–42). London, England: Bloomsbury Academic.

Milner J., & Milner, L. (2008). *Bridging English* (4th ed.). Upper Saddle River, NJ: Pearson Education.

Pollard, V. (2003). *From Jamaican creole to Standard English: A handbook for teachers.* Kingston, Jamaica: The University of the West Indies Press.

Rosenblatt, L. (1995). *Literature as exploration* (5th ed.). New York, NY: The Modern Language Association of America.

Senior, O. (2005). Colonial girls school. In M. McWatt, & H. Simmons-McDonald, (Eds.). *A world of poetry* (p. 20). Essex, NJ: Pearson Education.

Showalter, E. (2003). *Teaching literature.* Oxford: Blackwell Publishing Ltd.

Thiong'o, (1986). *Decolonising the mind: The politics of language in African literature.* London, England: Heinemann.

Zuber-Skerrit, O. (2011). Action research. In L. Cohen, L. Manion, & K. Morrison. (Eds.), *Research methods in education* (p. 345). Oxon, England: Routledge.

PART II

MOVING FROM THEORY TO PRAXIS: APPLICATION OF DECOLONIZING RESEARCH IN THE CARIBBEAN

CHAPTER 4

AN INDUCTIVE META-SYNTHESIS OF QUALITATIVE EDUCATIONAL RESEARCH IN THE ENGLISH SPEAKING CARIBBEAN: 1990–2016

Amanda K. Thomas

This study presents a philosophical and empirically driven investigation of three decades of qualitative educational research produced by the Schools of Education (SOE) across the three campuses of the University of the West Indies from 1990–2016. Meta-integrative considerations are utilized to find connections between the different modalities of qualitative research to generate substantive frameworks of Caribbean educational practice. In framing this study within Boaventura des Sousa Santos's (2012; 2002) sociology of absences and Walter Mignolo's (2011) coloniality systems of knowledge frameworks, I aim to produce a "critical spatial analytic" (Robertson, 2006, p. 2) that introduces a more regional worldview of teaching, learning, and

Decolonizing Qualitative Approaches for and by the Caribbean, pages 65–92
Copyright © 2019 by Information Age Publishing
All rights of reproduction in any form reserved.

education anchored within a contemporary Caribbean epistemology (Santos, 2012).

While the Caribbean has not "lagged behind" in qualitative research (Boxhill, Chambers, & Wint, 1997, p. 49), we must confront the reality that our modes of questioning and even the answers they provide, often continue to be modelled after Western ways of thinking and interpretation (Mignolo, 2011). In order to decolonise Caribbean educational practice, researchers must interrogate the Caribbean landscape using contextually driven methodological approaches, capable of informing a call to action towards educational transformation. The indigenization of qualitative inquiry, data collection and analysis can contribute towards the development of locally driven modes of inquiry and theoretical frameworks that better explain the "contradictions and complexities" (Henry, 2000, p. 62) shaping the institutions and ways of knowing of the Caribbean region and its people.

PHILOSOPHICAL FRAMEWORKS

Within the last two decades there has been an urgent call for decolonial shifts in intellectual focus, to recognize the importance and equality of knowledge produced within diverse geographical contexts. Local theory building begins through the localized epistemological construction of knowledge about the forms of educational transmission found within a local milieu (Santos, 2002). The coloniality systems of knowledge call for an interruption and eventual delinking from exogenously imposed worldviews, to foster emergent and transformational knowledge about local practices to promote relevant forms of representation and engagement (Robertson, 2006).

The logic of the sociology of absence is grounded in the search for what is missing to deconstruct existing forms of knowing and reconstruct alternatives (Santos 2002) capable of initiating shifts in the tide of academic inquiry. The following questions serve as "decolonial epistemic platforms" (Mignolo 2011, p. 189) which inform the modes of inquiry utilized for this chapter:

1. Who is the knowing subject and what is his/her material apparatus of enunciation?
2. What kind of knowledge/understanding is he/she engaged in generating and why?
3. Who is benefitting from, or taking advantage of, this knowledge or understanding?

For the first question, knowing subjects are interpreted as the scholars and researchers, practitioners and policy makers of the region. As knowing subjects, we must recognise that the methods informing knowledge production and are shaped by a geo-political, socio-cultural and epistemic dependency on our academic training (Mignolo, 2011). Our academic training gives us our credentialed backgrounds. Our credentialed backgrounds give us the authority to chart the future direction of regional development. However, these credentials are legitimized by the ranking of our educational institutions and the extent western epistemic privilege is articulated and advanced within these institutions. Our credentials are also legitimized by our ability to carry out historically acceptable forms of educational practice.

The second and third questions call for an interrogation of the forms of knowledge researchers are interested in generating and understanding. The qualitative research paradigm asserts that participants are knowing subjects. Varied interpretations of reality are gathered from participants to represent their known and lived experiences. However, the extent to which this is practiced, and whether the forms of knowing derived from participants are explicitly represented can be questioned. Ultimately qualitative researchers winnow participant data to suit their research questions and areas of interest.

The coloniality systems of knowledge encourage us to shift the ways we use our credentialed backgrounds to pursue educational progress "according to what is realistically best for us" (Mignolo, 2011, p. 132). Subsuming the tools of our training to "decolonized forms of reasoning," allow us to identify as knowing subjects and "decolonial thinkers" (Mignolo 2011, p. 123) who engage in various forms of methodological defiance to produce knowledge that serves the interests of all stakeholders in the education system.

While a variant of each question has been boom dropped[1] at different turning points in the written or verbal work of Stewart (2013; 2016), the late Dennis Brown (2013),[2] and Ramphall (1997), it has not fully resonated into actual practice. This chapter continues along a similar vein, to reclaim some measure of theoretical agency for the education sector in the Caribbean. The SOE journals of the University of the West Indies are targeted because their establishment marked positive steps in the direction of regional de-coloniality.

Mignolo's three decolonial platforms are used to produce analytic possibilities (Santos, 2002) that open up this body of work on education practice to various synthesis options for inductive meta-synthesis. These synthesis options can help envision the forms of practice and pedagogy needed to reclaim some of our inalienable rights to develop innovative solutions to the persistent problems in the education sector. The following research questions guide this study: What can Caribbean qualitative research reveal about Caribbean educational practices? What are the best synthesis options for meta-synthesizing Caribbean qualitative educational research? How can these synthesis options be applied to create a contextually relevant theoretical framework about the system process and outcomes of educational practices in the Caribbean?

METHODOLOGY

Meta-synthesis is an interpretive analytic technique for synthesizing a sample of studies that utilize qualitative designs. The initial procedures of meta-synthesis necessitate thoroughly reading through the findings of each study to understand how the epistemological, ontological and theoretical assumptions influenced qualitative methodology, and methods of data collection and analysis (Petticrew et al., 2013). By integrating evidence from different types of qualitative studies, meta-syntheses is a technique that demonstrates the power of many versus the power of one. Application of this inductive analytic method "sheds light on complexities within a specific discipline" (Petticrew et al., p. 1234)

Meta-synthesis uses a process of interpretive conceptual translation to recognize similar concepts within the results of sampled studies, despite the different words and terms of reference used (Thomas & Harden, 2008) and different reporting formats of qualitative data collection and analysis (Paterson, Thorne, Canam, & Jillings, 2001). The decolonial focus of this chapter compelled me to distinguish the primary research within each study from any perspectives that consciously or unconsciously shaped the ways phenomena were investigated, understood, and explained (Patterson et al., 2001) within this study.

Literature Search, Inclusion, and Exclusion Strategies

Delineation of literature search strategies, inclusion and exclusion criteria is necessary to allow for transparency and replication of decisions that guided the sample selection process. Five educational journals are published by the UWI Schools of Education. The *Journal of Education and Development in the Caribbean* (JEDIC) and the *Caribbean Journal of Education* (CJE) are published by the Mona campus, the *Caribbean Educational Research Journal* (CERJ) is published by the Cave Hill campus, and the St. Augustine campus publishes the *Caribbean Curriculum* and *Caribbean Teaching Scholar* journals.

I contacted journal editors from the Mona and Cave Hill campus and visited the St. Augustine SOE library to retrieve articles for this meta-synthesis.[3] Articles that utilized only qualitative modes of inquiry and designs were targeted as a body of contextually derived knowledge on Caribbean educational practices. Of the 569 articles accessed for review, 437 articles were eliminated as follows: 135 quantitative, 89 theoretical/historical, 53 mixed methods, 46 policy evaluations, 37 comparative studies, 27 literature reviews, 26 articles based on non-Caribbean contexts, 13 personal reflections, four methodological articles and four articles with unclear methodological approaches. Three duplicate articles published in different journals were also eliminated.

The remaining 132 articles that utilized qualitative designs were subjected to a second round of assessment for methodological quality using a partially ordered meta-matrix (Miles, Huberman, & Saldaña, 2014). This matrix was developed within the classifications and attributes function in NVivo 11 and allowed the researcher to condense relevant findings from each study and conduct comparative analysis of study quality to ensure trustworthiness and confidence in the management of such a complex qualitative dataset.

This resulted in the elimination of 8 additional articles without explicit descriptions of qualitative data collection and data analysis strategies. A final sample of 124 studies were available for analysis. Five articles from the CERJ, 18 from the JEDIC, 39 from the CJE, 45 from Caribbean Curriculum and 17 from the Caribbean Teaching Scholar. Figure 4.1 provides a graphic display of the sample selection process. Appendix 1 provides a complete listing of all 124 studies included in the final sample.

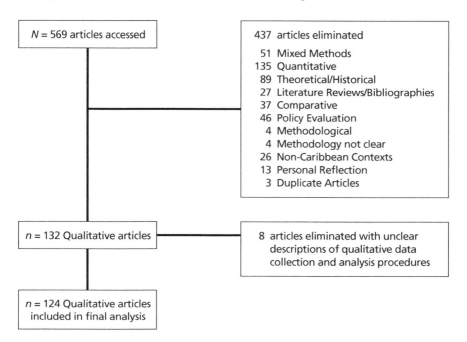

Figure 4.1 Sample selection process for inductive meta-synthesis.

Data Analysis and Synthesis Options

All 124 studies were uploaded into the qualitative data analysis software, NVivo v. 11 (QSR 2015), for coding and analysis. A process of inductive synthesis based on the analytic techniques of grounded theory were utilized (Hossler & Scalese-Love, 1989; Stall, Meadows, & Hyle, 2010). Inductive synthesis uses an emergent constant comparative method to guide the process of extracting information from aggregated results. Synthesis options were pursued based on different configurations of the data arranged in the meta-matrix. An intermediate sample was utilized for each synthesis option.

Although the concept intermediate sample is not present within the corpus of knowledge about qualitative non- probability sampling, I introduce this term within the context of this study to capture instances where the sampling process of this meta-synthesis underwent different arrangements, depending on the synthesis options used for analysis.

Synthesis options analyzed for this study include: chronological time frames, schools, classrooms and curriculum, Science Technology Engineering and Math (STEM) and language and literacy subject areas, the levels of education sequence, and education administration and leadership. Out of concern for theoretical saturation (Creswell, 2013), synthesis options with the largest intermediary samples were analyzed. The "systematically structured table"—Pettigrew et al., (2013, p. 1236)—provided in Table 4.1 presents the different synthesis options pursued, as well as the intermediate samples utilized during the coding process.

A sequential process of open, axial, and selective coding was applied to each synthesis option selected. During the first round of open coding, text segments were analyzed for categories of information or properties that represent multiple perspectives. The axial coding stage reassembled the data in new ways, focusing on "connecting intersecting categories, properties, processes or actions" (Creswell, 2013, p. 193) to integrate open codes into higher level categories (Corbin & Strauss, 2008). The memo and annotation functions were also utilized within NVivo 11 to explore relationships between concepts (Corbin & Strauss, 2008) and to capture the researcher's "internal dialogue" with the data.

During the final stage of selective coding, propositions were developed based on the inter-relationship of categories from the axial coding stage. These propositions were used to form a unified framework (Corbin & Strauss, 2007, p. 107) that represented the overall and underlying dynamics of the synthesis options selected. Member checking was pursued in collaboration with two colleagues proficient in inductive grounded theory analysis and qualitative data analysis in NVivo 11[4] for trustworthiness and reliability of coding and analysis.

TABLE 4.1 Synthesis Options and Intermediate Samples	
Synthesis Options	**Intermediate Samples**
Level of Education	
Early Childhood	5
Elementary	15
Secondary	35
Higher Education	38
Special Education	2
Research Designs	
Narrative	5
Ethnography	6
Case Study	35
Grounded Theory	4
Phenomenology	6
Qualitative Inquiry	54
Action Research	14
Subject Areas	
Business and Management	2
STEM	22
Foreign Languages	5
Literacy and Literature	24
Social Sciences	6
The Arts	3
Teacher Education	22
Education Administration and Leadership	10
Context	
Community	2
School	36
Classroom	71
Home	2
Policy	5

Limitations

Technical reports, published peer reviewed studies from international sources, and completed M.Ed., M.A., M.Phil. theses and doctoral dissertations from the UWI, other Caribbean universities, and non-Caribbean universities are not included in this study. This is significant since these studies constitute a body of untapped research relevant to this chapter.

This inductive meta-synthesis is explicitly grounded in philosophical arguments towards de-linking that typify the coloniality of knowledge and sociology of absences frameworks. Although attempts were made to eliminate theoretical references that shaped findings within texts, it is highly doubtful that this could be entirely achieved. Most meta-synthesized studies collected data within the Jamaican and Trinidadian contexts. As an outcome, the resulting propositions and contextual interpretations lack scholastic contributions from most of the islands that comprise the English speaking Caribbean.

FINDINGS

Framework of Triadic Imbalance

Data analysis within the various synthesis options led to the development of the *Framework of Triadic Imbalance* presented in (Figure 4.2). *Triadic imbalance* is a constant state of tension produced as an outcome of the lived experiences of students, teachers and administrators as they interact with the inconsistencies underlying the school and classroom context, teaching practice and student learning as three vital components within the Caribbean educational environment. Dashed lines are included as a design feature that illustrates varying levels of misalignment between school and classroom contexts, teaching practice and student learning. The theory of triadic imbalance is further explained by ten concepts and 15 grounded propositions. Table 4.2 outlines the 15 grounded propositions generated as a result of inductive data analysis procedures. Single and dual directional arrows illustrate interconnections between concepts and grounded propositions (Glaser, 1967). The discussion that follows offers a description of each proposition of its respective synthesis option to allow for greater understanding of the inductive process that led to the development of the framework of triadic imbalance of the underlying dynamics within the Caribbean educational environment.

Context: Schools and Classrooms

Teachers face persistent contextual challenges within school and classroom environments, including: unavailability of teaching aids, adverse physical conditions, and curricula elusiveness. *Curricula elusivesness* is defined as an inability to conceptualize local breakthrough replacements to curricula content at all levels of the education system. Curricula elusiveness is attributable to several factors. It is based upon consistent pattern of curriculum development without sufficient collaboration and input from

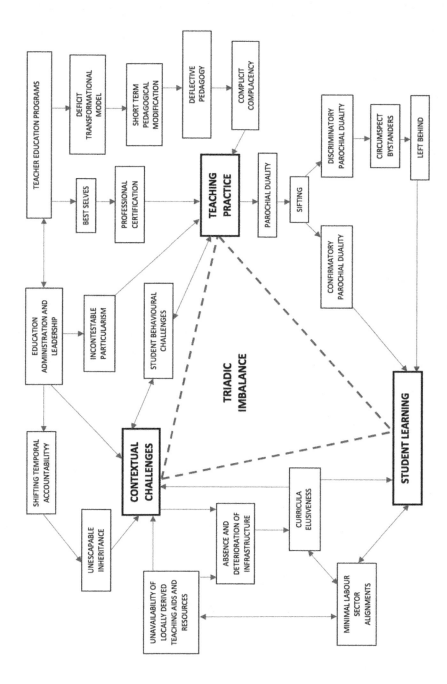

Figure 4.2 Framework of triadic imbalance.

TABLE 4.2   Synthesis Options and Grounded Propositions

Synthesis Options	Grounded Propositions
Context: Schools, Classroom STEM and Language and Literacy	Curricula elusiveness
Teacher education	Best selves, deficit transformational models, deflective pedagogy, complicit complacency
Secondary education	Parochial duality, sifting, confirmatory parochial duality, discriminatory parochial duality, circumspect bystanders, left behind
Higher education	Education for utility
Education administration and leadership	Shifting temporal accountability, incontestable particularism, unescapable inheritance

teachers, parents, the wider community, and students. Teachers frequently alluded to an inherent inflexibility of the syllabus towards creative teaching approaches to achieve intended results for language and literacy, and especially science and mathematics. There is an absence of large scale pedagogical innovation that incorporates locally based materials and supportive modes of social interaction. Additional characteristics of Caribbean curricula elusiveness are demonstrated when teachers are mandated to teach without fully understanding the process used to develop and deliver the curriculum. The full range of skills endorsed by the syllabus was not fully explored because teachers face administrative and societal pressures to teach for standardized tests, resulting in less skills transfer and a devoted focus on narrowing down curricula content.

Teachers and administrators are more likely to denounce the unavailability of much needed resources rather than the fact that most resources are imported. For the most part, teachers demonstrated limited adaptive strategies to cope with contextual challenges and the intensification of student behavioral problems. Another factor contributing to curricula elusiveness is the use and development of curricula with inadequate levels of contextual relevance. The application of a Caribbean aesthetic to curriculum, pedagogy and testing is, for the most part, missing. Most importantly, local curriculum socializes students, teachers and administrators to accept the educational process as presented, and never to reimagine it.

SUBJECT AREAS

Science, Technology, Engineering and Mathematics (STEM)

Curricula elusiveness was especially pronounced within the STEM curricula at all levels, specifically on account of the difficulties teachers faced with the conceptualization and design of the practical components. While teachers possess high levels of content training, their ability to disseminate the cultural nuances that foster indigenous development of STEM disciplines with local applications were limited.

Time constraints and pedagogical practices provided little opportunity for the exploration of student enquiries, especially when they were not related to the topic being discussed. Primacy was attached to getting back to the lesson. Teachers' responses were interpreted as a rejection of inquisitiveness, which is considered to be a desirable attribute for creativity in STEM. Classroom probing and student responses were dependent upon short term memory and the precise replication of textbook content. More attention was paid to structure and replication rather than curiosity, natural inquiry, exploration, and resultant discovery.

Students experienced problems making cognitive connections to STEM content. This contributed towards their partial understanding of and disinclination towards STEM. This facilitated being left behind in the classroom context. Although there is an underlying awareness that success at STEM is connected to students' wider educational achievement, few instructional attempts were made to find linkages between the different curricula, STEM curricula content and the wider environment.

Language and Literacy

Variants of Caribbean creole were presented as an impediment to classroom success. Caribbean creole is held in direct opposition to British grammar, reading and comprehension competencies. It is perceived as undermining, rather than being supportive of, student's ability to develop teachable literacy competencies. Although teachers typically complained about poor literacy and the weak reading skills of their students, most evidence of subject-wide collaboration and interventions to improve oral and writing skills were found at the lower levels of the education system.

This finding is connected to curricula elusiveness, since there is a direct disconnect between the modes of curricula delivery, communication, and expression that Caribbean students have been exposed to over time. During classroom interaction and in their community contexts, literacy is informal, iterative, and expressive. It includes hand talking and engaging in forms of open communication using the sights and sounds that typify their everyday experiences. While the literature and literacy curricula provide regional substantiation by focusing on Caribbean sporting heroes, writers, national festivals, historical figures, forms of expression and cultural orientations; these efforts may have limited impact, as they rarely attach significance to the dynamic challenges of students' everyday experiences.

LEVELS OF EDUCATION

Teacher Education

Although teacher training is integral to the development of a professional identity among student teachers, certification is the predominant value attached to in-service teacher education. In-service teacher training provided teachers with experience in presenting and practicing their *best selves* outside of their actual experience with the contextual and curricula challenges faced in elementary and secondary school environments. This is possible because the tertiary education setting is for the most part removed from these contexts.

Reported best practices within teacher education programs include: reflexive teaching, journaling and groupthink. Reflective teaching emerged as the most successful strategy utilized within teacher education programs to facilitate changes to pedagogical practice. Caribbean reflective teaching practice is defined as a process of historical and personal appraisals of the dominant aspects of teaching practice that leads to greater self-awareness and pedagogical modification.

The strategies learned worked well, allowing teachers to make important adjustments to their practice in the short term. However, most student teachers eventually viewed these strategies as ideal approaches with minimal long- term use or value in Caribbean classrooms. Application in the classroom setting is impeded by time constraints, contextual challenges and student behavioral problems. This pointed to an underlying *deficit transformational model* informing teacher education programs.

The deficit transformational model is based on student teachers' perception that in the long run, training programs are out of touch with the triadic imbalance present within the educational environment. The inherent contradiction observed between teacher training practice and classroom practice is that student teachers exhibit creativity and necessary pedagogical adjustments when confronted with ideal situations for certification. Short-term pedagogical modification is achieved, because teacher in-service training provides possibilities for pedagogical re-imaginings, which allow student teachers to generate a deeper understanding of the personal re-adjustments needed to sustain pedagogical modifications. This may be somewhat contradictory because the ideal situations afforded to student teachers within these programs are rarely afforded to students within the classroom context.

The possibility for longer- term gains from exposure to teacher training is impeded by a *deflective pedagogy*. Deflective pedagogy is teaching that redirects responsibility for sustaining key changes to classroom practice. It is a mode of instruction that allows teachers to minimize deeper consideration about their inability to meet the intended purpose or objectives of teacher education programs for the majority of students. This eventually leads to the development of an ethos of *complicit complacency*—an expectation that it is not feasible to sustain pedagogical modifications because of their experiences with levels of triadic imbalance within classroom and school contexts, teaching practice and student learning.

Higher Education

Consistent references to the need for greater alignment with programs and labor market aspirations are taken as an indicator of increasing levels of student self-advocacy in higher education. Caribbean students at this level agitated for an education system driven by competitiveness and a drive to overcome the challenges imposed by the high demand and scarce supply of jobs within Caribbean economies. Education for utility is a form of educational practice that confronts the limited options for employment and empowerment. Education for utility strategically trains graduates to gain a beneficial advantage upon initial entry into the labor market. It also represents a form of educational practice that enables meaningful professional advancement after graduation.

The main barriers to education for utility are demonstrated in the scant focus on the forms of skill transfer leading to knowledge generation. This stems from lecturers' perceptions, particularly at the undergraduate level, that local knowledge production among undergraduate students is an inconceivable ideal. Topics more aligned with practical needs were not given equal attention and emphasis. Students experienced consistent interfacing with outdated equipment and courses in need of upgrading.

Students acknowledged they were on the receiving end of a pedagogy that valued replication as both process and outcome. Higher education students face the challenge of using information recall as a learning strategy. Although information recall allows students to achieve classroom success at the primary and secondary levels, it becomes more difficult to replicate this model when faced with the increased workload and lower levels of teacher engagement that typify the higher education experience. Students become demoralized because they reject regurgitation of class information as an indicator of skill and competency. Frequent protestations against group assignments and student collaboration indicate the emergence of a new form of self-advocacy and individualized student identity.

Secondary Education

A process of *parochial duality* typified classroom experiences at the secondary level. Parochial duality is a process of student differentiation sustained by specific forms of pedagogical stimuli, norms, values and behaviors in the classroom environment. Parochial duality is reinforced through sifting as a form of teacher directed self-projection and scrutiny used to identity students who are and who are not inclined to accept socially acceptable forms of classroom behavior and models of classroom success. When sifting is activated during teaching practice it divides students into two contrasting groups with different experiences and outcomes within the education system.

Complementary parochial duality is demonstrated in the forms of acceptable behavior that teachers provide as guidelines for classroom success. Students who experience classroom success are more likely to be deferential and possessing of the ability to replicate and reproduce lessons as presented. These students receive various forms of positive feedback as well as psychological, social, and affective reinforcement that build their self-esteem and increase their level of integration into the school system. Students who conform to *confirmatory parochial duality* accept it as a successful pathway to scholastic achievement.

Discriminatory parochial duality is a process of conscious or unconscious sifting of students who are not inclined to accept socially acceptable forms of classroom behavior and models of classroom success. Students subjected to discriminatory parochial duality are more likely to feel alienated and are *left behind.* Left behind is a form of teacher and parent driven neglect for students who exist on the margins of classroom teaching, not as an active participant but as a *circumspect bystander.* Circumspect bystanders are students who are subjected to various levels of discriminatory parochial duality, are often ignored and left to their own devices. The classroom inquiry of students who thrive as a result of confirmatory parochial duality are more likely to be positively channeled and affirmed, while the non-normative class inquiry of circumspect bystanders is discouragingly sifted and rarely explored. Openly displaying this rationalization contributes to the development of students who are unsure of who they are and their purpose within the classroom setting.

Rote memorization is institutionalized at the classroom level by mutually reinforcing forms of student to teacher and teacher to student interaction. Classroom teaching is driven by the students who have accepted confirmatory parochial duality. Classroom success and positive feedback are based upon replicating or reproducing lessons as presented. Students who are at variance with the linear processing of information that typifies rote memorization are made to feel unintelligent, incapable and inept. There is an atmosphere of student protest against a pedagogy and mass educational environment that is non-responsive to their needs. Interpersonal problems occur between students and teachers because of incompatibility between student aspirations and the meanings transmitted via deflective pedagogy, complicit complacency, and discriminatory parochial duality.

Although most students express a desire for educational advancement, this desire is informed by the belief that education should translate into immediate economic returns. Male students are socialized to see themselves as income earners and providers at an early age for economic survival. Male students were also found to be naively at ease with the concomitant low labor market status and the vagaries of an uncertain future. They were also more likely than female students to rationalize that the costs of formal schooling do not outweigh the benefits of early entry into the labor market.

Teacher collaboration was found to be event specific and focused on coping with the challenges encountered in the school and class environment. Instances of collegial camaraderie are pursued primarily for personal support to cope with contextual challenges, and rarely for meaningful forms of student support, inter-subject and inter-class collaboration.

Educational Leadership

Leaders of educational institutions are predominantly male, with high levels of *inconte*stable *particularism* in the way they carry out their administrative functions. Incontestable particularism is defined as an overarching assertion of the rightness of leadership, based upon years of experience and the paying of dues within the education system. Incontestable particularism is focused on maintaining control of classroom and school environments, preference for compliant teacher personalities, and the ways pedagogical skills can be used to improve school performance on assessments and tests.

Shifting temporal accountability typified educational leadership and administration. Shifting temporal accountability repositions liability and the inability to respond to the challenges posed by triadic imbalance within school environments. Evidence of shifting temporal accountability is also displayed through historical attempts to institutionalize changes based upon imported best practices, and the large gaps in implementation and impact that result. References to an *unescapable inheritance* were used to explain the absence of meaningful change as an outcome of the policies and tenure of past administrators. While leaders were aware of strategies to create education for utility by formulating dynamic labor market and education sector alignments for students at all levels, they often vocalize a powerlessness to fully execute these strategies.

Discussion

Over time, significant capital investments and infrastructure have been utilized to expand educational institutions and teacher development programs that give some measure of epistemic privilege to exogenously driven educational practices. While these practices are endorsed as inherently benign, this privilege has produced enduring burdens of disparate and inconsistent outcomes. The 15 grounded propositions which inform the framework of triadic imbalance illustrate and explains the levels of inconsistency and incompatibility that continue to underlie the Caribbean educational landscape. The theory of triadic imbalance speaks to dynamics that activate tensions within school and classroom contexts, teaching practice, and student learning.

While the possibility exists that for some, this Caribbean educational framework may constitute a chaotic model (Stewart, 2016, p.16) it is meant to exist as a philosophically guided analytic tool that initiates dialogue and praxis for educational transformation. The methodological innovation utilized within the data collection and analysis phases is a direct outcome of the application of Mignolo's (2011) coloniality systems of knowledge and dos Santos (2012; 2002) absences frameworks as decolonial platforms. Application of these de-colonial options also enabled findings to attain epistemological connectivity with the original work of Orlando Patterson (1969), Walter Rodney (1974) and Elsa Goveia (1980) which serves to strengthen the explanatory capability of this framework.

Finding complementarity with different qualitative modes of inquiry allowed for greater clarification of the persistent weight(s) of history borne by Caribbean people (Brown, 2002) within the education system. The challenges of triadic imbalance have their genesis in the colonial plantation economy which "did not permit the development of industry and skills for labor market alignments beyond the plantation" (Rodney, 1974, p. 251). Caribbean societies were built upon systems of agricultural exploitation and subsistence, designed to extract maximum surplus value for the benefit of North-Atlantic economies. Epistemologically, the non-normative knowing of most Caribbean peoples was stymied, mystified, and ascribed little or no value. At its core, colonization was a debilitating and asymmetrical process characterized by minimal consideration of the competencies and abilities of the masses of field slaves to pursue local growth and expansion.

The parochial dualities, deflective pedagogy, and complicit complacency propositions demonstrate the distinct lack of awareness of the ways in which educational practices impact on student learning and future outcomes. Formal education through paternalism continues to promote static forms of learning and assimilation (Goveia, 1980). Parallel to this confirmatory parochial duality is reminiscent of the underlying historical character of docility and tractability that colonial subjects were expected to portray in order to survive the plantation. This historical characterization also enabled a small number of ex-slaves to "reap the benefits of instruction by Christian missionaries" (Rodney, 1974, p. 253).

The theory of triadic imbalance exists as a "critical spatial analytic" (Robertson, 2006, p. 2) that points to a Caribbean educational context that continues to promote irrelevant forms of engagement and sporadic evidence of educational inventiveness. This framework helps us to understand why a growing number of our young people join the ranks of the intellectually dispossessed, even after participating in and exiting the education system. These are the students who have never experienced sufficient exploration of their potential and capabilities.

The ability to make "the most rational use of materials and resources" (Patterson & ACLS, 1982, p. 172) that typify indigenous advancements continues to be impeded by curricula elusiveness, shifting temporal accountability and inescapable inheritance. This hinders progression to more utility-driven forms of educational practice. Disparities in the proportion and magnitude of the inductive propositions that underlie triadic imbalance within each institution, warrant termination of the tendency to apply "one size fits all" policies and assessments. Relinquishing tendencies toward incontestable particularism can afford us the freedom to pursue educational practice that "evolves out of the local environment," finds "connectivity with relevance," and "possesses a many sided versatility that maintains close links with the collective material and social life" of the region (Rodney, 1974, p. 239).

IMPLICATIONS AND CONCLUSIONS

Revisiting the discussion of "decolonial epistemic platforms" (Mignolo 2001, p. 189), post-synthesis revealed that the educational enunciation of administrators and teachers is often one of deep-seated opposition to ideas of compatibility between educational progress and Caribbean culture (Goveia, 1980). This is diametrically opposed to the epistemological foundation of Caribbean societies; that colonialism could not prevent Caribbean people from producing the forms of knowledge necessary for survival. Students are often more knowing of the cultural and contextual challenges within their environments. Learning to generate creative returns to escape persistent maldevelopment[5] are the forms of knowing students are interested in generating. When viewed through the rationalization of secondary school students who are left behind, the inability to activate student driven forms of knowing in the classroom context is understandable given the triadic imbalance and accompanying tensions within the education system.

Embarking upon this methodological exercise of de-coloniality makes it imperative to end this chapter by proposing a foundation upon which decolonial education can be pursued to bring balance and vitality to school and classroom contexts, teaching practices, and student learning—as three cornerstones of the Caribbean educational environment. To this end, I turned to the seminal work of (Stewart, 2013; 2016) on Critical and Inclusive Pedagogy (CIP) in the Caribbean context.

CIP is a mode of instruction that challenges "dominant ideologies" and stimulates transformational praxis (Haynes, 2016 p. 2) within the Caribbean secondary (Stewart, 2013) and higher education (Stewart, 2016) sequence. CIP is a pedagogical approach and redemptive strategy that encourages educational practices that "expose the relationship between knowledge and lived experience" (Haynes, 2016, p. 2) to "evaluate who is being included in, and excluded from the learning process when teaching fails to consider the varying social, psychological, physical, and/or emotional needs of students" (Haynes, 2016, p. 2), and the much needed institutional adjustments needed to effect significant change.

The rejection of this highly imbalanced educational environment by "historically marginalized students" (Tuitt, 2016, p. 206) in the Caribbean context is evidence of a critical consciousness (Freire, 1993) deserving of meaningful attention. Inclusive pedagogy can tap into the agency that students activate for survival, and reinforce the desire for dignity that informs individualized student identities. CIP activates pedagogical changes such as truth telling and radical honesty (Williams, 2016) and "creates transformative affirming and equitable learning environments" for all students, teachers, and administrators that allow them to "unlearn normative ideologies of teaching and learning" and "become architects of their own understanding" (Stewart, 2016, p. 18). Introduction of CIP into the education sequence can serve to deflect negative encounters with parochial duality that blocks both teachers and students from experiencing their actualized selves within the educational environment.

CIP is a teaching philosophy that is at once culturally relevant and emancipatory. It places students and teachers at the centre of the environments they occupy, and gives them a personal stake in the process of educational transmission. In the face of the persistent regional perception that inclusive education is a pedagogy for students with physical and cognitive disabilities, CIP exists as a timely yet complementary praxis that promotes greater advocacy for the use of inclusive education practices—to achieve greater reach within student populations and transcend socio-economic, historical, ontological, and epistemological barriers.

Appeals for education for utility cautions us to reposition the relationship between structure and agency (Ramphall, 1997), to uphold the holistic liberation of students and teachers as an end product and not a by-product of educational practice. In the long run the ability to institutionalize suitable corrective policies based upon an amalgamation of CIP with the findings of the triadic imbalance framework is ultimately dependent on the acceptance, interpretation, disregard, or refutation by practitioners and policy makers—which should not be ignored in the face of continuous epistemological agitations for meaningful participation and relevant action for material and collective empowerment.

NOTES

1. Afro-Caribbean slang describing the meaningful effects of a very strong performance on an audience as the artiste leaves the stage after the performance has ended.
2. Dennis A. V. Brown was a Jamaican lecturer at the University of the West Indies, St. Augustine campus from 1992-2014. He taught Development Studies courses at the Department of Behavioral Sciences. This article is dedicated to his memory and the forms of scholarship he tried to encourage in the region.
3. Special thanks to the librarian Dr. Simone Primus and library assistants at the University of the West Indies, St. Augustine campus SOE library who were instrumental in helping to retrieve all the journal articles utilized for this study.
4. Special thanks to Dr. Camille Huggins and Dr. Dylan Kerrigan at the University of the West Indies, St. Augustine campus for their expertise and review of the methodological approaches used.
5. The term *maldevelopment* coined by Samir Amin (1995) was meant to challenge the concept of underdevelopment in the Third World. Underdevelopment infers that specific regions have not achieved acceptable levels of modernization when following western standards. The term maldevelopment is better suited within the context of this study because it details the ways in which countries continue to apply and sustain contextually unsuitable and contradictory forms of growth and expansion.

APPENDIX A: LIST OF JOURNAL ARTICLES PROVIDING SOURCE DATA FOR META-SYNTHESIS

Caribbean Curriculum

Alleyne, S. (1993) Sharing the curriculum conceptions of excellence in secondary education in Trinidad and Tobago. *Caribbean Curriculum, 3*(2), 79–99.

Kuboni, O. (1994). Teachers' treatment of three types of knowledge in the design of primary science materials. *Caribbean Curriculum, 4*(1), 1–12.

Herbert, S. (1999). Urban students' ideas about the heated body. Implications for science education. *Caribbean Curriculum, 7*(1), 1–20.

Seunarinesingh, K. (2002). Managing a paradigm shift in language arts pedagogy. A case study of effective literacy practice. *Caribbean Curriculum, 9,* 47–64.

Worrel, P. (2004). Addressing cultural diversity in a creole space. The SEMP language arts curriculum. *Caribbean Curriculum, 11,* 1–22.

Rampersad, J., & Herbert S. (2005) Reflections of science teachers in an in service teacher education programme. *Caribbean Curriculum, 12,* 1–23.

Osborne, A. (2005) Graded examinations in solo steelpan performance. A Caribbean innovation in music education. *Caribbean Curriculum, 12,* 25–36.

James, C. (2005). Themes and metaphors in the autobiographical narratives of new sector secondary teachers in Trinidad and Tobago. A case study. *Caribbean Curriculum, 12,* 57–87.

Yamin- Ali, J. (2006). Meeting professional language standards in the classroom in Trinidad and Tobago. *Caribbean Curriculum, 13,* 23–44.

Cain, M., E & Hewitt-Bradshaw, I. P. (2006). Team teaching at the primary level. Insights into current practice in Trinidad and Tobago. *Caribbean Curriculum, 13,* 69–90.

Herbert, S., & Rampersad J. (2007). The promotion of thinking in selected lower secondary science classrooms in Trinidad and Tobago: Implications for teacher's education. *Caribbean Curriculum, 14,* 73–101.

James. C. (2007). Impacting struggling adolescent readers. A socio psycholinguistic study of junior secondary students in Trinidad. *Caribbean Curriculum, 14,* 1–30.

Griffith, A., & St. Hill, S. (2008). Addressing social participation as a major goal in social studies: A case study of a fifth form group pursuing the CXC/CSEC social studies programme in a Barbadian School. *Caribbean Curriculum, 15,* 1–23.

Maharaj- Sharma, R. (2008). Using role play to develop science concepts. *Caribbean Curriculum, 15,* 25–43.

Blackman, S. (2009). Learning is hard work and sometimes difficult. What pupils with dyslexia say about the difficulties they experience with learning at secondary school in Barbados. *Caribbean Curriculum, 16*(1), 1–16.

Herbert, S., Rampersad, J., & George, J. (2009). Collaborating to reform science education in context: Issues challenges and benefits. *Caribbean Curriculum, 16*(1), 17–39.

James, C. (2009). Using blogging as a teaching/ learning tool in a postgraduate teacher education programme at the University of the West Indies (UWI): An activity systems analysis. *Caribbean Curriculum, 16*(1), 71–92.

Yamin-Ali, J. (2009). Educational administration as a micro political exercise. *Caribbean Curriculum, 16*(1), 105–129.

Herbert, S. (2009). Secondary science teachers metaphors a case study, part 1. *Caribbean Curriculum, 16*(2), 1–31.

Herbert, S. (2009). Secondary science teachers metaphors a case study, part 2. *Caribbean Curriculum, 16*(2), 33–55.

Maharaj-Sharma, R. (2009). Lower secondary science student's misconceptions of ozone depletion and global warming. *Caribbean Curriculum, 16*(2), 57–71.

Barrow, D., & De Lisle J. (2009). A qualitative evaluation of the lower secondary SEMP science Curriculum of Trinidad and Tobago. *Caribbean Curriculum, 16*(2), 73–97.

Yamin-Ali, J. (2010). Context—The magic of foreign language teaching. *Caribbean Curriculum, 17,* 17–32.

Conrad, D. A., Paul, N. B., Charles, S., & Kirk, F. (2010). Special schools and the search for social justice in Trinidad and Tobago: Perspectives from two marginalized contexts. *Caribbean Curriculum, 17,* 59–84.

Abdul-Majeed, S. (2010). Don't treat me like I'm bad. Social competence and teacher roles in young children's social development at three primary schools in Trinidad. *Caribbean Curriculum, 17,* 85–114.

Maharaj-Sharma, R. (2011). What are student's ideas about the concept of electric current? A primary school perspective. *Caribbean Curriculum, 18,* 69–85.

Barrow, D. (2012). Student's image of the eleven plus: Implications for identity, motivation and education policy. *Caribbean Curriculum, 19,* 1–41.

Hewitt-Bradshaw I. P. (2012). Language issues in mathematics and science. An analysis of examiners reports on students' performance in Caribbean secondary education certificate examinations 2010–2011. *Caribbean Curriculum, 19,* 43–66.

Yamin-Ali, J., & Pooma, D. (2012). Honing a professional identity: The outcome of a teacher education programme. *Caribbean Curriculum, 19,* 67–90.

Ali, D., Augustin, D., Herbert, S., James F., Phillip, S., Rampersad, J., & Yamin Ali, J. (2012). Is anybody listening? Stakeholders perspectives on the in service diploma in education programme at the School of education, The University of the West Indies, St. Augustine Campus. *Caribbean Curriculum, 19,* 173–196.

Conrad, D., Forteau-Jaikaransingh, & Popova, D. (2013). Poetry to rapso: Localized narrative in the Classroom. *Caribbean Curriculum, 20,* 1–29.

Conrad, D. J., & De Four-Babb (2013). Improving teacher education through a self-study of practicum programmes: Conversations and reflections of two teacher educators. *Caribbean Curriculum, 20,* 53–75.

Cain, M., & Abdul-Majied, S. (2013). Teachers views of quality teaching/learning at the infant level in a new primary school. *Caribbean Curriculum, 20,* 161–185.

Harry, S., N., & Smith, T., L. (2013). What de teacher say? Talk as a mode of inquiry in Curriculum enactment in a technical vocational classroom. *Caribbean Curriculum, 21,* 19–45.

Seunarinesingh, K. (2014). Re-visiting writing in spite of teachers issues in teaching writing (Trinidad and Tobago) 20 years later. *Caribbean Curriculum, 22,* 35–66.

Maharaj-Sharma, R. (2014). Teaching integrated science through the use of interactive worksheets. *Caribbean Curriculum, 22,* 85–103.

Lee-Piggott, R. (2014). When teachers lead: An analysis of teacher leadership in one primary school. *Caribbean Curriculum, 22,* 105–132.

Hewitt-Bradshaw, I. (2014). Linguistic landscape as a language earning and literacy resource in Caribbean creole contexts. *Caribbean Curriculum, 22,* 157–173.

James, F. (2014). Leading school improvement through collaboration: An evidence based model. *Caribbean Curriculum, 22,* 175–207.

Dixon, R., & Mayne, H. (2015). Why yuh talking to yuhself? Exploring role identity through conversation analysis: Implications for curriculum and teaching. *Caribbean Curriculum, 23,* 1–22.

Popova, D., Conrad, D., Philip, L, Conrad, D., & Mohammed, A. (2015). Recollections and representations of folk in the classroom: Teacher perspectives. *Caribbean Curriculum, 23,* 49–78.

Figaro-Henry, S., & James, F. (2015). Mobile learning in the 21st century higher education classroom: Readiness, experiences and challenges. *Caribbean Curriculum, 23,* 99–120.

Birbal, R., & Hewitt-Bradshaw, I. (2016). First year university perspectives and experiences of the flipped classroom strategy in a technology course. *Caribbean Curriculum, 24,* 27–51.

Barras, D., Bitu, B., Geoffroy, S, Lochan, S, McLeod, L., & Ali, S. (2016). Social science teachers perceptions of transformatory learnings and the transfer of transformatory learnings from an initial in-service professional development programme at the University of the West Indies Trinidad and Tobago 2013–2014. *Caribbean Curriculum, 24,* 75–99.

Antoine, S., & Ali, S. (2016). Transfer and transitioning: Students experiences in a secondary school in Trinidad and Tobago. *Caribbean Curriculum, 24,* 141–178.

Caribbean Educational Research Journal

Dorian, B., & DeLisle, J. (2010). A qualitative evaluation of some teachers' concerns, and levels of use of the lower secondary SEMP science curriculum of Trinidad and Tobago. *Caribbean Educational Research Journal, 2*(1) 3–16.

Dennis, C., Paul-Fraser, N., Bruce, M., Charles, S., & Felix, K. (2010). Social justice and the education of students with disabilities: Perspectives from two marginalized Contexts. *Caribbean Educational Research Journal, 2*(1), 54–62.

Barrow, D. A., & Kent, N. N. (2015). Strategies teachers use in helping students overcome the eleven- plus barrier: A multi-site case study of high-stakes testing in Belize. *Caribbean Educational Research Journal, 3*(1), 2–17.

Braithwaite, B. (2015). Deaf perspectives on deaf education: An ethnographic study from Trinidad and Tobago. *Caribbean Educational Research Journal, 3*(1), 18–26.

Polius, A. (2015). Developing teacher reflexivity and communities of practice through the incorporation of new literacies in a content area methods course: A case study of student teachers' new literacies experience. *Caribbean Educational Research Journal, 3*(2), 62–75.

Caribbean Journal of Education

Bogle, M. (1997). Constructing literacy. Cultural practices in classroom encounters. *Caribbean Journal of Education, 19*(2), 179–190.

Bailey, B., & Brown, M. (1997) Reengineering the primary curriculum in Jamaica. Improving effectiveness. *Caribbean Journal of Education, 19*(2), 146–160.

Carter, B. (1998). Fostering learner autonomy among mature language learners. *Caribbean Journal of Education, 20*(1), 102–115.

Morris, J. (1999). Women in educational administration. Career choices and career paths. *Caribbean Journal of Education, 21*(1&2), 58–73.

Rampersad, J., & Herbert, S. (1999). Teacher's stories about an in-service teacher education programme: Perceptions of an impact. *Caribbean Journal of Education, 21*(1&2), 85–109.

Ezenne, A., & Cook, L. (2002). Virtual U online teaching and learning in higher education. *Caribbean Journal of Education, 24*(1), 63–73.

McLymont, E. (2002). The cognitive coaching approach: A universal approach to teaching and learning. *Caribbean Journal of Education, 24*(2), 133–149.

Berry, C. (2002). Learning opportunities for all: Teaching in multi-grade and mono-grade classrooms in the Turks and Caicos. *Caribbean Journal of Education, 24*(2), 101–129.

Lambert, C. T., & Down, L. (2003). Towards a profile of the Jamaican literary specialist. *Caribbean Journal of Education, 25*(1), 64–87.

Davis-Morrison, V., & McCallum, D. (2003). Educating for values, attitudes, and character development: Policy and practice in the formal curriculum in social studies and history. *Caribbean Journal of Education, 25*(2), 103–127.

Keller, C., & Mohammed, J. (2003). The qualitative research seminar. Reflections on an approach. *Caribbean Journal of Education, 25*(2), 128–145.

Miller, E. (2005). Partnership for computer assisted instruction in Jamaican Schools. *Caribbean Journal of Education, 26*(1–2), 120–161.

Newman, M. (2005). School leadership and social justice: Four Jamaican high school principals. *Caribbean Journal of Education, 27*(1), 3–18.

Lewis-Smikle, J. (2006). Literacy and learning through literature in the junior years: A prototype project. *Caribbean Journal of Education, 28*(1), 85–109.

Tucker, J., & Osborne, A. (2006) Play yuh Pan. Success challenges and he future of music education in Trinidad. *Caribbean Journal of Education, 28*(2), 126–144.

Johnson, J., & Carpenter, K. (2006). Home school relationships: Bridging educational gaps. *Caribbean Journal of Education, 28*(2), 163-185.

Yusuf-Khalil, Y., & Bailey, B. (2007). Implicit and explicit gender based violence in Caribbean educational institutions. *Caribbean Journal of Education, 29*(1), 65–90.

Clarke, C. (2007). Boys gender identity school work and teachers and parents gender beliefs. *Caribbean Journal of Education, 29*(1), 126–156.

Marguerite-Charles, S. (2007). We want justice! Student perspectives of gender justice in Caribbean schools. *Caribbean Journal of Education, 29*(1), 34–64.

Lee, N. (2008) A recycling and resource Centre for mathematics: Recycle for math's today preserve the environment today for tomorrow. *Caribbean Journal of Education, 30*(1), 136–159.

Francis, K. F. (2008). Writing with a purpose: Improving the writing performance of a group of grade eleven Spanish students at a non- traditional English school in Jamaica. *Caribbean Journal of Education, 30*(2), 295–322.

Stewart, M. (2010). Jamaican Creole alongside standard Jamaican English in the speech of two year olds from Urban Kingston. *Caribbean Journal of Education, 32*(2), 177–201.

Warrican, S. J. (2011). Exemplary principals leading with care. *Caribbean Journal of Education, 33*(1), 1–21.

Burns, S. (2011). Teacher in search of improved practice becomes a teacher researcher. *Caribbean Journal of Education, 33*(1), 22–37.

Down, L. (2011). Beginning teachers as change agents for sustainable development: Exploring the relationship between beginner teachers' concept of change agency and the concept of sustainability. *Caribbean Journal of Education, 33*(1), 40–60.

Collins-Figueroa, M, Down, L, Gentles C H, Newman, M & Davis Morrison, V. (2011). Concepts of professionalism among prospective teachers in Jamaica. *Caribbean Journal of Education, 33*(2), 176–200.

Wilson, L. (2011). Through the window of the doorway: Challenges faced by dance student teachers in developing pupils creativity in dance in Jamaica. *Caribbean Journal of Education, 33*(2), 259–275.

Wynter- Palmer J. (2013). Towards greater human capital development (HCD) policy relevance and coherence in TVET in Jamaica. *Caribbean Journal of Education, 35*(1), 56–92.

Philip, S. (2013). Cracking the poetry code: An exploration of teachers experiences in the classroom. *Caribbean Journal of Education, 35*(2), 147–153.

Reece- Peters, C. (2014). Teachers' self- disclosures: Insights into Mental health. *Caribbean Journal of Education, 36*(1&2), 182–198.

Stage, F & Cook, L (2014). Non- traditional paths to higher education in the Caribbean. *Caribbean Journal of Education, 36*(1&2), 1–18.

Tortello, R & Minott, C. (2015). Make time to play. *Caribbean Journal of Education, 37*(1&2), 77–101.

Walters, K. (2016). Language teacher or service representatives. *Caribbean Journal of Education, 38*(2), 1–17.

Kennedy, M. (2016). Systematicity in the acquisition of determination by three year old Jamaican children. *Caribbean Journal of Education, 38*(2), 18–42.

Jones, C. V. (2016). Planting the write seeds. *Caribbean Journal of Education, 38*(2), 68–96.

Taylor, M. (2007). The experience of teaching and learning in Jamaican creole. A phenomenological account. *Caribbean Journal of Education, 29*(2), 222–242.

Lacoste, V. (2007). Modelling the sounds of standard Jamaican English in a grade 2 classroom. *Caribbean Journal of Education, 29*(2), 290–326.

Maguerite Charles, S. (2007). We want justice! Students' perspectives of gender justice in Caribbean schools. *Caribbean Journal of Education, 29*(1), 34–64.

Yusu-Khalil, Y., & Bailey, B. (2007). Implicit an explicit gender based violence in Caribbean educational institutions. *Caribbean Journal of Education, 29*(1), 65–91.

Clarke, C. C. (2007). Boys gender identity, school work and teachers and parents gender beliefs. *Caribbean Journal of Education, 29*(1),126–160.

Caribbean Teaching Scholar

Brodie Walker, S N A (2012). An examination of the practical learning experiences of first year Clinical Psychology master's level students: A qualitative study. *Caribbean Teaching Scholar, 2*(2), 125–134.

Chase, T A. (2013). The BSc. Management (Marketing) programme at The University of the West Indies, Cave Hill, Barbados: Focusing on student feedback to improve service quality and student satisfaction. *Caribbean Teaching Scholar, 3*(1), 63–79.

McCallum, D. D. (2013). Journal writing as an active learning tool. *Caribbean Teaching Scholar, 3*(1), 23–39.

Worrell, P. (2013). Authenticity and student engagement: Experiences of using my eLearning in a journalism programme. *Caribbean Teaching Scholar, 3*(2), 153–166.

Noel, K V. (2013). Creating a faculty community from a distance. *Caribbean Teaching Scholar, 3*(2), 139–151.

Watson, D. (2013). Re-evaluating focus, forum and frontiers within the academic writing classroom. *Caribbean Teaching Scholar, 3*(2), 121–137.

Hickey, W., D., & Ross, S. (2013). Readiness for active student engagement: Principals' perceptions related to the challenges of hands-on activities in a district of Belize. *Caribbean Teaching Scholar, 3*(2), 111–120.

Bailey, K & Jagnanan, E. (2014). Internet-based technologies in social work education: Experiences, perspectives, and use. *Caribbean Teaching Scholar, 4*(1), 23–37.

Maharaj-Sharma, R. (2014). Student perceptions on physics teaching and its impact on science subject choices in Trinidad and Tobago High Schools. *Caribbean Teaching Scholar, 4*(1), 123–138.

Nathai-Balkissoon, M., & Balkissoon, S. (2014). WebQuest development in the blended classroom: What do students gain? *Caribbean Teaching Scholar, 4*(2), 99–122.

Richardson, A., & Blair, E. (2015). Understanding practical engagement: Perspectives of undergraduate civil engineering students who actively engage with laboratory practicals. *Caribbean Teaching Scholar, 5*(1), 47–59.

Mideros, D. (2015). The social dimension of FL listening comprehension: From theory to practice in higher education. *Caribbean Teaching Scholar, 5*(2), 111–124.

Amina Ibrahim-Ali. (2015). Defying established practice in the EFL classroom: The development of a theoretical framework for teaching and testing periphrastic verbs. *Caribbean Teaching Scholar, 5*(2), 95–109.

Ali, S., Barras, D., Bitu, B., Geofroy, S., Lochan, S., & McLeod, L. (2015). Did they learn anything? Experiences of social sciences teachers on an initial in-service post-graduate teacher education programme, 2013/14, at The School of Education, UWI, St. Augustine Campus, Trinidad and Tobago. *Caribbean Teaching Scholar, 5*(2), 63–78.

Feraria, F. (2016). Engendering curriculum pedagogy for alternative pathways to secondary education in Jamaica. *Caribbean Teaching Scholar, 6,* 81–99.

Roberts, N., & Watson, D. (2016). Re-imagining graduate supervision. *Caribbean Teaching Scholar, 6,* 27–42.

Yamin-Ali, J. (2016). Facilitating factors in programme renewal: Faculty's perspectives. *Caribbean Teaching Scholar, 6,* 43–61.

Journal of Education and Development in the Caribbean

Jennings, Z. (1999). Innovation with hesitation: Distance education in commonwealth Caribbean universities. *Journal of Education and Development in the Caribbean, 3*(2), 115–144.

Evans, H., Brown, M., Davies, R., & Tucker J. (2000). Becoming a teacher educator in Jamaica: Some initial findings. *Journal of Education and Development in the Caribbean, 4*(2) 93–106.

Mackenzie-Briscoe, B. O., & Rainford, M. (2001). Conceptual change in science education. The role of teachers and curricula. *Journal of Education and Development in the Caribbean, 5*(1), 23–32.

Rainford, M. (2002). Assessing Classroom learning in an integrated science classroom; Insights into the practices of a grade 7 teacher. *Journal of Education and Development in the Caribbean, 6*(1&2), 57–81.

Craig, D. R. (2007). Constraints on educational development: The Guyanese case study. *Journal of Education and Development in the Caribbean, 9*(1&2), 3–30.

Smikle, J. L. (2008). In-service teacher's response to a constructivist approach to literacy assessment. *Journal of Education and Development in the Caribbean, 10*(2), 103–120.

Lattibeaudineare, A. (2009). Choosing to remain in the teaching profession. A life history inquiry into three teachers experiences. *Journal of Education and Development in the Caribbean, 11*(1), 163–180.

Grantson, C. (2009). Information Communication technology ICT in Jamaica's primary schools. An examination of teacher's use of ICT in the Primary Education Support Project. *Journal of Education and Development in the Caribbean, 11*(2), 1–19.

Barret, S., & Newman, M. (2009). ICT based learning among adult learners in Non formal programmes: challenges and strategies. *Journal of Education and Development in the Caribbean, 11*(2), 34–59.

Herbert, S & Pierre, P. (2010). Finding culture space in the classroom in Trinidad and Tobago since independence. *Journal of Education and Development in the Caribbean, 12*(2), 70–103.

Nunez, E., Pringle, R., & Showater, K. (2010). The CSEC Biology Syllabus, the CSEC examinations and the teaching of biological evolution in Belize. *Journal of Education and Development in the Caribbean, 12*(2), 27–51.

Shannon-Webster, P., & Lewis-Smikle, J. (2011). Developing character education through children's literature and literature based instructional approaches: portraits from American and Jamaican elementary students. *Journal of Education and Development in the Caribbean, 13*(1&2), 35–53.

Richards, W. (2011). A critical multicultural analysis of Jamaican children's literature. *Journal of Education and Development in the Caribbean, 13*(1&2), 54–83.

Lewis-Fokum, Y. (2011). Examining the discourse behind the grade four literacy test. Evidence from two primary schools in Jamaica. *Journal of Education and Development in the Caribbean, 13*(1&2), 110–132.

Joseph, S., Jackman, M., & Moore, Z. (2012). An investigation into male perspectives of their educational experiences in Trinidad and Tobago. *Journal of Education and Development in the Caribbean, 14*(1), 65–98.

Blackman, S. (2012). Principal's roles in managing assessment curriculum and instruction in mainstream and special education in Barbados. *Journal of Education and Development in the Caribbean, 14*(2), 72–96.

Mitchell, B & Harry, S., N. (2012). The e-connect and learn curriculum change in Trinidad and Tobago. The voice of the teacher. *Journal of Education and Development in the Caribbean, 14*(2), 48–71.

Abdul-Majeed, S., DeLisle, J., Mohammed, R., Gayah-Batchsingh, A., & McMillian-Solomon, S. (2012). A multi-site case study of data driven decision making in early childhood centres of Tobago. *Journal of Education and Development in the Caribbean, 14*(2), 19–47.

REFERENCES

Boxhill, I., Chambers, C., & Wint, E. (1997). *Introduction to social research with applications in the Caribbean.* Kingston, Jamaica: The University of the West Indies Press.

Brown, D. (2013). The use of life narrative and Living Standard Measurement Survey data in the study of poverty in the Caribbean: A resolution of conflicting epistemologies. *Sociology Mind, 3*(3), 223–229.

Brown, D. (2002). *The weights of history. Some recent evidence of chronic poverty in Grenada.* Retrieved from http://www.open.uwi.edu/sites/default/files/bnccde/grenada/conference/papers/BrownD.html

Corbin, J., & Strauss, A. (2008). *Basics of qualitative research: Techniques and procedures for developing grounded theory* (3rd ed.). Los Angeles, CA: SAGE.

Creswell, J. (2013). *Qualitative inquiry and research design choosing among five traditions.* Los Angeles, CA: SAGE.

De Sousa Santos, B. (2002). Towards a Sociology of Absences and a Sociology of Emergence. *Revista Critica De Ciencias Sociais, 63,* 237–280.

De Sousa Santos, B. (2012). Public sphere and epistemologies of the South. *Africa Development, 37*(1), 43–68.

Freire, P. (1993). *Pedagogy of the oppressed.* New York, NY: Continuum.

Glaser, B., & Strauss, A. (1967). *The discovery of grounded theory: Strategies for qualitative research.* Chicago, IL: Aldine.

Goveia, E. (1980). *Slave society in the British Leeward Islands at the end of the eighteenth century* (Caribbean series, 8). Westport, CT: Greenwood Press.

Haynes, C. (2016). Introduction: Critical and inclusive pedagogy: Why the classroom is all it's cracked up to be. In F. Tuitt, C. Haynes, & S. Stewart (Eds.), *Race, equity and the learning environment: The global relevance of critical and inclusive pedagogies in higher education* (pp. 1–6). Sterling, VA: Stylus.

Henry, A. (2001). Looking two ways: Identity, research and praxis in the Caribbean community. In B. Merchant, & A. Willis (Eds.), *Multiple and intersecting identities in qualitative research* (pp. 61–68). Mahwah, NJ: Erlbaum.

Mignolo, W. (2011). *The darker side of western modernity: Global futures, decolonial options, languages, empires, nations.* Durham & London: Duke University Press.

Miles, M. B., Huberman, A. M., & Saldaña, J. (2014). *Qualitative data analysis: A methods sourcebook* (3rd ed.). Los Angeles, CA: SAGE.

Paterson, B., Thorne, S., Canam, C., & Jillings, C. (2001). *Meta-study of qualitative health research: A practical guide to meta-analysis and meta-synthesis.* Thousand Oaks, CA: SAGE.

Patterson, O., & American Council of Learned Societies (ACLS). (1982). *Slavery and social death: A comparative study* (ACLS Humanities E-Book). Cambridge, MA: Harvard University Press.

Patterson, O. (1969). *The sociology of slavery: An analysis of the origins, development, and structure of Negro slave society in Jamaica.* (1st American Ed., Studies in society). Rutherford, NJ: Fairleigh Dickinson University Press.

Petticrew, M., Rehfuess, E., Noyes, J., Higgins, J., Mayhew, A., Pantoja, T., Shemilt, I., & Sowden, A. (2013). Synthesizing evidence on complex interventions: How meta-analytical, qualitative, and mixed-method approaches can contribute. *Journal of Clinical Epidemiology, 66*(11), 1230–1243.

Ramphall, D. (1997). Postmodernism and the re-writing of Caribbean radical development thinking. *Social and Economic Studies, 46*, 1–30.

Robertson, S. L. (2006). Absences and imaginings: The production of knowledge on globalization and education. *Globalization, Societies and Education, 4*(2), 303–318.

Rodney, W. (1974). *How Europe underdeveloped Africa.* Washington, DC: Howard University Press.

Stall-Meadows, C., & Hyle, A. (2010). Procedural methodology for a grounded meta-analysis of qualitative case studies. *International Journal of Consumer Studies, 34*(4), 412–418.

Stewart, S. (2013). *What in de dark must come to light. Extra lessons in post-secondary education in Jamaica.* Unpublished doctoral dissertation. Proquest.

Stewart, S. (2016). Advancing a critical and inclusive praxis. Pedagogical and curriculum innovations for social change in the Caribbean 9–22. In F. Tuitt, C. Haynes, & S. Stewart (Eds.), *Race, equity and the learning environment: The global relevance of critical and inclusive pedagogies in higher education* (pp. 9–22). Sterling, VA: Stylus.

Thomas, J., & Harden, A. (2008). Methods for the thematic synthesis of qualitative research in systematic reviews. *BMC Medical Research Methodology, 8*, 45. http://doi.org/10.1186/1471-2288-8-45

Tuitt, F. (2016). Inclusive pedagogy: Implications for race, equity and higher education in a global context. In F. Tuitt, C. Haynes, & S. Stewart (Eds.), *Race, equity and the learning environment: The global relevance of critical and inclusive pedagogies in higher education* (pp. 205–221). Sterling, VA: Stylus.

Williams, B. (2016). Radical honesty. Truth-telling as pedagogy for working through shame in academic spaces. In F. Tuitt, C. Haynes, & S. Stewart (Eds.), *Race, equity and the learning environment: The global relevance of critical and inclusive pedagogies in higher education* (pp. 71–82). Sterling, VA: Stylus.

CHAPTER 5

UNPACKING EDUCATIONAL POLICY AND PRACTICE IN JAMAICA THROUGH CRITICAL DISCOURSE ANALYSIS

A Theoretical Framework and Methodology

Yewande Lewis-Fokum

What drew me to Critical Discourse Analysis (CDA) was the way in which it provided a lens through which to view and critique how those in authority frame education policy. There are key moments in history when it is important to reflect upon that which is often taken for granted, or on policy changes which appear insignificant and benign but bear significant impact on teaching and learning. Put another way, there are times when "things are changing or going wrong. What is significant about these moments is that they provide opportunities to deconstruct the various ways aspects of practices, particularly language practices ... are often naturalized

Decolonizing Qualitative Approaches for and by the Caribbean, pages 93–113
Copyright © 2019 by Information Age Publishing
All rights of reproduction in any form reserved.

and therefore difficult to notice" (Woodside-Jiron, 2011, p. 157). I am of the view that CDA offers both a theoretical framework and a methodology through which to examine the sometimes taken-for-granted intersections between language, power, and social practices, especially in the realm of education policy and practice. Such research is valuable in postcolonial nations steeped in a history of power imbalance, as inequities still haunt social institutions such as education.

Research investigating the relationship between language and society is not new and has been explored by various methods in the fields of anthropology, linguistics and the social sciences. In this chapter, we will look specifically at Critical Discourse Analysis or CDA, which has been defined as a "contemporary approach to the study of language and discourses in social institutions" (Luke, 1997, p. 1). The CDA qualitative approach attempts to examine language use and social behaviors not as separate effects, but as processes that are intricately related and cannot necessarily be studied as separate processes for investigation (Fairclough, 2001; Foucault, 1999; Gee, 2005; Hall, 2001). In other words, "a central point discourse researchers make is that language is constructive. It is constitutive of social life. Discourse builds objects, worlds, minds and social relations. It doesn't just reflect them" (Wetherell, 2001, p. 16). Language is not a transparent medium that simply reflects behavior, but is itself constructing action in every utterance, whether verbal or written. As we explore CDA, we will describe its disciplinary lineage, identify some criticisms, explain its usefulness as a methodology for studying issues of power in postcolonial nations; describe a sample study conducted in Jamaica; provide a brief discussion of the sample study through a decolonizing lens; and conclude with some key points from the chapter.

BACKGROUND TO CRITICAL DISCOURSE ANALYSIS[1]

It was not until the 1980s/1990s that Critical Discourse Analysis emerged as a full-fledged theory and methodology. Its genealogy is in fact multidisciplinary, having borrowed heavily from linguistics and poststructuralist theories (Luke, 1997; Rogers, 2004). The linguistic work of John Gumperz, William Labov, Michael Halliday and Gunther Kress in the 1970s and 1980s challenged the ideas of Ferdinand de Saussure. Saussure (1985) espoused the view that language form was distinct from language function, and emphasized the structure/system of language (langue) above language-in-use (parole). Wetherell (2001) terms these challenges as the "*social turn in linguistics.*" In a similar vein, there was a concomitant *linguistic turn in the social sciences* in the 1950s (Luke, 1997). Alongside this was the changing paradigm from structuralism (for example, Emile Durkheim) to post-structuralism (for example, Michel Foucault) in the 1970s and 1980s. During this period, the work of Mikhail Bakhtin (1981), with his emphasis on speech genres, and Foucault's (1999) work on power, for example, became more influential within academia in the United States.

Social Turn in Linguistics

With the social turn in linguistics in the 1980s, the relationship between language form and language use was no longer perceived as arbitrary (Saussure, 1985); neither was language merely viewed as a transparent medium. Rather, as demonstrated in the works of Gumperz (2001), for instance, the speaker's form correlated with the social context, hence the decision to code switch between contexts. Halliday's (1978) work demonstrated how speakers made utterances with different purposes in mind—ideational, interpersonal or textual. Within the field of critical linguistics, Kress (2001), among others, went on to suggest that variations in power also determined language use. Here the work of Foucault was also influential as he brought to the fore the idea that institutional discourse carried with it the power to effect change, mainly by constricting behavior (Hall, 2001; Foucault, 1999). From a methodological perspective, this social turn in linguistics in the late 1970s/80s propelled new forms of investigating language such as conversation analysis and later CDA. No longer was the unit of analysis only language bits (whether the phoneme, syllable, or clause) but included utterances above that, the discourse (essay, newspaper article, speech).

Linguistic Turn in the Social Sciences

As early as the 1960s there was what Luke (1997) describes as the "linguistic turn in the social sciences." Similarly, Paget Henry (2000), an Afro-Caribbean researcher, explains that with the linguistic turn in the social sciences, "language . . . emerged as a distinct domain of human self-formation, with distinctly linguistic explanations of human behavior that . . . fundamentally altered the relations between language and the established disciplines" (p. 234). Meanwhile, the continued educational underachievement of ethnic minorities and lower socioeconomic groups in the United States had stirred research interest in the educational opportunities of different groups within the population (Ogbu, 1981). Debates within sociolinguistics and the ethnography of communication over the educational inequalities of minorities and lower socioeconomic groups had emerged in part as a result of these troubling issues. Moreover, developments in the civil rights movement in the US in the 1950s/60s created a "heightened awareness of the critical role of education, and very importantly, language and literacy education, for improving the quality of life of the vernacular-speaking masses" both in the United States and overseas (Craig, 1999, p. 12). Strong interest in dialects grew in the 1970s and 1980s in the United States, the Caribbean, as well as in other postcolonial nations (Craig, 2014; Labov, 1969; Myers-Scotton, 1993).

Changing Educational Environment in the 1970s and 1980s

Many of the educational research studies during the 1970s and 1980s used discourse analysis of face-to-face conversations within the microcosm of the classroom to address the questions of underachievement (Cazden, 2001). While these studies provided detailed descriptions of language-in-use in the classrooms and supplanted cognitive psychologists' "deficit" model hypothesis (Bernstein, 1972) for explaining student performance, they failed to take into account the larger social variables that contributed to such low academic performance (Foley, 1991; Ogbu, 1981). Large-scale migration from developing countries to the United States in the 1960s meant an influx of heterogeneous students from different countries, speaking different languages within the educational institutions of the United States (Luke, 1997). Bilingual education soon became a prominent field of study. By the time the millennium rolled around, educators were also faced with media texts (Fairclough, 1995); hybrid cultural identities (Holland, Lachiotte, Skinner, & Cain, 2000); changing structures of work and economy based on demands of the information age (The New London Group, 1996); as well as higher expectations for literacy (Brandt, 2001; Crystal, 1995).

As the 1980s approached, the context was therefore ripe for the development of Critical Discourse Analysis. CDA assumed that the challenges in education could be examined through careful review of language, discourse, and texts: "Educational institutions could be seen as complex sites constructed by and through discourses expressed in various texts—from policy statements and textbooks to face-to-face talk in classrooms" (Luke, 1997, p. 4). CDA also insisted on the connection between the microcosm of the classroom/local contexts and the larger macro-social structures:

> The outstanding task for Critical Discourse Analysis, then, is to provide detailed analysis of cultural voices and texts in local educational sites, while attempting to theoretically and empirically connect these with an understanding of power and ideology in broader social formations and configurations. (Luke, 1997, p. 5)

Critical Discourse Analysis, however, is still new to the Caribbean. Certainly, in the area of linguistics, there has been research using conversation analysis. Two that come to mind are Shields-Brodber's (1998) examination of the female voice on radio talk-show programmes in Jamaica, and Walters's (2016) investigation of how customer service representatives respond to speakers of Jamaican Creole (JC) and Jamaican English (JE). Devonish's (1986) work on bilingual language rights has been important in contesting certain colonial ideologies about language. Critical pedagogy has also been discussed to some extent by Bryan (2010) in her work on teaching English in a Creole-speaking environment in relation to the role of the teacher. In her discussion, Bryan (2010) speaks about "the location of the teacher in the early formation of post-Emancipation societies and the sense in which the country's development was linked to the belief in education's emancipatory power i.e., its potential for effecting change in society" (p. 155). In more recent times, the works of Waller (2006a, 2006b & 2009) and Lewis-Fokum (2017, 2011) have explicitly applied the theoretical and methodological framework of CDA to investigate social problems in Jamaica. Waller's work examined the role of discourse within the information & communication technology (ICT) industry, while Lewis-Fokum's work explored discourses behind the changed administration of the Grade Four Literacy Test (G4LT) and its impact on schools. Nevertheless, to date the use of CDA to investigate issues within education is limited, and therefore many opportunities exist to use this methodology in the Caribbean.

CRITICISMS OF CRITICAL DISCOURSE ANALYSIS

As with any other area of study, Critical Discourse Analysis has both its share of supporters and critics (Breeze, 2011). Some of the criticisms of CDA include its lack of objectivity, inadequate rigor, imbalance between social theory and linguistic method, and the extraction of discourse from its social context (Rogers, 2004, p.14). Rather than allowing the evidence to be revealed from the data analysis, critics claim that critical discourse analysts project their biases onto the data. This is because, as Tyrwhitt-Drake (1999) argues, critical discourse analysts are more committed to their "dogma" regarding political and societal change. Toolan (1997) suggests that there is also a lack of standardization in its methods, and that the more robust descriptions stem from linguistic and discourse analysis within CDA rather than its more impressionistic elements, such as hybridity. Toolan (1997) adds, "too often, an elaborate theoretical and interpretive superstructure is built upon the frailest of text-linguistic foundations" (p. 93). Perhaps the most severe critique of CDA, however, is what some authors suggest is its arrogance in claiming to change society by uncovering social injustices (Tyrwhitt-Drake, 1999).

To the contrary, Rogers (2004) describes CDA as rigorous, but mentions that each analyst adopts his or her own approach to the study at hand. Thus there is CDA as interpreted by Gee, Fairclough or Kress (Rogers, 2011, pp. 11–14). Like any other qualitative study, researchers include triangulation and member checking to enhance the trustworthiness of the data analysis. Gee's (2005) measures of validity add another layer of rigour. Knowledge of CDA's multidisciplinary genealogy, as outlined earlier, should also help analysts realize that no one discipline, even CDA, can provide the solution to the many research challenges of society. Solutions to "wicked problems" are seldom understood or alleviated in a sustainable manner by one method or way (Van Meter, Blair, Swift, Colvin, & Just, 2012). Indeed, one of the legacies of post-structuralism is the idea that multiple interpretations exist (Glesne, 2006). As such, Wells (1986) states that:

> The evidence is never so complete or so unambiguous as to rule out alternative interpretations. The important criteria in judging the worth of a story are: does it fit the facts as I have observed them and does it provide a helpful basis for future action? (p. xiii)

CDA WITHIN A POSTCOLONIAL LENS

Perhaps these very "weaknesses" of CDA, if explored from a postcolonial lens, might actually be strengths. If postcolonial theory is defined as a "conceptual reorientation towards the perspectives of knowledge, as well as needs, developed outside the west... [about] developing the driving ideas of a political practice morally committed to transforming conditions of exploitation and poverty" (Young, 2003, p. 6), then CDA is an appropriate methodological tool that can offer much within postcolonial thought. After all CDA aims to do these very things, that is, to deconstruct knowledge and assumptions that have been taken for granted, and which therefore have the potential to sustain status quos that may disempower rather than empower various groups of people. Yet, to claim that CDA in and of itself as a research method can lead to complete change or provide the solution to many of the "wicked problems" that continue to exist within postcolonial societies would be misleading.

CDA can help to unmask unequal power structures by investigating the intricate relationship between language and society. This can lead to a type of mental emancipation. However, I contend that, especially within postcolonial civilizations, change must also involve reconstruction. It is not sufficient to deconstruct assumptions, it is also important to appreciate how persons survive and thrive within and in spite of the status quo. This brings to mind the work of Holland, Lachiotte, Skinner and Cain (2000) in examining the tensions between individual agency and socio-historical determinism. Interestingly too, one of the emerging trends in CDA has been positive discourse analysis (PDA). Rogers and Wetzel (2013) describe PDA as, "not a new approach but a shift in analytic focus" (p. 62). For example, in a study conducted by Moses and Kelly (2017), they "utilized both positive and critical discourse analysis lenses to provide research that not only deconstructs power but also identifies positive ways in which students make room for themselves within academic settings" (p. 393). Martin (2004) best sums it up by saying that through positive discourse analysis we have the potential of "uncovering the past and designing the future" (p. 12).

It is this "uncovering the past and designing the future" that most intrigues me. From a postcolonial theoretical framework, CDA can be used as a methodological tool to help uncover the past through investigations of how colonial language was used and still shapes society and how society in turn shapes language and thought. The analytical shift towards positive elements within discourse or ways of being, doing and knowing can also help researchers to understand how persons thrive in spite of oppressive systems. However, that would be only one step in the process of change. Many of the challenges in postcolonial societies are deep-rooted and complex, and there is rarely one fool-proof solution. Therefore, despite our finite knowledge, and our wrestling with ambiguities when solving these "wicked problems," we can design possibilities. Even if we adopt a decolonizing discourse, we must also create, through participatory action-research, indigenous interventions that are beneficial and sustainable for generations to come (Craig, 1980; Friere, 2000; Paris, 2011). Is it possible then, to think of another shift within the analytical focus of CDA, that is, of decolonizing discourses and design methods, to add a dimension of action-research by educators?

Usefulness of CDA to Postcolonial Caribbean Contexts

As a theoretical and methodological framework, CDA is useful in understanding the relationship between language and society in postcolonial nations; specifically, explorations of power and how it is used to create, constrict and control our lives. Take for example, Jamaica, which was a British colony from 1655 to 1962, a period of 307 years. During the period of slavery, 1655 to 1834, when the Africans were considered property (chattel) and not humans, no education was provided for the slaves, and power was exerted through discourse and by brutal force. After Emancipation in 1834, when the Africans were rebranded as humans (as opposed to property), education was provided based on the model of education for the poor British masses (Drayton, 1990a, 1990b). The children of the ex-slaves received elementary education through the all-age schools, which ended at grade nine and was not always the best quality (Evans, 2009). A higher standard of education was available for the wealthy whites and brown privileged classes at both elementary and secondary schools. These secondary schools were better equipped, and would later be called traditional high schools.

As a result of this colonial history, therefore, Jamaica has inherited an education system that is marked by inequity. This inequity is evident in terms of a lack of access to good quality secondary schools (though that has changed significantly), and in the quality of education provided among the different categories of elementary and secondary schools. In terms of access, as indicated, Jamaica has improved tremendously, as at the elementary level there is almost universal enrollment (PREAL & CaPRI, 2012, p. 8). More students from public elementary schools also have greater access to better quality high schools which are better resourced (Evans, 2009). In terms of quality, however, improvement has been steady but slower. For example, on the national elementary school leaving exam, the Grade Six Achievement Test, students from private fee paying elementary schools consistently outperform students from most public elementary schools (PREAL & CaPRI, 2012, p. 11). The same is true for the Grade Four Literacy Test (Lewis-Fokum & Colvin, 2017). This trend is similar at the high school level, where traditional high schools consistently outrank many non-traditional schools on Caribbean Secondary Examination Certificate (CSEC) exams administered by the Caribbean Examinations Council (CXC) (Spencer-Ernandez, 2011). In light of these nagging issues of inequity in Jamaica's education system, Critical Discourse Analysis, therefore, provides a useful framework to unearth, deconstruct, and query how power is used through institutional discourse to improve or retard equity within the education system.

Caribbean educators and linguists have certainly done solid work to explore, document and problematize how education, and the English language, were used as instruments of socialization during the post-Emancipation and colonial periods. Turner (1987), writing about education in Jamaica between 1867–1911, states that:

> Like the British government, the Jamaican government recognized that social stability required not only indoctrination in values such as order, regularity of work and industriousness, but also acceptance by the different social classes of their ascribed statuses and roles. This it was believed, could also be achieved through schooling. (p. 61)

While these values are useful, the unfortunate intent was for the children to return to the plantations to work, rather than to create their own enterprises. Moreover, could the "acceptance [of] the different social classes" explain why it is so difficult to improve the quality of many non-traditional schools? Not surprisingly, it must be noted that children from low-income households largely attend these non-traditional secondary schools.

More specifically, the language of English was described as the "most important agent of civilization" (Drayton, 1990b, p. 200). There was a de facto language policy in which English was superior to all languages, including the other European languages in the colony, the African languages that the ex-slaves brought with them, and the Creole that was birthed out of the brutal contact among the languages on the plantations (Bryan, 2004; Drayton, 1990a & 1990b). While for decades there was the assumption that English was morally and intellectually superior to Creole, many linguists have taken this to task including Craig (2014), and Devonish (1986). While Devonish has advocated for bilingual language rights in Jamaica, others like Bryan (2010) and Pollard (1998) have wrestled with the challenge of teaching literacy in English (the official language) to predominantly Creole-speaking children within the framework of transitional bilingualism as advocated in the draft Language Education Policy (MOE, 2001).

With all the challenges of inequity that still haunt our postcolonial education system in terms of school types and English literacy differences, CDA can therefore be a helpful methodological tool to help deconstruct long-held oppressive assumptions. With a positive lens, one can also look for "good practices" in which students, teachers and schools thrive, despite the socio-historical odds against them. If one then adds action-oriented constructive interventions to a CDA research study, new options can be created—such as designing new possibilities and new discourses for ways of knowing, and enacting behaviors within education that empower students, teachers, and schools. In this way, I contend, CDA can be even more emancipatory.

SAMPLE STUDY: HOW CRITICAL DISCOURSE ANALYSIS IS USED IN THIS STUDY

The sample study I use to show how Critical Discourse Analysis can be employed in examining issues of language, power and educational policy transformation was based upon a study I conducted in Jamaica between 2009 and 2010. In this study, *Literacy in elementary school in Jamaica: The case of the Grade Four Literacy Test*, I documented the events surrounding the change to the administration of the Grade Four Literacy Test in Jamaica from a classroom-based assessment to a high-stakes test (Lewis, 2010). I was motivated to research this educational change because of the influence of two factors:

- A research paper written by Woodside-Jiron (2011), who traced the changes made to the reading policy in the state of California between 1995 and 1997. Woodside-Jiron (2011) used CDA as her methodology and examined policy documents, newspaper and magazine articles, as well as audio/video clips from radio and television presentations by key figures in education and research, in order to investigate how consensus was crafted to effect significant changes in the way reading was taught in California.

- The growing trend towards an accountability-by-testing agenda, which gained momentum in the early 2000s. I was curious to see the extent to which teachers and the public would resist or accept the changed administration of the G4LT, and how the new high-stakes test would impact on the behavior of teachers and students at the classroom level.

As with Woodside-Jiron's (2011) study, I wanted to find out how consensus was crafted from the policy-making institutional level of government right down to the day-to-day situational conduct of the classroom. Out of these interests I designed the following overarching research question: *How did the Grade Four Literacy Test, which was once a classroom-based assessment for a decade, become a national high-stakes exam in 2009?* This stem question was then broken down into three sub-questions, of which I will focus on two:

1. How did the discourse about the Grade Four Literacy Test change between 1999 and 2009 in specific government documents and in the print media?
2. What did schools, and particularly teachers, do to prepare students who failed the nationalized Grade Four Literacy Test in June 2009 and had to retake the test in December 2009?

THREE MAJOR CONSIDERATIONS WHEN CARRYING OUT YOUR CDA RESEARCH

There are three major steps that I would recommend when conducting Critical Discourse Analysis research: (a) choose which CDA approach is a good fit for your research study, (b) decide which data sources will provide information to answer your research questions, and (c) plan your data collection and analysis with consistency as the key element.

Getting a Good Fit: Selecting an Appropriate CDA Approach

One of the first steps is to select the approach to CDA that is most appropriate for what you want to investigate. In the case of the G4LT study

(Lewis, 2010), a blend of CDA from James Paul Gee and Norman Fairclough seemed like a good fit for what I wanted to study. While Fairclough, a British linguist, is explicit in his focus on class based struggles; Gee, an American linguist, is much more focused on how language gets used to perform certain activities and identities. Both CDA theorists, however, focus on issues of power. Fairclough's (2001) three-tiered approach to his analysis involving *description, interpretation,* and *explanation* was useful in answering the first research sub-question. In terms of *description,* Fairclough focuses on language form—analyzing how vocabulary, grammar and textual structures are used to cement an idea, for example, in a policy document. When ideas become naturalized, through discourse at the situation, institution and society levels, *orders of discourse* become common sense assumptions or ideologies. In turn, these ideologies either sustain existing social orders or create new orders of discourse. Fairclough's general *interpretation* is that there is always a struggle between the elite and the masses, with the former desiring to hold onto the prevailing orders of discourse on the one hand, and the masses either conceding or resisting those discourses on the other hand. To summarize then, an analyst using Fairclough's CDA will describe the textual cues at the descriptive level, attempt to interpret the assumptions behind the text/discourse, and then explain the effects, social determinants and ideologies of the particular orders of discourse under investigation.

As I also wanted to understand the impact of the changed G4LT at the classroom level, Gee's (2005) version of CDA, especially his work related to activities and identities, seemed a good fit. From Gee's perspective, discourse is about recognizing certain ways of being, doing and knowing as indexed by a particular pattern of activities or identity. For example, a new set of activities become established when, as a result of the changed administration of the G4LT to a high-stakes test, teachers and students start doing practice tests on a regular basis. Or, take for instance; the new *identities* cast upon schools dependent on what percentage of their students have mastered the G4LT. To explore this research focus on 'new identities', the research would then explore the data under a combination of questions from Gee's seven building tasks: significance, activities, identities, relationships, politics (distribution of social goods), connections, and sign systems and knowledge.

To extend this research from a postcolonial lens, I would need to include primary or secondary literature on education in the postcolonial era; and by combining critical and positive discourse analysis, I would also be able to highlight positive instances of agency. Thereafter, I would have to determine the extent to which the research project would be emancipatory. In the following two sections, I will share how I could have extended the original research to include a greater focus on decolonizing discourse and design.

Getting Data at the Three Different Levels

Based on the research questions, I was interested in retrieving data from government documents, the media, and from schools. Fairclough's three-tiered framework of the different context levels (situation, institution and society), and his three-part analysis (description, interpretation, and explanation) helped me to conceptualize and organize the data sources for the study.

As a methodological approach, CDA allows for flexibility in that it can be married with other methods. Since I not only wanted to examine text materials (policy documents and newspaper articles), but also the effects of the new high-stakes G4LT on schools, I used a case study approach as well. Waller (2006b) describes the case study as an "examination of halted reality...It allows snapshots of moments in an ongoing process...which the researcher interprets with the aim of explaining the phenomenon under investigation" (p. 15). By gathering multiple sources of data from government documents, newspaper articles, classroom observations of literacy teaching, and interviews from school staff and students, the researcher can add to the rigour of the research via triangulation. In other words, each data point within the contexts of the societal, institutional and situation level is a layer of data that can either strengthen a particular interpretation or refute it. Even within the context of the situation, multiple sources of data collected within the classroom, (for example, via interviews and observations), help the researcher to triangulate the data. These layers of data add to the depth of the qualitative study.

If I were to extend this research from a postcolonial lens, I would also focus on the quality of teaching and learning occurring at each school. Although teaching and learning were highlighted in the original study, much more work needs to be done to examine the following areas: the discourse of how instructional time is used, interrupted, and how much learning really takes place with such malleable timetables; the group of students who, although they passed the G4LT, were reading below the grade five level; and the set of students who consistently failed the minimum competency G4LT on multiple sittings and were later transferred to Alternative Secondary Transitional Education Programme (ASTEP) schools. Combining CDA with a micro-ethnographic methodology would help to uncover ineffective practices; highlight instances of agency; and help to build the basis of information necessary for a contextually-relevant and participatory action-research with a greater emancipatory/transformational impact.

Organization, Consistency and Asking Further Questions

There are multiple types of discourse data that can be collected in a CDA study. In the G4LT study, three types of discourse data were collected:

written texts, oral texts from audiotaped interviews, and behaviors or ways of doing things. In other studies, visuals can also be collected. How does one analyze all of this data? One of the first steps is to reduce the data into manageable portions. Having collected 262 newspaper articles and selected four government documents, my first job was to sort them in terms of date and relevance. While I read all the articles and government documents, I only analyzed those newspaper articles or sections of the government documents which were highly relevant according to the research focus. Thereafter, I described each type of discourse data in a recursive yet consistent way.

For the four government documents, I used for example, Fairclough's intertextuality as a CDA construct, to trace how bilingual education was spoken about or not spoken about in the portions of the document related to discussions about literacy, especially at the grade four level. Or, take for example, the classroom observation data. I wrote detailed observation notes of how the teacher taught and how the students responded during a literacy lesson. After this, I created a table with the following headings worded as questions based on Gee's (2005) building tasks: *What are the sub-activities that make up these schemata? Assuming the G4LT is a social good, how is it made relevant here in this classroom lesson?* I would then use the observation notes to fill in the related portion of the table. These are examples of analysis at the descriptive level. I would then interpret what I had described based on the research questions. After completing the description and interpreting the different types of discourse data, I then tried to explain these based on the CDA theoretical framework and the research literature.

From a postcolonial lens, there are further questions I would have asked in the analysis. For example: Are there intertextual links between this particular contemporary government document and another document from the colonial era, or from the research literature, about colonial education? In what ways are new sponsoring relationships similar or different from colonial relations of the past? What are the complexities that are included, simplified or overlooked within this government document? What has this document achieved in terms of reform despite its oversimplification of the problem? What could be the intended and unintended effects of this policy? In what ways are students, teachers and schools thriving in spite of inequities within the education system? With the help of the participants, what types of interventions could be crafted to bring forth sustainable change?

REFLECTIONS ON CDA AS A DECOLONIZING APPROACH TO RESEARCH

Globally, and certainly within postcolonial contexts, social justice issues plague our societies and are worth studying as a means of providing sustainable solutions. I present three arguments for applying CDA as a de-colonizing approach within the education arena. Incorporated throughout the discussions are themes related to the work of deconstructing negative colonial assumptions, the importance of highlighting agency, and the idea of designing more emancipatory action research.

Improving Social Justice

As previously mentioned, Jamaica has inherited a bifurcated education system from its colonial heritage. The implication of this is that education becomes a social justice issue as some students, due to their social class positions, experience a better quality of education than others. Certainly, literacy in Jamaica, with the assumption that it is the ability to read and write in English, is a key social justice issue—especially given the thorny relationship between Jamaican Creole and Jamaican English. Using CDA allowed me to trace how the discourse about bilingual education became silenced over time in successive government documents. In the Literacy Improvement Initiative of 1999, there was discussion about how to teach literacy in English given the language situation where two languages, JC and JE, compete for space. By the time the Competence-based Transition (CBT) policy came into effect in 2008, there was no discussion of such language issues. This latter document focused on the change in administration of the G4LT from a classroom-based assessment to a high-stakes test, the need to identify students who were struggling, and the formation of the ASTEP. While on paper ASTEP was to be a clear-cut solution to help improve literacy levels, what it also showed was how our education system—particularly our literacy teaching—was biased against JC speaking boys from poor working-class backgrounds, who made up the majority of ASTEP[2] students (Davis, 2004; Lewis-Fokum & Colvin, 2017; Thaffe, 2011).

Having selected an issue, the researcher also has to decide if he/she will frame the study as more prescriptive/emancipatory, or descriptive. Waller (2006b) describes this distinction as the difference between a normative and a critical approach:

> The former is an attempt to understand the configurations of a discourse operating within standard status-quo space. The latter is specific to deconstructing hegemonic relations of power in and over discourse and how this undermines social justice and may be considered anti-status quo, challenging the status-quo so to speak. (p. 8)

The design and scope of the G4LT study was not emancipatory, but descriptive. If a literacy intervention was conducted during or after the exploratory CDA research, then one could have described the study as emancipatory. For example, if I had returned and discussed my recommendations to the principals and we were to design an intervention to meet the context of the school, this would have been emancipatory. The aim of this intervention would be to move beyond test-preparation to help both teachers and students reimagine themselves as developing bilinguals with the capacity to speak, read and write in JE for a variety of purposes beyond the walls of the school, while affirming their JC mother tongue.

Equalizing Power in Society

CDA studies should be critical, that is, they should examine issues of power in society. One definition of power is *having the authority to get things done*, or as Fairclough (2001) puts it, "power in discourse is to do with powerful participants controlling and constraining the contributions of non-powerful participants" (pp. 38–39).

On the one hand, I find Fairclough's definition useful, especially in his three-tiered elaboration of how the powerful constrain the powerless in terms of contents, social relations and the subject positions people can occupy. For example, in relation to the G4LT study I could have asked the following questions: How does the discourse of the education ministry regarding the G4LT constrain the activities of schools and teachers preparing students to take the literacy test? What subject positions are constructed for students and schools as a result of the discourse about the new administration of the G4LT?

On the other hand, I find Fairclough's (2001) perspectives on power somewhat deterministic. Fairclough does mention that "power is won, held and lost in social struggles" (p. 61). However, this perspective is usually overshadowed by his greater emphasis on the powerful capitalist classes overpowering those on the margins of society (p. 26–30). Within the G4LT study I chose to explore multiple facets of power such as the following: how power, as evidenced by discourse, circulates and permeates all levels of society; how bureaucratic power can constrain others, but also be productive in terms of creativity and individual response (Foucault, 1999). This reflects more of the positive discourse slant currently emerging (Moses & Kelly, 2017). Hence, the focus of the study was more about the ways in which individuals and institutions exist within powerful discourse models, and less about how one group oppresses another. This is not to diminish, however, the significant ways in which powerful bureaucracies constrain the behaviors of those with less power.

Indeed, Gee (2008) asserts that "nobody looks at the world other than through lenses supplied by language or some other symbol system" and that "we are all both 'beneficiaries' and 'victims' of ideology" (p. 29). In other words, ideology sums up the ideas we use to make sense of the world; and these assumptions can both constrain and liberate us. Power also takes the form of sponsorship, that is, agents who "enable, support, teach, and model, as well as recruit, regulate, suppress, or withhold, literacy—and gain advantage by it in some way" (Brandt, 2001, p. 19). For instance, the Ministry of Education has the authority to change the Grade Four Literacy Test. Academics have the authority to make contributions to the construction of literacy policies. Funding agencies, especially international donors with valuable foreign currency, have the authority to shape literacy projects. Other literacy sponsors, such as UNESCO, have the global power to set the agenda for literacy worldwide. And finally, at least within the scope of this study, power manifests itself through linguistic/cultural capital (Bourdieu, 1977), or what Gee (2005) has identified as one aspect of the work of discourse, that is, pattern recognition. In other words, "people engage in such work [pattern recognition] when they try to make visible to others (and to themselves, as well) who they are and what they are doing" (p.29). Based on their retaking and passing of the G4LT, the students I observed were therefore trying, with the support of their teachers, to be recognized as literate. Yet, Gee warns us that who we are and what we are, "are creations in history and change in history"—meaning that we are also, at least, partial products of our social and historical circumstances (p. 41).

Reinforcing Identity

If a researcher wants to investigate themes of identity, then CDA should be considered. One of the first decisions to be made is to figure out what aspect of identity will be addressed in the study. Gee (2000, 2005), for instance, focuses on the ways in which language is used to enact certain social activities and social identities. Fairclough (2001) examines identity from the perspective of subject position, that is, the social roles that individuals occupy in relation to different discoursal types (Fairclough, 2001, p. 31). As such, in the G4LT sample study the following questions could be posed: What are the subject positions constructed for students and teachers within the discourse of government documents and the media in relation to the G4LT? Another dimension of "subject position" is the way in which "subject" can be defined: either as "someone who is under the jurisdiction of a political authority, and hence passive and shaped," or as the "subject of a sentence," in which case the individual displays agency and action (Fairclough, 2001, p. 32). From this perspective then, individuals do have some level of agency in changing their subject positions, although this is limited by social structures.

CONCLUSION

Quoting from Paris (2011), "research is always part me-search as well" (p. 20). So, in this paper I have tried to share my own wrestling with the complexities of improving/transforming our education system. I have identified two major problems—the vast differences in quality of education provided, and the challenge of teaching English effectively to a large Creole-speaking student population. In the original G4LT study, CDA allowed me to examine and critique the link between policy and classroom/school practice in the changed administration of the G4LT test. A decolonizing focus would have allowed me to make explicit the intertextual link between the current bifurcated education system and old colonial assumptions.

By incorporating critical and positive discourse analyses, one is further able to highlight how individuals and groups are controlled by, and yet create ways to resist and thrive in spite of the status quo. This is not to say that we should tolerate the systems which undermine our development. Rather, despite our finite capacity, we have the power to imagine different future possibilities. By combining critical and positive discourse analysis within a postcolonial lens, we can begin to design a future that is indigenous, participatory, and sustainable.

NOTE

1. This chapter on Critical Discourse Analysis is based on a study conducted by the author for her doctoral dissertation entitled Literacy in elementary school in Jamaica: The case of the Grade Four Literacy Test (2010).
2. ASTEP no longer exists. Currently, there is an Alternative Pathways to Secondary Education (APSE) program.

REFERENCES

Bakhtin, M. (1981). *The dialogic imagination: Four essays.* Austin: University of Texas Press.

Bernstein, B. (1972). A sociolinguistic approach to socialization with some reference to educability. In J. Gumperz, & D. Hymes, *Directions in sociolinguistics: The ethnography of communication* (pp. 465–497). New York, NY: Holt, Rinehart & Winston.

Bourdieu, P. (1977). *Reproduction in eduaiton, society and culture.* London, England: SAGE.

Brandt, D. (2001). *Literacy in American lives.* Cambridge: Cambridge University Press.

Breeze, R. (2011). Critical discourse analysis and its critics. *International Pragmatics Association, 21*(4), 493–525.

Bryan, B. (2004). Reconciling contradictions and moving for change: Towards a language education policy for Jamaica. In M. Brown, & C. Lambert, *Transforming the educational landscape through curriculum changes* (pp. 163–187). Kingston, Jamaica: IOE.

Bryan, B. (2010). *Between two grammars: Research and practice for language learning and teaching in a Creole-speaking environment.* Kingston, Jamaica: Ian Randle.

Cazden, C. B. (2001). *Classroom discourse: The language of teaching and learning.* Portsmouth, NH: Heinemann.

Craig, D. (1980). Langauge, society and education in the West Indies. *Caribbean Journal of Education, 7*(1), 1–17.

Craig, D. (1999). *Teaching language and literacy: Policies and procedures for vernacular situations.* Georgetown, Guyana: Education and Development Services.

Craig, D. (2014). Bidialectal education: Creole and Standard in the West Indies. In J. Allsopp, & Z. Jennings, *Language education in the Caribbean: Selected articles by Dennis Craig* (pp. 37–80). Kingston, Jamaica: UWI Press.

Crystal, D. (1995). *The Cambridge encyclopedia of the English language.* Cambridge: Cambridge University Press.

Davis, R. (2004). *Task force on educational reform: Jamaica–A transformed education system.* Kingston, Jamaica: Ministry of Education.

Devonish, H. (1986). *Language and liberation: Creole language politics in the Caribbean.* London, England: Karia Press.

Drayton, K. (1990a). Politics of textbooks: School books and the making of the colonial mind. *First Biennial Inter-campus Conference on Education.* Kingston: UWI, Cave Hill.

Drayton, K. (1990b). 'The most important agent of civilization': Teaching English in the West Indies, 1838–1986. In J. Britton, R. E. Shafer, & K. Watson, *Teaching and learning English worldwide* (pp. 200–225). Clevedon, London: Multilingual Matters.

Evans, H. (2009). *Six Jamaican educators.* Kingston, Jamaica: Arawak Publications.

Fairclough, N. (1995). *Media discourse.* London, England: Hodder Arnold.

Fairclough, N. (2001). *Language and power.* London, England: Longman.

Foley, D. (1991). Reconsidering anthropological explanations of ethnic school failure. *Anthropology & Education Quarterly, 22*(1), 60–86.

Foucault, M. (1999). The incitement to discourse. In A. Jaworski, & N. Coupland, *The Discourse Reader* (pp. 514–522). London, England: Routledge.

Friere, P. (2000). *Pedagogy of the oppressed.* New York, NY: Continuum.

Gee, J. P. (2000). Identity as an analytic lens for research in education. *Review of Research in Education, 25,* 99–125.

Gee, J. P. (2005). *An introduction to discourse analysis: Theory and method.* New York, NY: Routledge.

Gee, J. P. (2008). *Social linguistics and literacies.* New York, NY: Routledge.

Glesne, C. (2006). *Becoming qualitative researchers: An introduction.* Boston, MD: Pearson Education.

Gumperz, J. (2001). Interethnic communication. In M. Wetherell, S. Taylor, & S. J. Yates, *Discourse theory and practice: A reader* (pp. 138–149). London, England: SAGE.

Hall, S. (2001). Foucault: Power, knowledge and discourse. In M. Wetherell, S. Taylor, & S. J. Yates, *Discourse theory and practice* (pp. 72–81). London, England: SAGE.

Halliday, M. A. (1978). *Language as social semiotic: The social interpretaion of language and meaning.* Baltimore, MD: University Park Press.

Henry, P. (2000). *Caliban's reason: Introducing Afro-Caribbean philosophy.* New York, NY: Routledge.

Holland, D., Lachiotte, W., Skinner, D., & Cain, C. (2001). *Identity and agency in cultural worlds.* Cambridge, MA: Harvard University Press.

Kress, G. (2001). From Saussure to critical sociolinguistics: The turn towards a social view of language. In M. Wetherell, S. Taylor, & S. J. Yates, *Discourse theory and practice: A reader* (pp. 29–38). London, England: SAGE publications.

Labov, W. (1969). *The study of nonstandard English.* Champaign, IL: National Council of Teachers of English.

Lewis, Y. (2010). *Literacy in elementary school in Jamaica: The case of the Grade Four Literacy Test.* University of Iowa, Iowa: Unpublished Doctoral Disssertation.

Lewis-Fokum, Y. (2011). Examining the 'Discourse' behind the Grade Four Literacy Test: Evidence from two primary schools in Jamaica. *Journal of Education and Development in the Caribbean, 13*(1&2), 110–132.

Lewis-Fokum, Y., & Colvin, C. (2017). Tracing the Discourses of accountability and equity: The case of the Grade Four Literacy Test in Jamaica. *Changing English: Studies in Culture and Education, 24*(1), 11–23.

Luke, A. (1997). *International encyclopedia of sociology of education.* Oxford, England: Pergamon Press.

Martin, J. R. (2004). Positive discourse analysis: Solidarity and change. *Revista Canaria de Estudios Ingleses, 49,* 179–202.

MOE. (2001). *Language Education Policy draft.* Kingston, Jamaica: Ministry of Education, Youth & Culture. Retrieved from http://dlpalmer.weebly.com/uploads/3/5/8/7/3587856/language_education_policy.pdf

Moses, L., & Kelly, L. B. (2017). The development of positive literate identities among emerging bilingual and monolingual first graders. *Journal of Literacy Research, 49*(3), 393–423.

Myers-Scotton. (1993). *Social motivations for codeswitching: Evidence from Africa.* Oxford, England: Clarendon Press.

Ogbu, J. U. (1981). School ethnography: A multilevel approach. *Anthropology & Education Quarterly, 12*(1), 3–29.

Paris, D. (2011). Thoughts on langauge, literacy and culturally sustaining pedagogy in Jamaican and U.S. contexts. *Journal of Education and Development in the Caribbean, 13*(1&2), 19–34.

Pollard, V. (1998). Code switching and code mixing: Language in the Jamaican classroom. *Caribbean Journal of Education, 20*(1), 9–20.

PREAL & CaPRI. (2012). *Prisms of possibility: A report card on education in Jamaica.* Retrieved from http://archive.thedialogue.org/PublicationFiles/JamaicaRCPREALshortversion.pdf

Rogers, R. (2004). *An introduction to Critical Discourse Analysis in education.* Mahwah, NJ: Erlbaum.

Rogers, R. (2011). *An introduction to Critical Discourse Analysis in education* (2nd ed.). New York, NY: Taylor & Francis.

Rogers, R., & Wetzel, M. M. (2013). Studying agency in literacy teacher education: A layered approach to positive discourse analysis. *Critical inquiry into language studies, 10*(1), 62–92.

Saussure, F. d. (1985). The linguistic sign. In R. E. Ennis, *Semiotics: An introductory anthology* (pp. 24–46). Bloomington: Indiana University Press.

Shields-Brodber, K. (1998). Hens can crow too: The female voice of authority on air in Jamaica. In P. Christie, B. Lalla, V. Pollard, & L. D. Carrington, *Studies in Caribbean Language II* (pp. 187–203). Port of Spain, Trinidad: The Multemedia Production Centre.

Spencer-Ernandez, J. (2011). Transitioning from GSAT to CSEC: A longitudinal study on the impact of literacy development of students in Jamaican primary school on their performance in CSEC English A. *Journal of Education and Development in the Caribbean, 13*(1&2), 133–161.

Thaffe, N. (2011, October 12). ASTEP being overrun by boys–report. *The Gleaner.* Retrieved from http://jamaica-gleaner.com/gleaner/20111012/lead/lead93.html

The New London Group. (1996). A pedagogy of multiliteracies: Designing social futures. *Harvard Educational Review, 66*(1), 60–93.

Toolan, M. (1997). What is critical discourse analysis and why are people saying such terrible things about it? *Language & Literature, 6*(2), 83–103.

Turner, T. A. (1987). The socialisation intent in colonial Jamaican education 1867–1911. In R. H. King, *Education in the Caribbean: HIstorical pespectives* (pp. 54–87). Kingston, Jamaica: Faculty of Education, UWI.

Tyrwhitt-Drake, H. (1999). Resisting the discourse of critical discourse analysis: Re-opening a Hong Kong case study. *Journal of Pragmatics, 31*(8), 1081–1088.

Van Meter, K., Blair, E., Swift, A., Colvin, C., & Just, C. (2012). An introduction to sustainability service-learning course for the creation of sustainable citizens to engage wicked problems. *Journal of Service-Learning in Higher Education, 1,* 30–49.

Waller, L. (2006a). *ICTs for whose development? A critical analysis of the discourses surrounding an ICT for Development Initiative for a group of microenterprise entrepreneurs operating in the Jamaican tourist industry.* University of Waikato, New Zealand: Unpublished Doctoral Dissertation.

Waller, L. (2006b). Introducing Fairclough's Critical Discourse Analysis methodology for analyzing Caribbean social problems: Going beyond systems, resources, social action, social practices and forces of structure or lack thereof as units of analysis. *Journal of Diplomatic Language, 3*(1), 21–45.

Waller, L. (2009). *The role of discourse in ICT for development: Lessons from Jamaica.* . Berlin, Germany: VDM Verlag Dr. Muller.

Walters, K. (2016). Language teacher or service representative?: The corrective conversational practices of customer service representatives in Jamaica's public entities. *Caribbean Journal of Education, 38*(2).

Wells, G. (1986). *The meaning makers: Children learning languages and using language to learn.* Portsmouth, New Hampshire: Heinemann.

Wetherell, M. (2001). Themes in discourse research: The case of Diana. In M. Wtherell, S. Taylor, & S. J. Yates, *Discourse theory and practice: A reader* (pp. 14–28). London, England: SAGE.

Woodside-Jiron, H. (2011). Language, power, and participation: Using critical discourse analysis to make sense of public policy. In R. Rogers, *An introduction to Critical Discourse Analysis* (pp. 154–182). New York, NY: Routledge.

Young, R. J. (2003). *Postcolonialism: A very short introduction.* Oxford, England: Oxford Press.

CHAPTER 6

A MISSING PART OF THE WHOLE

Poor Performance in Mathematics in the Caribbean: Lessons from a Qualitative, Microgenetic, Decolonizing Study on Fraction Learning

Lois George

In 2013 I was a young, glassy-eyed researcher from the island of Dominica (different from the Dominican Republic) ready to embark on my first major piece of empirical research. Through this research I hoped to contribute knowledge to the learning and teaching of mathematics that would ultimately result in improving students' performance in one aspect of the Number strand in the primary school curriculum. My intentions were very ambitious—I saw myself as a trailblazer, hoping to harness the power of research to revolutionise the teaching and learning of mathematics in Dominica and the Caribbean region.

In the Caribbean, poor student performance in mathematics at the primary and secondary levels of education has been an issue of major concern

Decolonizing Qualitative Approaches for and by the Caribbean, pages 115–137

TABLE 6.1 Percentage of Students Working at or Above Grade 2 and 4 in Number Concepts and Computation From 2000–2012 in Dominica

Year	At/above grade level	
	Grade 2	Grade 2
2000	24.18	NA
2001	23.76	NA
2002	29.84	34.29
2003	33.31	37.46
2004	31.18	36.48
2005	31.62	41.74
2006	33.33	43.54
2007	37.13	48.25
2008	30.53	35.25
2009	29.42	40.1
2010	32.45	34.3
2011	41.18	NA
2012	42.48	NA

Note: NA = Data not available.
Source: Ministry of Education and Human Resource Development, 2011.

for some time. Pass rates in annual national or regional assessments do not generally exceed 60% (Caribbean Development Bank, 2016). This is exemplified in the data from Dominica presented in Table 6.1, which show the percentage of students working at or above Grades two and four in the "number concepts and computation" section of the Grades two and four National Assessments from 2000–2012.

An inspection of the data reveals that well over 50% of Dominican students, from as early as Grade two, show a pattern of unsatisfactory performance in this key foundational strand in the mathematics curriculum. Table 6.2 shows a similar pattern of mathematics performance across the Caribbean region, displaying the percentage of candidates receiving a passing grade (Grades I, II, III) in the May/June offering of the Caribbean Secondary Education Certificate (CSEC) mathematics examinations, administered by the Caribbean Examinations Council (CXC) from 2006–2016. Table 6.2 shows that over the ten-year period, the average percentage pass rate is 40.48%.

The subject of mathematics has pride of place within the school curriculum. It remains a compulsory subject up to the secondary school level of education; and within the school timetable it is afforded the most time, along with English Language. Additionally, it is widely accepted that knowledge of mathematics is fundamental to educational and economic success

TABLE 6.2 Percentage Pass in CSEC May/June Mathematics Examinations From 2006–2016

Year	Total # of candidates sitting exam	% of candidates receiving grades			
		I	II	III	Total
2016	85,017	11.62	11.31	21.38	44.31
2015	85,042	14.81	17.2	24.84	56.85
2014	91,089	10.16	13.95	25.60	49.71
2013	94,187	6.04	9.49	19.59	35.12
2012	NA	NA	NA	NA	34.00
2011	89,977	6.92	9.71	18.53	35.16
2010	88,373	7.95	11.8	21.29	41.04
2009	83,129	7.8	11.42	20.06	39.28
2008	80,421	7.76	11.71	21.27	40.74
2007	79,769	5.57	9.02	18.97	33.56
2006	78,697	6.00	9.43	20.08	35.51

Note: NA = Data not available
Source: Caribbean Examinations Council, 2006–2016.

in contemporary society (Siegler et al., 2012). Consistent with this assertion, the mathematics syllabus of the Caribbean Examinations Council (2015), the main body administering external examinations within the Caribbean region states:

> Mathematics promotes intellectual development, is utilitarian, and applicable to all disciplines. Additionally, its aesthetics and epistemological approaches provide solutions fit for any purpose. Therefore, Mathematics is the essential tool to empower people with the knowledge, competencies and attitudes which are precursors for this dynamic world. (p. 1)

Since scores of students perform poorly in mathematics, however, it stands to reason that very few students are able to harness its power. One consequence of this is that many students may actually be disempowered from a psychological, vocational and utilitarian perspective, since limited knowledge of mathematics has in effect closed the doors of learning and vocational opportunities to them (Claessens & Engel, 2013; Siegler et al., 2012). While data from the Caribbean related to the socioeconomic and racial portrait of poor performance in mathematics is not available, empirical research such as the work of Secada, Fennema, Adajian, and Byrd (1995) has found that mathematics has a wider "gap" across socio-economic and racial lines than any other academic subject. In any other facet of society, the terms *educational injustice* or *social injustice*, would apply; but the discipline of mathematics presents an interesting case, where many have come to accept, consciously or otherwise, that perhaps mathematics is a subject only accessible to a privileged few. The latter notion, however, has been disputed by a number of scholars (for example, Boaler, 2015; Devlin, 2000) who assert that all people are capable of learning mathematics.

MATHEMATICS EDUCATION RESEARCH IN THE CARIBBEAN

While the issue of poor performance in mathematics is unsatisfactory, it has proven difficult to address. One of the main aims of research within the Social Sciences, under which education is subsumed, is to provide insights into problematic issues and to propose possible solutions for addressing these issues. A search for research work centred on mathematics education in the Caribbean, from 2007 to 2017, revealed that there are very few empirical research studies. As far as I could find, it appears that within this timeframe there were less than 20 studies published, with most adopting a quantitative or mixed methods research design. These studies focused on the use of technology to improve mathematics achievement (Kalloo & Mohan, 2011; Warner, 2009; Wintz, 2009), gender and school differences (Bailey, 2008), and the impact of teacher expectations on student performance (P. George, 2013). Of the studies reviewed, one study adopted a qualitative approach (Junor Clarke, 2007) and focused on the experiences and perceptions of teachers as they investigated the incorporation of computer technology in their mathematics teaching.

From the literature I examined, it appears that while some research has been conducted in mathematics education, the field seems to be in a fragmented, embryonic phase. Furthermore, I found it is interesting that while students are a major stakeholder group in the learning/teaching process, alongside Ministries of Education, teachers, parents, employers and industries, their voices articulating – how they see themselves as learners of mathematics, how they learn mathematical concepts/topics and the extent to which mathematics is meaningful to them, – within the mathematics education research discourse in the Caribbean are noticeably silent.

In my view, this mirrors a form of marginalisation, similar to the failure to recognise indigenous belief systems and knowledge when studying indigenous peoples (Smith, 1999), or the denial of access, participation, and power to research projects which directly impact some groups, such as disabled people (Goodley & Runswick-Cole, 2012). It is on this premise that the notion of decolonising research methods that deconstruct power and privilege to a few, to benefit knowledge, communities and participants, becomes applicable to the domain of mathematics education research, an area in which it has rarely been applied before. In this chapter, I adopt the description of "decolonisation" put forward by Goodley and Runswick-Cole (2012). They explicate that in their attempts to listen to children, they use decolonizing approaches to research that subvert traditional researcher-led, top-down models which have denied marginalized groups access, participation and power to research ventures; and "work with the complex and expert knowledge of these groups, as necessary resources for the generation of theories and practices" (p. 215).

Taking into account the dearth of qualitative research in the Caribbean, the potential of mathematics to empower learners, and students' long-standing, unsatisfactory mathematics performance, I posit that the domain of mathematics education can benefit from adopting decolonising, qualitative research approaches that prioritise the perspective of the learner of mathematics. Consistent with this, Williams (2014) suggests that in order to achieve the goal of improving mathematics education, there is a need to "focus on the act of learning as we study other aspects of . . . instruction" (p. 8), which include the curriculum, a supportive learning environment, a cohesive educational infrastructure and skilled teaching. It is against this backdrop, that this chapter examines how using a qualitative research strategy, I employed an exploratory, microgenetic research design (L. George, 2017) to gain significant insights into children's understanding of a key topic area in the mathematics curriculum—fractions. Based on this examination, I discuss three main lessons learned from conducting this type of research and possible future directions for research in mathematics education in the Caribbean.

BACKGROUND TO THE STUDY

The Microgenetic Research Design

Understanding how individuals learn and grow in their knowledge of different mathematical content is central to helping students improve their understanding of this content and assisting teachers to facilitate learning. Notwithstanding this, observing and analysing the changes which occur during the learning process is difficult, because this includes describing children's thinking at junctures within the learning process, as well as explaining *how* and *why* the changes take place (Luwel, Siegler, & Verschaffel, 2008). The microgenetic research design evolved from the need to address the aforementioned difficulty and the recognition by researchers of the inadequacy of existing research designs such as longitudinal, cross-sectional, and teaching experiments, which only "provide a snapshot of the events surrounding change, without describing the process itself" (Flynn, Pine, & Lewis, 2006, p. 152).

Three characteristics which define the microgenetic approach include:

(a) Observations span the entire period from the beginning of the change to the time at which it reaches a relatively stable state. (b) The density of observations is high relative to the rate of change of the phenomenon. (c) Observed behaviour is subjected to intensive trial-by-trial analysis, with the goal of inferring the processes that give rise to both quantitative and qualitative aspects of change. (Siegler & Crowley, 1991, p. 606)

When this approach is adopted, a learner engages in similar tasks over a relatively short time period. This quickens the process of change, resulting in highly frequent observations of a learner's verbalisations and actions and the increased likelihood that the change is captured by a researcher while it is occurring. Typically, a learner's engagement with tasks is unguided, which means that there is no explicit teaching of the concepts/procedures being observed.

This highly concentrated examination of the learning process has several advantages and disadvantages. One strength is that changes in reasoning/approaches/strategies can become visible very near to when they occur which allows for the understanding of the change process and the discovery of natural development and learning trajectories (Resing, Bakker, Pronk, & Elliott, 2017). In addition, this allows "for differentiating between substantive conceptual change and the existence of multiple conceptions" (Brock & Taber, 2017, p. 47). By contrast, the collection and analysis of the rich data resulting from these observations are time- and effort-consuming. This is due to the high density of observations and demands associated with the fine-grained analysis of data that are essential for capturing change over a period of transition and the specific nature of transition phases (Flynn et al., 2006). Consequently, a small number of participants, sessions, or both, typify microgenetic studies (Siegler, 2006).

The microgenetic approach has been applied to many content domains and age groups, for example, construction-analogy (Resing, Bakker, Pronk, & Elliott, 2016), analogical reasoning (Siegler & Svetina, 2002), cooperative play (van der Aalsvoort & van der Leeden, 2009), strategy discovery and choice in locomotion (Berger, Chin, Basra, & Kim, 2015). As it relates to research in mathematics, the microgenetic approach has been used in investigating: mathematical equivalence (e.g., Fyfe, Rittle-Johnson, & DeCaro, 2012), numerical–spatial relations in a number board (e.g., Laski & Siegler, 2014), strategies for single-digit multiplication (e.g., Van der Ven, Boom, Kroesbergen, & Leseman, 2012).

Microgenetic investigations may adopt a qualitative, quantitative, or mixed research strategy, but qualitative studies are far less prevalent than their quantitative counterparts. Some examples of empirical studies in the field of mathematics which adopted a microgenetic approach are: Voutsina

(2012) who explored changes in 5–6 year old children's problem solving strategies when solving a multiple-step additive task; the study of Schoenfeld, Smith, and Arcavi (1993) which investigated a single student's learning of various aspects of simple algebraic functions; and Saada-Robert (1992) who examined the development of numerical representations.

Overview of Fractions

The research on which this chapter is based focused on fractions, which is an important component of the mathematics curriculum from a theoretical, educational and practical perspective (National Mathematics Advisory Panel, 2008; Siegler, Fazio, Bailey, & Zhou, 2013). Fractions provide students first opportunity to learn that many properties of whole numbers do not extend to all types of numbers (Siegler, Thompson, & Schneider, 2011). They are also an integral part of everyday life (Fuchs et al., 2013) and play a pivotal role in most subjects in a school's curriculum (Gabriel, Coché, Szucs, Carette, & Rey, 2013). Additionally, proficiency in fractions is considered essential for performing optimally in the domains of measurement, algebra, and geometry in secondary school mathematics (Department for Education, 2011).

While the importance of fractions has been widely recognised by researchers and educators alike, there is a general consensus, globally, that students have difficulty in learning this topic (Siegler & Pyke, 2013). One of the reasons for this is that fractions represent a multi-faceted construct consisting of five sub-constructs (Kieren, 1988; Middleton et al., 2015). This means that one fraction can have five different meanings depending on the context. An example of this can be seen in some of the many interpretations of the fraction ¾ given in the list below:

- a shape divided into four equal pieces with three pieces shaded (*part-whole*)

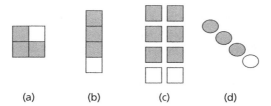

(a)	(b)	(c)	(d)

- the amount that each person receives when three pizzas are shared among four friends (*quotient*)
- find ¾ of sixteen balls (*operator*)

- for every three boys in the class there are four girls (*ratio*)
- the number represented by the arrow on the number line

(*measure*).

Considering that the fraction construct consists of multiple sub-constructs, a full understanding of fractions can only be obtained if all the fraction sub-constructs are included in fraction instruction (Kieren, 1993; Lamon, 2012). In Dominica and the wider Caribbean, the part-whole is the first and sometimes the only fraction sub-construct that children explicitly learn in the classroom. Consequently, in view of:

1. the importance of examining how one fraction sub-construct develops from existing fraction knowing;
2. the fact that the part-whole fraction sub-construct is still predominantly the first sub-construct that children learn in school;
3. the scarcity of studies, globally, which focus on the development of knowledge starting from the part-whole notion;

The main research question on which this chapter draws (L. George, 2017) is: *What strategies do Year 5 (aged 9–10) children who have only been taught the part-whole fraction sub-construct use to find the fraction associated with solving partitive quotient problems in general and in a sequence of problem-solving sessions?*

DESIGN AND METHODS

In order to explore the development of the partitive quotient from existing part-whole knowledge, video-recorded, one-to-one task-based interviews (Maher & Sigley, 2014) were used as the main data collecting tool (see Figure 6.1).

The data collection took place over a six-week period in the first term of the academic year. During this time, nine (three girls and six boys) middle- to high-attaining Year 5 children (aged 9–10 years) from Dominica engaged in solving eight partitive quotient problems which they had not encountered before. Five children (two girls and three boys) were selected from one Year 5 class at a government-run primary school located in the Western district of Dominica, and four children (one girl and three boys) were selected from a private primary school, also located in the Western district of Dominica. Opting to conduct a small-scale study, with a small number of research participants is consistent with key objectives of microgenetic studies, which include high density of observations and trial-by-trial analysis of the observations (Siegler & Crowley, 1991).

Figure 6.1 Research participant engaged in solving a partitive quotient problem.

Partitive quotient problems incorporate sharing situations relating to varying numbers of people and continuous items, such as pizzas or cakes. The tasks for this study were modified from earlier empirical work (e.g., Charles & Nason, 2000; Lamon, 2005; Streefland, 1991). Table 6.3 presents the number of items and people involved in the sharing situations across the eight tasks, T01–T08 and an example of a task prompt.

TABLE 6.3 Example of Task								
Tasks	**T01**	**T02**	**T03**	**T04**	**T05**	**T06**	**T07**	**T08**
Number of items	2	4	3	4	2	3	2	3
Number of people	3	3	5	6	7	6	5	8

Share five rectangular pizzas among three children so that each child gets the same amount of pizza and no pizza is left over. How much pizza would each child get? (**First solution**)

After the child gives the first solution, how else can you share the same five pizzas among the three children? (**Subsequent solutions**)

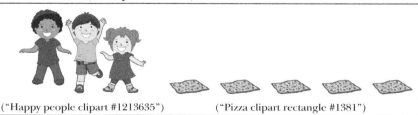

("Happy people clipart #1213635")   ("Pizza clipart rectangle #1381")

The research participants generally engaged in solving two partitive quotient tasks weekly, depending on whether they were available due to obligations at school. Interviews did not exceed 30 minutes in duration. The rectangular region model was selected to represent pizzas and cakes in the tasks, since existing research (e.g., Keijzer & Terwel, 2001), showed that children worked with less difficulty with this model, when compared to the circular model. During each interview (see Appendix A), I prompted children to describe and explain their strategies by asking questions such as: "How did you figure that out?" and "How do you know?" After providing a solution to the problem, children were prompted to think of other ways to share the items. To elicit different solutions, I also asked the question: "How else can you share [number of items] among [number of people]?"

Data Analysis

For this study, a detailed, microgenetic analysis of strategies used by the children in finding the fraction related to solving the partitive quotient problems, entailed the coding of observed strategies and tracing of changes in strategy use on a trial-by-trial basis. This resulted in a detailed description of how children's approaches developed across the eight task-based interviews (for a detailed discussion of the findings pertaining to strategy development for this study see L. George, 2017). This analysis was undertaken after all the data had been collected.

An illustration of the coding of the research data in this manner is presented next. The coding is based on the excerpt of David, a student engaged in solving the problem of sharing two cakes among three children (see Appendix B). In the excerpt, the underlined section shows David's verbalisation and actions as he quantified each person's share. David counts the total number of pieces in the two rectangles which represent the cakes and finds this to be six. This six becomes the denominator of the fraction. The numerator of two represents the number of pieces that he gave to each person after partitioning as per the following verbalisation: "This child gets one" [writes 1 in the first partition of the first rectangle] and "I'm going to do the same thing I did for the first cake, for the second cake" . . . "and then each kid gets another piece." [Writes 1, 2, 3 in each of the three partitions while speaking].

For the analysis reported in this chapter, video recordings, associated transcripts of individual task-based interviews, and the written work (e.g., drawings, partitioning of diagrams, workings) of the children were carefully examined, to identify the strategies used for finding the fraction. The next three sections discuss lessons learnt from adopting the qualitative, microgenetic research design.

LESSON ONE: SURVIVING THE DATA COLLECTION AND ANALYSIS PROCEDURES

The use of a decolonizing approach to data collection proved demanding but rewarding. One lesson learnt is that the use of the one-to-one task-based interview involved adopting a new lens through which to see knowledge, as well as learning new techniques in conducting research. In this regard, I had to privilege and prioritize children's ways of working by learning how to listen to them without imposing my own way of doing and seeing onto their thinking. I had to ask neutral questions such as: "How did you figure that out?" and "How do you know?, that sought to uncover their thinking, but not lead them down any particular path. Empson and Jacobs (2008) comment that "listening effectively and responding to children's mathematical thinking is surprisingly hard work" (p. 257), and that research shows that extended amounts of time are required to become proficient at this. In this regard, to become competent in conducting one-to-one task-based interviews with children, I conducted a pilot study before the main study data collection of the research. Before these data collection periods, I also conducted ongoing practice with children of my friends and colleagues, and even with colleagues themselves. I videotaped some sessions so that I could review and reflect on them. Additionally, I used a task-based interview protocol, which served as a guide for conducting interviews, yet allowed for flexibility in questioning based on what the research participant said. All the aforementioned involved the investment of time, effort and money that ultimately led to the successful completion of the research project.

Some of the children in this study also appeared to have to adopt new ways of working within the learning setting. The excerpt in Appendix C shows an example of this, where Jack engages with the task of sharing fairly two cakes among three children. In this excerpt, the sections underlined show two instances where Jack is seeking direction as to what to do, and an assurance this his answer is right. Jack, like many other children in the Caribbean, was accustomed to teacher-centred ways of learning, where the teacher was the dispenser of knowledge and he was the receiver. By the third task, however, I did not have to ask Jack or the other research participants to repeatedly tell me what they were thinking or to find other ways of sharing the items. They approached their tasks with confidence and eagerness. An important lesson stemming from this point is that when there has been a longstanding imbalance of power between the groups involved in utilising the decolonising research approach, sufficient time must be allowed for all parties to learn and adjust to new ways of operating. This lesson goes beyond the research setting to the classroom as well. Boaler (2015) underscores the importance of children exploring mathematical tasks before formal methods are introduced, as it develops their creativity and their ability to solve problems.

A related lesson learnt is that the individual or group that has traditionally held the power in the setting must also explicitly demonstrate through words and actions that they are relinquishing/sharing power/control, and that the perspective of the researched is valued. Appendix D presents an excerpt of another research participant, Gabriel, engaged in the same problem as Jack. In this excerpt, I use verbalisations such as "do you think there are different ways?," "not necessarily, it is up to you" and "could you show me what you mean?," to achieve the aforementioned.

Regarding data analysis for my research, I encountered two main challenges. Data analysis proved to be extremely time consuming, a key limitation of a microgenetic design due to the high-density observations (Shaffer & Kipp, 2013). This is also consistent with decolonising approaches to research, where the researcher works with the complex data obtained from these researched individuals or groups, as necessary resources for the generation of theories and practices. The data analysis for this study took approximately one year, which was a third of the time for the total research project. In choosing this design, the researcher must ensure that he or she can allocate this time to the analytic process, cope with the mental and psychological demands that data analysis over such a long period of time requires, and that the use of this design is best for the specific set of research questions.

The fact that I had only previously worked with quantitative data made qualitative data analysis, from a philosophical perspective, extremely uncomfortable and challenging. At the core of any research study are beliefs and assumptions about how a researcher looks at, interprets, and acts in the world (Denzin & Lincoln, 2011). These assumptions and views are characterised by epistemological (knowledge), ontological (reality) and methodological considerations, which together comprise a researcher's paradigm—a basic set of beliefs that guide action (Guba, 1990). The interpretivist paradigm was an obvious choice on which to base my research, since it was wholly in line with all the elements of the research process (for example, research strategy, design, methods, research phenomena/questions, theory). Despite this, and most likely because of my extended immersion in a positivist paradigm typically associated with subjects such as Mathematics and Science, I found that during data analysis, I struggled with some of the notions associated with qualitative research, such as: there is not necessarily a right or wrong finding; there is not just one plausible explanation for given data, as another researcher could apply a different analytic lens and come away with a different picture than that which I had conceptualised and proposed. As I reflected on the previously mentioned, I realised that I unconsciously felt that having one right answer placed me on a secure footing and afforded me a power in knowing that I was indisputably right. While one can argue that the power (and by extension the privilege) of being right has its place in research, from my study (relating to how children learn the partitive quotient), this does not hold to be necessarily true. In fact, some of my research findings challenged longstanding "right" explanations for one strategy for finding the fraction in solving partitive quotient problems and provided some alternate pictures than currently exist in empirical literature of children's solving of this type of problem over time.

As it relates to this philosophical conflict, or any others that a researcher may encounter in conducting qualitative research, the main strategy is not to pretend that it does not exist, but to confront and address the issues.

LESSON TWO: ADDRESSING THE ISSUE OF RESEARCHER INFLUENCE HEAD ON

In empirical research, trustworthiness of the findings presented and conclusions made is a significant consideration. In postcolonial Caribbean countries, we have been taught to believe that research should be objective, and the field of mathematics wholly embraces the objectivity of research. This ingrained perspective makes the subjectivity of qualitative research markedly problematic. In conducting qualitative research, particularly interviews, the influence of the interviewer on the person being interviewed is inescapable (Maxwell, 2005), since the researcher is part of the world that is being studied, even when attempts to minimise the influence are made. A lesson learnt regarding this is linked to advice provided by Maxwell (2005). He suggests that researchers should focus on how they influenced what the research participant said, and how this affected the validity of the inferences drawn from the data collected. For my research, I found that although some questions, such as "Why did you do this?," asked during the task-based interview, seemed to prompt some children to rethink a present solution (see Appendix A), and could therefore be considered researcher influence, this revisiting of previous work is in keeping with what would occur as a learner's understanding of a mathematical concept/topic grows. It also parallels what occurs in a typical classroom setting where children are engaged in learning. This therefore reinforces the richness and authenticity of the research data and findings, even as it confirms that the findings are relevant to children's actual learning, although the data was collected outside the classroom setting, where formal learning typically occurs.

In some research situations which use a decolonising qualitative approach (such as the present study), there is an imbalance of power between the researcher and the researched (Cohen, Manion, & Morrison, 2011). This has the potential to influence research participants' behaviour and/or events. Consequently, many consider this to be a form of researcher influence and a limitation of qualitative research.

This ethical issue of how to counter the unequal power between an adult researcher and child participants (Punch, 2008) was a key consideration in my research. Ginsburg (1997) clarifies this issue, stating that most children have had no experience with one-to-one interviews, and so probably focus on the interviewer's status as an adult. In general, this means "an adult who is powerful, knowledgeable and who must be obeyed" (p. 110). In addition, a child may believe that classroom rules apply to the interview, which typically means that children expect to be "tested" about their knowledge, and that right answers are positive, while wrong ones are negative (see Appendices C and D). To address this issue, I followed Ginsburg's (1997) advice, based on his extensive experience in interviewing children. Some of the suggestions made by Ginsburg (1997) include: establish trust, make informal contact, explain the purpose of the interview, use the child's language, be warm and supportive, encourage effort and verbalisation, and monitor affect. Specific examples of how I incorporated these suggestions within my research beyond those discussed in the previous section, include: attempting to "develop a relationship of trust and mutual respect" that allowed "an intimacy centred on the child's thought" (p. 113), even before the interviews commenced. I spent up to a week in the research participants' classroom for the children to become familiar with my presence. I also interacted with them during the break and lunch periods, to develop some level of comfort before the task-based interviews were conducted. At the start of each task-based interview, each child was asked if they were happy to engage in solving fraction problems. They were also reminded that I was interested in how they solve problems, and not whether the answers were right or wrong.

LESSON THREE: EMPOWERMENT OF THE RESEARCHER AND THE RESEARCHED

Thus far in this chapter, the issue of power and empowerment has been discussed from the perspectives of the qualitative research approach, the researcher, and the subject of mathematics. As this chapter concludes, it seems fitting to again focus on what I consider to be a missing element in the discussion on improvement of mathematics education in the Caribbean—the learner's perspective. By conducting this qualitative microgenetic study, I, as a researcher, was able to empower children by providing the means whereby they could add to a discourse concerning mathematics learning—an area of study which wholly concerns them, but from which they have largely been excluded.

The microgenetic approach and the task-based interviews used to collect the data also served a decolonising role, because they placed the researcher in a position to observe and listen closely to children's problem-solving approaches, thereby privileging their verbalisations and ways of working above that of the researcher. To this point, Lamon (2001) states that it is surprising that students who divide a unit into fourths and designate three of them, obtaining a value of 3/4, cannot make the leap to recognise that when dividing three pizzas among four people, each will receive 3/4 of a pizza. I maintain that this "taken-for-granted" attitude by teachers and mathematics education researchers about how children should conceptualise mathematical concepts, versus how they are actually conceptualising them, is disempowering and could possibly impede progress in understanding children's learning and conceptualisation of fractions. I further assert that the teaching of fractions, and perhaps other topics in mathematics, is also hampered if teachers and curriculum planners do not privilege children's ways of working, and use it as a springboard to plan for their instruction.

While I am fully aware that the children who participated in my study felt very proud and excited to be included as research participants, I do not think that the elements of empowerment that I articulate here were apparent to them. In my research, I did not explicitly explore how the children felt and the specific meaning of the research for them; this could be a useful focus for future research.

One main objective of decolonising qualitative research is to empower vulnerable research participants, but the researcher's role in facilitating this process can also provide a key lesson. It is important to note, however, that the act of conducting decolonising qualitative research in which children are the research participants is insufficient to fully empower children, who are typically "recipients of knowledge" within the teaching/learning setting, to become participants in knowledge creation. A more significant element of empowerment is the responsibility that the researcher holds in crafting a reliable picture of what the children have said and done. I achieved this by providing thick descriptions from the research data related to what I have discussed. Additionally, the researcher who aims to give children (or any disempowered or vulnerable group) a voice has a responsibility to actively seek out, take up, or create opportunities to disseminate the findings of research to the researched group and to other relevant parties in different forums; such as online forums, workshops, conferences, and book chapters. In my opinion, it is only when all these elements have been attended to that my research can be said to have had an empowering effect.

CONCLUSION

The potential of mathematics to empower learners to thrive scholastically, vocationally, and in everyday living; and the persistent problem of poor mathematics performance of most Caribbean students in primary and secondary school—creates an unequal power dynamic which decolonising research approaches typically address. This chapter has highlighted that there is a need for this type of research in mathematics education; and the application of the notion of decolonisation to mathematics education could potentially contribute to solving a longstanding educational problem. It has also underscored the urgent need to focus the Caribbean's research voice in mathematics education and add it to the existing international discourse.

I have asserted throughout this chapter that learners need to be more centrally situated in the discourse related to improving the learning and teaching of mathematics within the Caribbean. The qualitative, microgenetic research design is a unique research approach that allows this to be accomplished. The fine-grained data collection and analysis processes that are characteristic of this approach not only provide keen insight into how children learn mathematics, but also invariably place the primary focus on the researched instead of the researcher, and in so doing empowers the former. This research wholly exemplified this strategy.

As it relates to future research, I suggest that we can focus on the adoption of the microgenetic method for investigating the learning of other mathematics concepts and topics which have been notoriously difficult to learn and teach, such as geometry or other sub-topics subsumed under number. Other aspects of mathematics education research can also benefit from using decolonizing qualitative methods. Some of these areas include exploring various dimensions of learners' mathematical identities that are currently not considered when choosing curricular content or pedagogical approaches, such as how learners of mathematics see themselves and the extent to which mathematics is meaningful to them.

APPENDIX A

Kenny: So, I can share the cake into four pieces. Four cakes. [Partitions the first diagram into four.]
Researcher: Please tell me why you chose four?
Kenny: Because... [Looks at diagrams, touching the pencil to different parts of each diagram.]. Not four.
Researcher: Not four? Why not four?
Kenny: Because when I, if I cut all the cakes into four pieces and I share them among the three people, one slice would be left over. And then, I would have to share, share one and—we must share all the cake so that each person gets the same amount and that no cake can be left over.

APPENDIX B

David: [Looks at paper with the written task and diagrams and places pencil on the diagram of one child.] Wait! Actually, since there are three children and two cakes I'm going to separate the cakes into thirds, cause there are chi-, two children. [Looks at paper with the written task and diagrams while speaking.] The cake into thirds. [Partitions the first diagram into three using vertical lines.]

And so then... make the thirds.
David: [Points to the picture of the first child.] This child gets one [writes 1 in the first partition of the first diagram], [points to the picture of the second child], this child gets one [writes 2 in the second partition], [points to the picture of the third child], the other child gets another one and then [points to the picture of the third child again] this child gets another one, [writes 3 in the third partition], gets one. [Looks at the partitioned diagram.] So now that I have shared [touches each of the three partitions in turn with pencil] the—first cake to ev–, everybody gets an equal, everybody gets equal. [Looks at partitioned diagram while speaking.]
So now I have to separate the second cake. [Points to second diagram with pencil.] So, what I have, since the first cake was, am, separated equally, I'm going to do the same thing I did for the first cake, for the second cake. The rule is

that I put this one into thirds as well [partitions the second diagram into three using vertical lines], and then each kid gets another piece.

[Writes 1, 2, 3 in each of the three partitions while speaking.]

So then, each person would get [counts quietly pointing to each partition in turn with the pencil], one, two, three, four, five, six, so it would be two out of six. So two-sixths.

Researcher: [Points to line on paper.] Go ahead and write your fraction here.

David: [Writes 2/6.]

APPENDIX C

Researcher: Here is our task for today. Share two cakes among three children so that each child gets the same amount of cake. How much cake would each child get if each person gets the same amount of cake and no cake is left over?

Jack: Am, [Long pause].

Researcher: Please, tell me what you are thinking.

Jack: [Partitions first rectangle into three]. So, miss that is one, two and three. *Miss do it for the second one too?*

Researcher: *It is really up to you [smiles].*

Jack: [Partitions the second rectangle into three]. [Long pause while looking at paper]. That is one, two and three. [Long pause while looking at paper]. So, one piece of cake for one child, another piece for another child and that, the third piece is for the third child. And for this one [points to picture of second person] the first piece for the first child, the second piece for the second child, and the third piece for the third child.

Researcher: So, one piece would be what fraction?

Jack: *One piece would beeee, um, . . . miss, a half?*

Researcher: *I'm not sure, can you please tell me?*

Jack: Miss a half.

Researcher: How else can you share the two cakes, the two rectangular cakes?

APPENDIX D

Gabriel: The one third, each child gets two-thirds.

Researcher: *Please tell me how you got two-thirds?*

Gabriel: I got two thirds from the three here and each child gets two. And then there's one left over but you still have like three more, so you could take one more from that and you give the child and there's two more, so you give the other child.

Researcher: Okay. So, could you write down your fraction here, please? Okay. How else can you share the same two cakes among three children?

Gabriel: [Pause]. Like different ways?

Researcher: Different ways? *Do you think there are different ways?*

Gabriel: There might be but—

Researcher: *So, let's explore that.*

Gabriel: Okay, well so you have to use both the cakes? They have to get from both the cakes?

Researcher: *Not necessarily, it is up to you how you decide to share the cakes.*

Gabriel: Okay. I think that one cake will be finished if each of them gets one but then you have another cake left over.

Researcher: *Could you show me what you mean?*

REFERENCES

Bailey, B. (2008). *Explaining gender differences in school performance throughout the Caribbean.* Retrieved from http://bit.ly/2l2m4hD

Berger, S. E., Chin, B., Basra, S., & Kim, H. (2015). Step by step: A microgenetic study of the development of strategy choice in infancy. *British Journal of Developmental Psychology, 33*(1), 106–122. doi:10.1111/bjdp.12076

Boaler, J. (2015). *Mathematical mindsets: Unleashing students' potential through creative math, inspiring messages and innovative teaching.* San Francisco, CA: Jossey-Bass.

Brock, R., & Taber, K. S. (2017). The application of the microgenetic method to studies of learning in science education: Characteristics of published studies, methodological issues and recommendations for future research. *Studies in Science Education, 53*(1), 45–73.

Caribbean Development Bank. (2016). *Solving the problem of mathematics education in the region.* Retrieved from http://www.caribank.org/news/solving-problem-mathematics-education-region

Caribbean Examinations Council. (2006–2016). *CSEC May/June entry and performance data.* Retrieved from http://www.cxc.org/category/annual-reports/

Caribbean Examinations Council. (2015). *Caribbean Secondary Education Certificate (CSEC) mathematics syllabus.* Retrieved from https://www.cxc.org/SiteAssets/CSEC_Mathematics_Syllabus_with_Specimen_Papers.pdf

Charles, K., & Nason, R. (2000). Young children's partitioning strategies. *Educational Studies in Mathematics, 43*(2), 191–221. doi:10.1023/A:1017513716026

Claessens, A., & Engel, M. (2013). How important is where you start? Early mathematics knowledge and later school success. *Teachers College Record, 115*, 1–29.

Cohen, L., Manion, L., & Morrison, K. (2011). *Research methods in education* (7th ed.). London, England: Routledge.

Denzin, N. K., & Lincoln, Y. S. (2011). *The SAGE handbook of qualitative research* (4th ed.). Thousand Oaks, CA: SAGE.

Department for Education. (2011). *The framework for the national curriculum. A report by the expert panel for the national curriculum review.* Retrieved from http://dera.ioe.ac.uk/13207/1/NCR-Expert%20Panel%20Report.pdf.

Devlin, K. J. (2000). *The math gene: How mathematical thinking evolved and why numbers are like gossip.* New York, NY: Basic Books.

Empson, S. B., & Jacobs, V. R. (2008). Learning to listen to children's mathematics. In D. Tirosh & T. Wood (Eds.), *Tools and processes in mathematics teacher education* (pp. 257–281). Rotterdam, The Netherlands: Sense.

Flynn, E., Pine, K., & Lewis, C. (2006). Time for change? *Psychologist, 19*(3), 152–155.

Fuchs, L. S., Schumacher, R. F., Long, J., Namkung, J., Hamlett, C. L., Cirino, P. T., Changas, P. (2013). Improving at-risk learners' understanding of fractions. *Journal of Educational Psychology, 105*(3), 683–700. doi:10.1037/a0032446

Fyfe, E. R., Rittle-Johnson, B., & DeCaro, M. S. (2012). The effects of feedback during exploratory mathematics problem solving: Prior knowledge matters. *Journal of Educational Psychology, 104*(4), 1094–1108. doi:10.1037/a0028389

Gabriel, F., Coché, F., Szucs, D., Carette, V., & Rey, B. (2013). A componential view of children's difficulties in learning fractions. *Frontiers in Psychology, 4*, 1–12. doi:10.3389/fpsyg.2013.00715

George, L. (2017). *Children's learning of the partitive quotient fraction sub-construct and the elaboration of the Don't need boundary feature of the Pirie-Kieren theory.* (PhD), University of Southampton, Retrieved from https://eprints.soton.ac.uk/411237/1/Lois_George_Thesis_Final_submission_29_03_2017_.pdf

George, P. (2013). Made for mathematics? Implications for teaching and learning. In D. Leslie & H. Mendick (Eds.), *Debates in mathematics education.* New York, NY: Routledge.

Ginsburg, H. P. (1997). *Entering the child's mind: The clinical interview in psychological research and practice.* New York, NY: Cambridge University Press.

Goodley, D., & Runswick-Cole, K. (2012). Decolonizing methodology. In A. Azzopardi & S. Grech (Eds.), *Inclusive communities: A critical reader* (pp. 215–232). Rotterdam, The Netherlands: Sense.

Guba, E. G. (1990). *The paradigm dialog.* Newbury Park, CA: SAGE.

Happy people clipart #1213635. Retrieved from http://clipart-library.com/clipart/BcaE8Bqdi.htm.

Junor Clarke, P. (2007). Exploring the use of computer technology in a Caribbean context: Views of preservice teachers. *International Journal of Education and Development using Information and Communication Technology, 3*(1), 23–38.

Kalloo, V., & Mohan, P. (2011). An investigation into mobile learning for high school mathematics. *International Journal of Mobile and Blended Learning, 3*(3), 59–76. doi:10.4018/jmbl.2011070105

Keijzer, R., & Terwel, J. (2001). Audrey's acquisition of fractions: A case study into the learning of formal mathematics. *Educational Studies in Mathematics, 47*(1), 53–73. doi:10.1023/A:1017971912662

Kieren, T. E. (1988). Personal knowledge of rational numbers: Its intuitive and formal development. In J. Hiebert & M. Behr (Eds.), *Number concepts and operations in the middle grades* (Vol. 2, pp. 162–181). Reston, VA: National Council of Teachers of Mathematics.

Kieren, T. E. (1993). Rational and fractional numbers: From quotient fields to recursive understanding. In T. Carpenter, E. Fennema, & T. Romberg (Eds.), *Rational numbers: An integration of research* (pp. 49–84). Hillsdale, NJ: Erlbaum.

Lamon, S. J. (2001). Presenting and representing: From fractions to rational numbers. In A. A. Cuoco (Ed.), *The roles of representation in school mathematics—2001 Yearbook* (pp. 146–165). Reston, VA: National Council of Teachers of Mathematics.

Lamon, S. J. (2005). *Teaching fractions and ratios for understanding: Essential content knowledge and instructional strategies for teachers* (2nd ed.). Mahwah, NJ: Erlbaum.

Lamon, S. J. (2012). *Teaching fractions and ratios for understanding: Essential content knowledge and instructional strategies for teachers* (3rd ed.). New York, NY: Taylor & Francis.

Laski, E. V., & Siegler, R. S. (2014). Learning from number board games: You learn what you encode. *Developmental Psychology, 50*(3), 853. doi:10.1037/a0034321

Luwel, K., Siegler, R. S., & Verschaffel, L. (2008). A microgenetic study of insightful problem solving. *Journal of Experimental Child Psychology, 99*(3), 210–232. doi:10.1016/j.jecp.2007.08.002

Maher, C. A., & Sigley, R. (2014). Task-based interviews in mathematics education. In S. Lerman (Ed.), *Encyclopedia of Mathematics Education* (Vol. 1, pp. 579–582). Dordrecht, The Netherlands: Springer.

Maxwell, J. A. (2005). *Qualitative research design: An interactive approach* (2nd ed.). Thousand Oaks, CA: SAGE.

Middleton, J. A., Helding, B., Megowan-Romanowicz, C., Yang, Y., Yanik, B., Kim, A., & Oksuz, C. (2015). A longitudinal study of the development of rational number concepts and strategies in the middle grades. In J. Middleton, J. Cai, & S. Hwang (Eds.), *Large-scale studies in mathematics education* (pp. 265–289). Switzerland: Springer International.

Ministry of Education and Human Resource Development. (2011). *Key results of grade 2 and 4 national assessments.* Roseau, Commonwealth of Dominica: Ministry of Education and Human Resource Development. Retrieved from http://bit.ly/2HIdFpM

National Mathematics Advisory Panel. (2008). *Foundations for success: The final report of the National Mathematics Advisory Panel.* Retrieved from Washington, DC: https://www2.ed.gov/about/bdscomm/list/mathpanel/report/final-report .pdf

Pizza clipart rectangle #1381. Retrieved from http://moziru.com/explore/Pizza% 20clipart%20rectangle/#.

Punch, S. (2008). Researching childhoods in rural Bolivia. In K. Tisdall, J. M. Davis, & M. Gallagher (Eds.), *Researching with children and young people: Research design, methods and analysis* (pp. 89–96). Thousand Oaks, CA: SAGE.

Resing, W. C. M., Bakker, M., Pronk, C. M. E., & Elliott, J. G. (2016). Dynamic testing and transfer: An examination of children's problem-solving strategies. *Learning and Individual Differences, 49*, 110–119. doi:10.1016/j.lindif.2016.05.011

Resing, W. C. M., Bakker, M., Pronk, C. M. E., & Elliott, J. G. (2017). Progression paths in children's problem solving: The influence of dynamic testing, initial variability, and working memory. *Journal of Experimental Child Psychology, 153*, 83–109. doi:10.1016/j.jecp.2016.09.004

Saada-Robert, M. (1992). Understanding the microgenesis of number: Sequence analyses. In J. Bideaud, C. Meljac, & J.-P. Fischer (Eds.), *Pathways to number: Children's developing numerical abilities* (pp. 265–282). Hillsdale, NJ: Erlbaum.

Schoenfeld, A. H., Smith, J. P., & Arcavi, A. (1993). Learning: The microgenetic analysis of one student's evolving understanding of a complex subject matter domain. In R. Glaser (Ed.), *Advances in instructional psychology* (Vol. 4, pp. 55–175). Hillsdale, NJ: Erlbaum.

Secada, W. G., Fennema, E., Adajian, L. B., & Byrd, L. (1995). *New directions for equity in mathematics education.* Cambridge, England: Cambridge University Press.

Shaffer, D., & Kipp, K. (2013). *Developmental psychology: Childhood and adolescence* (8th ed.). Belmont, CA: Wadsworth.

Siegler, R. S. (2006). Microgenetic analyses of learning. In D. Kuhn & R. Siegler (Eds.), *Handbook of child psychology* (6th ed., Vol. 2, pp. 464–510). New York, NY: Wiley.

Siegler, R. S., & Crowley, K. (1991). The microgenetic method: A direct means for studying cognitive development. *American Psychologist, 46*(6), 606. doi:10.1037/0003-066X.46.6.606

Siegler, R. S., Duncan, G. J., Davis-Kean, P. E., Duckworth, K., Claessens, A., Engel, M., & Chen, M. (2012). Early predictors of high school mathematics achievement. *Psychological Science, 23*(7), 691–697. doi:10.1177/0956797612440101

Siegler, R. S., Fazio, L. K., Bailey, D. H., & Zhou, X. (2013). Fractions: The new frontier for theories of numerical development. *Trends in Cognitive Sciences, 17*(1), 13–19. doi:10.1016/j.tics.2012.11.004

Siegler, R. S., & Pyke, A. A. (2013). Developmental and individual differences in understanding of fractions. *Developmental Psychology, 49*(10), 1994–2004. doi:10.1037/a0031200

Siegler, R. S., & Svetina, M. (2002). A microgenetic/cross-sectional study of matrix completion: Comparing short-term and long-term change. *Child Development, 73*(3), 793–809. doi:10.1111/1467-8624.00439

Siegler, R. S., Thompson, C. A., & Schneider, M. (2011). An integrated theory of whole number and fractions development. *Cognitive Psychology, 62*(4), 273–296. doi:10.1016/j.cogpsych.2011.03.001

Smith, L. T. (1999). *Decolonizing methodologies: Research and indigenous peoples.* New York, NY: Zed Books.

Streefland, L. (1991). *Fractions in realistic mathematics education: A paradigm of developmental research* (Vol. 8). Dordrecht, The Netherlands: Kluwer Academic.

van der Aalsvoort, G. M., & van der Leeden, R. (2009). The microgenetic emergence of cooperative play in 6-year-olds developmentally at-risk. *International Journal of Educational Research, 48*(4), 274–285. doi:10.1016/j.ijer.2010.01.001

Van der Ven, S. H., Boom, J., Kroesbergen, E. H., & Leseman, P. P. (2012). Microgenetic patterns of children's multiplication learning: Confirming the overlapping waves model by latent growth modeling. *Journal of Experimental Child Psychology, 113*(1), 1–19. doi:10.1016/j.jecp.2012.02.001

Voutsina, C. (2012). A micro-developmental approach to studying young children's problem solving behaviour in addition. *The Journal of Mathematical Behaviour, 31*(3), 366–381. doi:10.1016/j.jmathb.2012.03.002

Warner, S. (2009). *Mathematics lessons for slower learners in secondary schools in the Caribbean using the LAMS platform.* Paper presented at the Proceedings of the 4th International LAMS & Learning Design Conference, Sydney, Australia.

Williams, S. R. (2014). Reflections on a portrait of our field. In K. R. Leatham (Ed.), *Vital directions for mathematics education research* (pp. 1–14). New York, NY: Springer.

Wintz, P. (2009). Making quality education accessible to all through technology: A case study on accelerating quality delivery of the mathematics curriculum by re-tooling mathematics classrooms with only one computer. *International Journal of Education and Development using Information and Communication Technology, 5*(3), 72–84.

CHAPTER 7

REFLECTION, DIALOGUE, AND TRANSFORMATION THROUGH PARTICIPATORY ACTION RESEARCH

Experiences of Jamaica's Change From Within Programme

Therese Ferguson

"Much of the culture of our schools, like much of the culture of our societies, needs to be transformed" (Down, 2015, p. 157). Speaking within the context of the global sustainability crisis, Down (2015) points to evidence that many schools in the Caribbean region are grappling with issues such as underperformance in regional examinations, drop-outs, alcohol and drug abuse, and high levels of violence. The reculturing of schools towards sustainability, therefore, is a necessary global and regional imperative which has implications for wider societal development. Similarly, it is an important issue in Jamaica, where issues such as school violence present

Decolonizing Qualitative Approaches for and by the Caribbean, pages 139–158
Copyright © 2019 by Information Age Publishing
All rights of reproduction in any form reserved.

a troubling phenomenon (Down, Lambert, & McPherson-Kerr, 2005; King, 2002; Pottinger, 2012; Ministry of Education, 2012).

The literature highlights various factors that shape school culture, with leadership being a critical one (e.g., Deal & Peterson, 2009; Evans, 2001). This includes the leadership exhibited by principals as well as by other school stakeholders such as management and administrative staff, teachers, parents, and students. In addition to leadership, there are other important elements. A significant corpus of ideas comes from Senge and his conceptualisation of what he terms the "learning organisation." Senge (2006) highlights five disciplines that must be cultivated for organisations to engage in a process of continual learning and transformation: mental models, dialogue, personal mastery, shared vision, and systems thinking—critical factors to the shaping of school culture. The notion of mental models speaks to those deeply entrenched assumptions or generalisations that influence our understanding of the world. Senge emphasises the need for all individuals involved in the change process to reflect upon and challenge their mental models in order for new ways of thinking and as a natural corollary, change, to take place. As Fullan (cited in Stolp & Smith, 1995, p. 72) articulates, "The very first place to begin change is within ourselves." Similarly, dialogue and team learning also lead to shared meaning and understanding, both of which underpin commitment to action and change.

As Down's (2015) discussion indicates, school cultural change towards cultures of peace (and wider sustainability values) is integral for Caribbean nations such as Jamaica. As the literature on school culture illustrates, reflection, dialogue, and collaborative learning and action are critical in this reculturing process. The Change from Within (CfW) programme in Jamaica has sought to address violence and indiscipline within schools through an internal process, driven by a Participatory Action Research (PAR) approach that facilitates dialogue, reflection and participation, all precursors to school and wider societal change.

In this chapter, the PAR process utilised by the CfW programme will be shared. The discussion will highlight in particular how reflection, dialogue, participation, and transformation are facilitated by the approach. Two of the programme's components—the Circle of Friends and training—will be drawn on as examples, given that the change process is an ongoing and dynamic one for the schools involved in the current phase of the programme.

To organise the discussion, I will begin by offering an overview of PAR in relation to both conventional and action research. I will also share examples of how action research approaches have been utilised to support school (cultural) change. I will then describe the CfW programme, before moving on to the substantive focus of the paper, the ways in which the CfW programme's PAR approach supports sustainable change within schools and the wider society. I will end with some lessons learnt from the schools' engagement with PAR.

Before proceeding, I wish to openly state that I occupy multiple roles as the new CfW Programme Leader since January 2016—academic research-er, and "outsider" to the schools and their communities. Whilst I am ex-tremely passionate about the programme and protective of its foundations, I also am able to view the programme through the lenses of newcomer and outsider.

CONVENTIONAL, ACTION, AND PARTICIPATORY ACTION RESEARCH

Some of the concerns about conventional research are that it is primarily researcher driven, with the researcher as the individual who defines the problem to be investigated and the methodological approach, then analy-ses and disseminates the findings. The researcher is viewed as expert in this model, and undertakes research *on subjects*, exhibiting a hierarchical de-marcation between the two. There is a gap between the theoretical knowl-edge generated and the action that results from that knowledge. Finally, the benefits from the research mainly accrue to the researcher and the wider academic community.

Action research differs from this traditional approach and addresses sev-eral of these concerns. Action research has its traditions in various disci-plines (Berg, 2001); these include psychology, community development, and education (McNiff, 2014). Greenwood and Levin (2007) define action research as "social research carried out by a team that encompasses a profes-sional action researcher and the members of an organisation, community, or network ("stakeholders") who are seeking to improve the participants' situation" (p. 3). Koshy, Koshy, and Waterman (2011) articulate that "the purpose of action research is to learn through action that then leads on to personal or professional development" (p. 4). Notions of professional de-velopment, collaboration in the research process, and action are important elements of this research approach, and can be seen in the stages outlined by Berg (2001):

1. Identifying the research question(s)—these questions must be deemed important by the stakeholders involved.
2. Gathering the information to answer the question(s)—this can be through a range of methods such as observation, interviews, and documents.
3. Analysing and interpreting the information—"this involves exami-nation of the data in relation to potential resolutions to the ques-

tions or problems identified during the first stage of the research process" (Berg, 2001, p. 182).

4. Sharing the results with the participants—this is a significant aspect of fostering inclusion, participation, and empowerment of individuals, and can be done through various means, ranging from focus groups to informal meetings to institutional or community meetings.

Kemmis and McTaggart (2005) highlight the cyclical nature of the approach, describing the process as a "spiral of self-reflective cycles" of planning, acting, observing, and reflecting (p. 276). Thus, knowledge gained from previous cycles informs the process.

A number of writers use the terminology "action research" and "participatory action research" synonymously. There is the contention, however, that action research, with its origins in the "North," carries an underlying hegemonic approach to research. In other words, Western scientific worldviews underlie conventional research and some generations of action research. Additionally, some argue that these approaches primarily benefit the academic community and the researcher himself or herself (Swantz, 1996). Another critique of action research is that the emphasis is on "professional problem-solving," and that it retains the traditional notion of research with respect to defining the research problem, defining the sample and methodology, and interpreting and reporting the findings (Noffke, 1997, p. 311). Thus, whilst concerned with action, issues of wider structural and social change are left unaddressed (Noffke, 1997). For these theorists, research has to encompass both participatory and action oriented roles, more accurately represent the cultures of marginalised communities, and serve as mechanisms for wider social change, addressing issues of social equity and justice (Mertens & Cram, 2016; Swantz, 1975; Tandon, 2002).

PAR arose in response to these imperatives, with its origins in the social movements of countries such as India, Brazil, and Tanzania (Fals-Borda, 1999; Kemmis & McTaggart, 2005), and draws on both action and participatory research approaches.

Fals-Borda (1995) outlines four guidelines for PAR:

- Do not monopolise your knowledge nor impose arrogantly your techniques but respect and combine your skills with the knowledge of the researched or grassroots communities, taking them as full partners and co-researchers. That is, fill in the distance between subject and object;
- Do not trust elitist versions of history and science which respond to dominant interests, but be receptive to counter-narratives and try to recapture them;

- Do not depend solely on your culture to interpret facts, but recover local values, traits, beliefs, and arts for action by and with the research organisations; and
- Do not impose your own ponderous scientific style for communicating results, but diffuse and share what you have learned together with the people, in a manner that is wholly understandable and even literary and pleasant, for science should not be necessarily a mystery or a monopoly of experts and intellectuals."

From this, several important aspects of PAR can be identified. Firstly, the democratisation of the research process through the recognition of voices that might previously have been marginalised or gone unnoticed are prioritised, and the legitimisation of forms of knowledge that might not historically be viewed as valid, such as indigenous or local knowledge (Fals-Borda, 1995; 1999; 2013). This also means that research needs to be undertaken and communicated in a manner that is culturally appropriate and understandable (Fals-Borda, 1999). Secondly, there is the belief that researchers and participants are not discrete, opposing entities but people whose views should jointly be taken into account (Fals-Borda, 1999). Finally, PAR is meant to be social, participatory, practical and collaborative, emancipatory, critical, reflexive and dialogic, and transformative with respect to both theory and practice (Kemmis & McTaggart, 2005). A number of these elements are also congruent with Senge's (2006) ideas about the learning organisation and, by extension, school cultural change.

ACTION RESEARCH FOR SCHOOL CULTURE CHANGE

Action research has been used successfully in a variety of educational contexts. Kourkoutas, Eleftherakis, Vitalaki, and Hart (2015) describe action research to enhance the resilience of children at risk in four urban primary schools in Crete, Greece. The programme sought to help parents and teachers develop strategies both at home and in school to support the social, emotional, and academic resilience of children deemed to be at-risk. Through action research, parents and teachers reported enhanced understanding of children's difficulties and ability to respond to these challenges. Wood and Govender (2013) share on an action research project in South Africa, which formed part of a larger Integrated School Improvement and Development project. Ten of the 27 schools involved in the larger project participated in the action research component, with facilitators guiding the participants—principals, deputy principals, and heads of departments—in the process. This involved identifying aspects of their schools that they wished to improve, reflecting on the social and educational contexts of their schools, acting to improve the situation, evaluating the actions, and identifying lessons learnt to inform future practice. Researchers found that participants' practice was positively changed as a result of the action research process, more democratic and inclusive leadership styles emerged, and positive changes in school climate also resulted. Additionally, as the two case studies of action research shared by the researchers showed, actions taken resulted in positive changes, such as promoting a culture of reading and a more positive (as opposed to corrective) approach to school discipline.

Higgins (2005) documents action research undertaken at Caversham Primary School in New Zealand to address issues of bullying through the Eliminating Violence Programme. The programme sought to develop a school culture that includes elements of collegiality, open communication, inclusivity, participation, and consistent procedures and policies. Drawing on the action research process, school stakeholders were called to survey the school community as part of an initial reflective cycle on the school's culture and violence. The survey results then informed the development and implementation of a plan to address issues; this plan included various initiatives such as improving the school's physical environment, instituting clear rules and procedures, having staff see themselves and act as role models, and addressing the wider social and emotional needs of students and their families. At the end, the programme was then evaluated and changes made to inform the next phase of the cycle. As a result of the action research process employed, the school experienced a change from the previous school culture to one characterised by respect, kindness, and non-violence.

Action research also has been utilised by academics in the Caribbean. Although not explicitly termed as action research, Lewis-Smikle (2006) utilised the approach as part of a research team developing a prototype programme—the Literature-Based Language Arts Project (LBLAP)—to address issues surrounding the ways in which literacy is taught. The team worked in three primary schools in St. Andrew, Jamaica. Workshops were held with personnel from regional institutions working in the area of literacy as well as with teachers and administrators in the project schools. Through the project activities and the support workshops, students' literacy was enhanced. Lee (2009) also utilised action research with a team of both pre- and in-service teachers to find solutions to various issues, including: teachers' requests for more resources for mathematics teaching, improved teaching practice, and students' poor performance in mathematics. This is addressed through her EnviroMath approach to teaching and learning in mathematics which supports the creation of mathematics resources and professional development of mathematics teachers whilst simultaneously promoting environmental stewardship. Lee chronicles the cyclical nature of the action research undertaking, how all participants had a voice in the undertaking, and how "collaboration, teamwork and partnership" allowed much to be accomplished through the project. She states:

> The action research process provided opportunities for more frequent inter-actions with the participants and a greater level of collaboration that allowed me to understand the meanings and reasons behind their beliefs and their classroom practices. This was important because the experience gave me direction and guidelines for addressing some of their professional development training needs. (Lee, 2009, p. 116)

Lee shares that: "The recycling activities have resulted in the production of various kinds of inexpensive teaching/learning resources, in good supply, that satisfy curriculum standards, and help make mathematics more meaningful for students" (Lee, 2008, p. 157).

It is now time to offer some details about the CfW programme before we turn to examine the PAR approach.

THE CHANGE FROM WITHIN PROGRAMME

There have been various initiatives in Jamaica to address issues of violence and indiscipline within schools and the wider society, including formal programmes such as Peace and Love in Schools (PALS), as well as initiatives focused on parenting, youth mentorship, and communities (Gardner et al., 2008; Ward, Gordon-Strachan, Carr, & Ashley, 2006). One of the school-based initiatives is the CfW programme, which has been in existence since 1992, and has been implemented by the School of Education (SoE) at The University of the West Indies since 2002.

The CfW Programme has its genesis in the change processes embarked upon by four inner-city schools in the parishes of Kingston, St. Andrew, and St. Catherine; these were internally driven change processes using existing positives within the schools as the foundation for transformation in areas such as academics, parental involvement, and staff and student self-esteem. Subsequent research carried out on the programme (Sewell, Chevannes, & Morgan, 2003) identified eight key components that provided the impetus for the changes (see Box 7.1).

BOX 7.1 CHANGE FROM WITHIN COMPONENTS

1. Empowering school leaders. Early research findings highlighted the empowerment of school leaders as an important factor in the change processes within schools. Capacity-building initiatives to enhance leadership at all levels (e.g., students, teachers,

principals) empower others and encourages collaboration in the change process.

2. Building on existing good practices. Utilising existing "positives" within schools to promote and sustain change is integral. For instance, schools with strong sports or performing arts programmes have utilised these elements to promote attendance and punctuality, and foster discipline.

3. Utilizing new pedagogies. Schools have drawn on elements, such as the Jamaican culture and students' interests to teach in creative ways that engage students in the learning process, and build self-confidence and self-esteem. For instance, schools have utilised their football field or farm to teach concepts such as velocity and angles in subjects such as science and mathematics. Additionally, reggae music from various artists, such as Bob Marley and Jimmy Cliff, was utilised to build self-esteem amongst staff and students.

4. Mentoring (of all school stakeholders). Mentoring of children is fostered to encourage holistic care and development of children beyond the school walls. Additionally, mentoring of teachers and principals as part of leadership development is undertaken.

5. Involving parents and the wider community. The change process is dependent on all school stakeholders. Forums such as the Parent-Teacher Association and workshops for parents are amongst the mechanisms utilised to promote ownership of the change process and involvement by all school stakeholders. For example, parents have beautified and maintained school campuses in the absence of school personnel.

6. Involving children in decision-making. The participation of children in decision-making enhances self-esteem, confidence, and ownership of the change process. Consultation with students over lunch menus and the institution of a regular hour where students' concerns can be heard and addressed have been some initiatives of schools.

7. Training staff and students. Special training initiatives for staff and students in areas identified by the schools themselves are organised and delivered. Areas of staff training have included time management, health, and team-building. Students have received training in areas such as etiquette, social skills, and leadership.

8. Building a shared "Circle of Friends" with other schools. The Circle of Friends, a support network of principals and other school leaders, has been identified as the most successful aspect of the programme, offering support, guidance, and partnership in the change process.

After an approximate four-year hiatus, the CfW programme resumed in the year 2016. Currently, eleven schools—six primary and five high schools—are involved in the programme. In this new period of CfW, the emphasis has been on the following:

- Building a Circle of Friends amongst the eleven schools. The Circle of Friends meets on a monthly basis and involves principals, vice-principals, and others deemed as having leadership potential, such as guidance counsellors and teachers. During these meetings, challenges, successes, and best practices are shared, and professional and personal support offered.
- Organising and delivering capacity-building workshops for management and teaching staff on priorities identified by the schools themselves, in areas such as: teachers with special responsibilities, conflict resolution, safeguarding the child, interpersonal relationships, stress management, and teaching methodologies.
- Coaching of students deemed at risk or in need of special support.
- Researching and documenting aspects of the programme to inform the on-the-ground implementation of the change processes in the schools.

Within this new phase of implementation, there is a four-member team comprised of the programme leader based within the SoE, a founding member of CfW and former programme leader, an ESD consultant, and an accredited master coach. Whilst these team members support the schools, it is the schools themselves that take ownership of and drive the change process.

CfW and Education for Sustainable Development (ESD)

When the CfW programme resumed in 2016, it did so under an ESD thrust, so that the programme's methodology could be utilised to foster the knowledge, values, skills, and behaviours consistent with sustainability. Given the programme's foundational focus on promoting peace within schools and, by extension, societies, this ESD thrust was simply made more explicit in this new phase. Additionally, engagement in lifelong learning, taking responsibility for and learning to change, systemic thinking, and critical, problem-solving, decision-making, and reflective skills are all part of ESD (Tilbury, 2011; Wals, 2009); these are all facilitated through the capacity-building initiatives, as well as the PAR approach which drives action to address real-life problems.

With this ESD focus, the programme is responding to both international and national imperatives. The Sustainable Development Goals (SDGs) adopted by the world community in 2015 seek to enhance quality of life for the global populace. The programme specifically contributes to SDGs Four and Sixteen in particular, which speak to ensuring inclusive and quality education and lifelong learning, and promoting just, peaceful, and inclusive societies. Further, Jamaica's National Education Strategic Plan: 2011–2020 (NESP) has amongst its priority areas safety and security, and student performance (Ministry of Education, 2012). The programme also works to address Goal Two of Vision 2030 Jamaica, which speaks to a secure, cohesive, and just society (PIOJ, 2009). Thus, the programme and its use of PAR methods is driving school and wider societal change through its engagement of both school and community stakeholders.

CfW Methodology

The methodology of the CfW programme operates on three distinct yet interrelated levels (Sewell et al., 2003). The first level utilised a PAR approach, which "involved the engagement in and ownership of the programme by all the constituents. These were the community, the students, the teachers, the administration, and the parents. The main activities included observation, documentation, discussion and analysis" (Sewell et al., 2003, p. 9). The researchers further state that at this level, "participants were empowered to take initial initiatives and conceptualise, plan, and implement strategies using a large knowledge base generated by research findings and rich experiences shared during meetings" (Sewell et al., 2003, p. 9).

At the second rung of the methodology, various strategies for promoting change and building collaboration and cooperation were implemented to build participants' social skills and enhance interpersonal relationships. The aim was to create a positive school climate of respect, trust, enhanced self-esteem, and minimal conflict. The third level used the CfW methodology to build institutional capacity through various workshops, training initiatives, and meetings. Significantly, at this level, participants were encouraged to "identify and own the problems and challenges within their respective schools, to generate workable solutions, map plan(s) for action and implement strategies" (Sewell et al., 2003, p. 10).

It is important to note several key elements. As indicated, the eight principles that characterise the programme were not externally imposed by academic researchers, but were unearthed by academics exploring the four inner-city schools already experiencing successful transformation. Thus, these programme elements had their foundation in the schools themselves, and the communities in which they were situated. The names of the programme and particular elements were also derived from participants. The name "Change from Within" stemmed from the fact that the transformations taking place in the schools were driven "from within" the schools, as well as from within the stakeholders themselves. Additionally, the name "Circle of Friends" also emerged from the original four schools in which the programme had its genesis.

Programme components drew on elements within the Jamaican culture that were relevant to participants. For instance, the use of elements such as reggae music, sports, the performing arts, and farming to engender change are significant cultural aspects of the schools, communities, and the wider Jamaican society. As highlighted, the CfW approach is a participatory one, as the school stakeholders themselves own and direct the change process. Each school has its own particular context in which it operates, utilising its own internally based positives to drive the process. Indeed, the schools themselves have identified the approach as one of PAR. Significantly, Fals-Borda (1999) proposes that for addressing issues such as violence, the PAR methods are the best fit, due to the local, relevant knowledge that can be gathered and used to inform change.

In the next section, we turn to our substantive look at how the use of PAR methods promote dialogue, reflection, and transformation (personal, professional, and institutional) within the schools.

CFW'S CIRCLE OF FRIENDS

One of the core components of the CfW programme is the Circle of Friends (see Box 7.1). The Circle is a support and capacity-building group for school leaders, who are critical to the process of school culture change (Deal & Peterson, 2009; Evans, 2001; Stolp & Smith, 1995). Deal and Peterson (2009), for instance, point out that the role of leaders is a central one in shaping school culture through the articulation of important values, communication of the school's vision, and recognition of student and staff accomplishments. Additionally, another reason for their critical role is that they need to model the change envisioned. Johnson (2011) underscores the importance of school administrators using action research to model the need for continuous learning, personal and professional reflection, and the importance of collaboration—all of which are aspects of positive school cultures.

In the beginning years of the programme, the Circle was primarily comprised of the principals of CfW schools. As the programme evolved, however, the Circle expanded to include vice-principals and others identified as having leadership potential who could benefit from the Circle, such as guidance counsellors and senior or head teachers. This evolving nature of the Circle exemplifies how schools themselves modify the programme components to accord with their own experiences and internal needs; for example, the change that some schools make to the programme name—one high school, for instance, has called it a 'Friendship Circle'. In the current programme phase, the Circle meets on a monthly basis and engages in various activities including:

- sharing of challenges, solutions, and best practices;
- visioning and reflection;
- sharing of school and personal milestones; and
- engaging in icebreakers and games with reflective dimensions.

These processes are facilitated by the four-member programme team. Past research has identified the Circle as one of the most meaningful and successful aspects of the programme (Down et al., 2005). Recent qualitative research has also identified the professional and psychosocial benefits of the Circle.

The Circle is part of the CfW's PAR approach, with members identifying areas of focus (practical issues or problems) and engaging in reflection and dialogue. The core concept that drives CfW is the need for the change to be internally driven, in other words, for the school stakeholders themselves to identify areas of change, initiate change, and monitor change.

In the current phase of the CfW, this process began at one of the early Circle meetings in 2016 during which Circle members were asked to identify areas of change that they felt were critical within their schools. Leaders were asked to think about (reflect on) what was taking place within their schools and come to the next monthly meeting with this "list"—this afforded them an additional month to observe and reflect on the situations in their schools. In subsequent meetings, the areas of focus (or change) were identified by the schools themselves, as opposed to being externally imposed upon by the programme team.

Additionally, through Circle dialogue, alongside informal conversations between Circle members and programme team members on visits to the schools, CfW Circle members are called to engage in reflective processes on the change efforts. Leaders share what they have been doing to engage in and support the change processes initiated, what is working well, and also what is not working so well. Members of the Circle find these dialogic and reflective processes useful as they are able to reflect professionally (on actions implemented) and personally. As one Circle member, a high school Principal, shared:

> It has developed our capabilities to deal with the struggles, through collegiality, so we meet with other people and we get to find out that the problem I thought was me alone who had it, and was insurmountable, that somebody else has had it and has found a way to get around it.

This sentiment underscores the importance of the dialogic and team learning element facilitated by the Circle. In terms of the reflection promoted by the Circle, this participant also indicated:

> I feel what we have not done enough of, as administrators, we have not done enough of meeting the children where they are at. What we have assumed is, that they come with a particular structure and when they do not reach us where we expect for them to, we very often write them off. And so what we need to do in this twenty-first century and beyond is to find ways, to meet the children where they are, that is how I see it. That is how 'Change from Within' has helped me to see it.

Thus, this Principal is voicing the way in which the Circle has helped him to reflect upon and challenge his own mental models, the ways in which he sees children and, as a result, their potentialities.

The Circle also empowers participants to become a "Community of Practice" as they share information with one another, learn from one another and, as a consequence, develop both personally and professionally. This is evidenced from the sentiments of the high school principal expressed above, where he speaks of collegiality and how dialogue has developed his and other members' abilities to deal with issues. Another Circle member, a primary school guidance counsellor shared, "Through the Circle of Friends, we have a kind of a network, where we can call on each other." Additionally, another principal shared how the Circle has empowered her to work collaboratively, for instance, in drafting her primary school's action plan: "I don't write the school action plan on my own, so . . . in August, writing the new plan, inviting everyone as a staff, in development sessions, and I ask them to write sections of the plan within a community. . . ."

CAPACITY-BUILDING

Capacity-building of all school stakeholders is an important element of the CfW programme (see Box 7.1). This is undertaken through the Circle of Friends, as well as through mentorship and specially organised training initiatives for various school stakeholders. In the current phase of the programme, management and teaching staff of the schools participated in a series of five training workshops during the 2016–2017 school year that focused on the areas of need identified by the schools. Areas of focus included the duties of teachers with special responsibilities, conflict management and restorative justice, safeguarding the child, interpersonal relationships, project-based learning and the use of the arts and silence in teaching and learning.

All of the workshops incorporated the action research cycle, calling participants to engage in planning, action, observation, and reflection. Due to the fact that the stakeholders are not a homogenous group of persons, dialogue and communication is critical to the success of the process (Greenwood & Levin, 2007. All of the workshops therefore also utilised activities to support communication and dialogue. The workshop on conflict management and restorative justice will serve as an illustration.

This two-day workshop, held in November 2016, was facilitated by two members of the programme team, one of whom is a trained restorative justice practitioner who has worked in community and school contexts. Participants were asked to begin by reflecting on the following questions:

- What is your definition of conflict?
- How does conflict manifest itself in your environment, school, and classroom?
- How does it impact learning?
- How do you respond?
- Are you happy with your responses?
- Who is involved in these conflicts?

One primary school principal later shared an anecdote with me, relating that at the close of the workshop, one teacher voiced aloud her reflective thoughts about her role in conflicts and the changes that she needed to make, as she and colleagues walked from the workshop venue to the parking area. This illustrates the potent power of reflection as a tool for personal (as well as professional and institutional) change.

After participants discussed these questions, facilitators looked at options for addressing conflict. Schools were asked to share their own initiatives to address conflicts, borne out of their own experiences; they shared a Courtesy and Respect Campaign, the use of "Transformation Sessions" to replace detentions, creating the role of Detention Officer amongst students, the institution of a special uniform for school prefects, and gender-based devotions. The facilitators then took participants through the use of restorative justice circles as another option for addressing conflicts. Facilitators outlined the pillars and principles of restorative justice, and the guidelines for facilitators of these circles. This was then followed by mock circle exercises based on various scenarios, to allow individuals to become oriented to the use of the circles and the roles of facilitators.

Facilitators then took attendees through a strategic planning cycle, inclusive of a SWOT (Strengths, Weaknesses, Opportunities, Threats) analysis. Participants worked in groups divided according to their schools, to identify an area or issue for which conflict management is needed and to strategically plan how new initiatives would be implemented. This exercise was not shared with the wider group as it was recognised that schools might have particular issues that they wished to address internally. This component can be seen as the "planning" aspect of the action research cycle.

Post-workshop feedback revealed that participants appreciated the opportunity to dialogue and reflect. Teaching and management staff shared sentiments such as "the interactive sessions with teachers from other schools was meaningful." Some also noted that the practical exercises in the workshop "were good as we were actively involved, and presenting [on group activities] provided us with the opportunity for participants to learn from each other." It is important to remember that throughout this workshop, facilitators asked participants to draw on their own lived experiences in outlining their definitions of conflict, how conflict manifests itself, how it impacts learning, and solutions. Whilst schools were introduced to the concept of restorative justice circles, there was no imposition of the practice upon the schools. Individuals were encouraged to continue building on existing strategies that were working and/or to try strategies that had been shared by other schools. Some participants did, however, indicate that they would try the restorative justice circles, stating: "the restorative justice circle was and is very meaningful to me and is one that I would implement at my school" and, "I will be able to go back to my school and use the tools and skills learnt, especially the circle."

Schools were encouraged to undertake the "action" component of the cycle and implement their action plans post-workshop. At one of the CfW primary schools, use of the restorative justice circle was implemented. For instance, Peace Day in March 2017 was held under the theme 'Simmer Down—Let's Talk it Out' (Ferguson & Chevannes, 2018). Members of the school's guidance committee organised and presented a dramatic item in order to introduce restorative justice circles. The committee used the scenario of a child cheating on a test and being "tattled" on by another, resulting in a dispute between the two children. The enactment illustrated the restorative justice circle as an alternative to physical altercations. The school guidance counsellor has also been using the restorative justice circle to address conflicts with children.

At one of the high schools, some of the workshop attendees held a series of staff development workshops to orient the wider school population to the use of the restorative justice circles. There are further plans to incorporate the use of restorative justice circles into the school's five-year strategic plan for 2017–2022, which includes a section focused on interpersonal relationships and the use of the restorative justice circles, will be adopted for use in staff conflicts. Restorative justice circles are also being incorporated into the school's Behaviour Modification Programme as a mechanism for dealing with conflicts prior to their escalation.

Post-workshop visits to the CfW schools found that participants also had been engaging in the observation aspect of the action research cycle, with some schools noting certain issues with the restorative justice circle. As an example, participants from one of the primary schools attempted the restorative justice circle to address a school conflict, but noted that the intervention did not work due to the fact that (i) it was a deep-rooted issue; (ii) time was a constraint; and (iii) due to the nature of an issue, an impartial facilitator was needed.

As was the case with the evolution of the Circle of Friends, some schools modified their use of the restorative justice circle, suggesting, for instance, the creation of a list of resource persons from the other CfW schools who could serve as restorative justice circle facilitators to ensure an impartial process. This action (utilising the restorative justice circle), observation (of the process of using the intervention), and subsequent troubleshooting (through the identification of an alternative means of implementing the restorative justice circles), is an important illustration of the cyclical nature of action research.

CONCLUSION

In both the past and present iterations of the CfW programme, PAR has been and continues to be an integral part of transformation within schools and, by extension, the wider society. The approach offers benefits, including enhancement of participants' collaborative, communication, problem-solving, critical-thinking, and reflective skills, sense of efficacy and empowerment, and attitudes towards change (Berg, 2001; Greenwood & Levin, 2007; Ferrance, cited in Johnson, 2011). This has been experienced by participants in both the past and present phases of the programme. All of this contributes to the overall capacity building of participants and, by extension, the sustainability of the change process.

The programme and its PAR approach support ESD and, by extension, the SDGs adopted by the worldwide community, as well as important policy imperatives outlined by Jamaica in its NESP and Vision 2030 goals. The programme not only fosters sustainability values such as peace, respect, and tolerance; it also contributes to the sustainability of education, as the positive changes brought about in areas such as attendance, punctuality, discipline, and academic achievement are internally driven and embedded within the programme's schools and, as a result, more sustainable.

As this discussion concludes, I would like to share a few lessons learnt from both phases of the programme, based on my own observations as an academic researcher and on feedback from participants in the past and present phases of the programme.

One of the critical lessons learnt and reinforced, is the need for participants to collect data to inform the "action" component of the research and to document the process. These two aspects have been ongoing challenges within the previous and current phases of the CfW programmes. The CfW schools have always been encouraged to collect data and engage in the documentation of their own experiences with implementing change processes. This was underscored by researchers working in the first substantive phase of the programme, with academicians encouraging principals to keep daily or weekly journals to document the process of change in the schools. Individuals, however, reported challenges, such as finding the time to keep a journal or unease with writing in journals (Sewell et al., 2003). This was a learning experience, with the realisation that the schools themselves should decide upon the means of documentation most relevant for them, whether journal writing, audio recording of experiences, documentation by an interviewer (e.g., postgraduate research assistant) or other means (Sewell et al., 2003).

In September 2017, three new schools joined the CfW programme. The programme team has offered, through the Circle of Friends, an informal series of sessions on PAR, looking at issues such as the importance of data, means of collecting data, the action research cycle, and areas that could benefit from data. These aspects were discussed using a quiz format, with Circle members working in teams and two members of the programme team serving as the "quizmasters" facilitating this process. This was a fun, interactive way of emphasising the importance of documenting the process of change in order to monitor and trace the schools' experiences. Schools drew on their own experiences, for instance, reflecting on and dialoguing about what "data" means to them, diagramming their own conceptualisations of the action research cycle, and identifying tools that they themselves would use to collect data. Additionally, schools identified ways that they would document the change process, such as through the use of videos.

Another important lesson has been the importance of providing opportunities for dialogue and reflection. Whether it is through the dialogic process that takes place during the Circle of Friends meetings or the collaboration and interaction that is encouraged as part of capacity-building activities, the importance of team building and collaboration has been noted. This reinforces the literature on school culture which speaks to elements such as relationships, collaboration, continual learning, and participation as being signifiers of positive school cultures and drivers of change.

The need to ensure participation and collaboration, and to hear all voices is also critical. The CfW methodology has always included all school stakeholders in the change process. CfW training and capacity-building initiatives, inclusive of mentoring and the Circle of Friends, have always responded to issues identified by the schools. The success experienced to date has been as a result of collaboration, the different mechanisms created to allow participants to share their perspectives, and responsiveness to the particular contexts in which the schools are situated and operating.

The CfW programme must be driven by leadership. There are 11 schools involved in the current phase of the programme. From my observation, the schools in which change is being driven in a collaborative and sustained process are those with strong leaders—leaders who attend the Circle of Friends meetings, training workshops, and who (based on perspectives shared by teachers and other staff members) support teachers, staff, and students in their attempts to drive change.

Cultural change does not happen overnight; time must be allowed for the PAR process to take shape and for transformation to happen. Additionally, reflective, dialogic, and participatory processes can also benefit from the allocation of space and time.

This discussion highlights the potential of PAR approaches, and the importance of the reflection, dialogue, and participation that it facilitates in school culture change. The examples shared in this chapter illustrate the beginning steps that the current CfW schools have taken in the present phase, which began in 2016. It is hoped that the experiences shared, along with lessons learnt, will be useful for those interested in the transformative potential of PAR. Moreover, it is hoped that these experiences will stimulate schools in the region to explore PAR as an approach to reculture schools towards sustainability. As Down (2015) forcefully yet simply articulates, a school culture of sustainability, inclusive of the principles of peace and justice, an environmental ethic, and a futures perspective, is critical for humanity's and society's survival.

ACKNOWLEDGMENTS

I would like to thank Mrs. Pauletta Chevannes, one of the founding members of the CfW programme and a former programme leader, for her thoughts on this manuscript. I also express admiration for the schools in the current phase of the programme for their commitment to the process of personal, professional, and school transformation.

REFERENCES

Berg, B. L. (2001). *Qualitative research methods for the social sciences*. Boston, MA: Allyn and Bacon.

Deal, T. E., & Peterson, K.D. (2009). *Shaping school culture: Pitfalls, paradoxes, and promises*. San Francisco, CA: Jossey-Bass.

Down, L. (2015). Transforming school culture through education for sustainable development (ESD). *Journal of Eastern Caribbean Studies, 40*(3), 157–167.

Down, L., Lambert, C., & McPherson-Kerr, C. (2005). *Violence in schools and the change from within project*. Kingston, Jamaica: Institute of Education.

Evans, H. (2001). *Inside Jamaican schools*. Kingston: University of the West Indies Press.

Fals-Borda, O. (1995). *Research for social justice: Some North–South convergences*. Retrieved from http://comm-org.wisc.edu/si/falsborda.htm

Fals-Borda, O. (1999). Kinsey Dialogues Series #1: The origins and challenges of participatory action research. *Participatory Research and Practice, 10*. Retrieved from http://scholarworks.umass.edu/cgi/viewcontent.cgi?article=1010&context =cie_participatoryresearchpractice

Fals-Borda, O. (2013). Action research in the convergence of disciplines. *International Journal of Action Research, 9*(2), 155–167.

Ferguson, T., & Chevannes, P. (2018). The change from within program: Bringing restorative justice circles for conflict resolution to Jamaican schools. *Childhood Education: Innovations, 94*(1), 55–61.

Gardner, J. M., Henry-Lee, A., Chevannes, P., Thomas, J., Baker-Henningham, H., & Coore, C. (2008). *Violence against children in the Caribbean: A desk review*. Retrieved from https://www.researchgate.net/publication/300078841_Violence _against_Children_in_the_Caribbean_A_Desk_Review

Greenwood, D. J., & Levin, M. (2007). *Introduction to action research: Social research for social change*. Thousand Oaks, CA: SAGE.

Higgins, N. (2005). Changing school culture through action research and leadership. *Waikato Journal of Education, 11*(2), 17–36.

Johnson, C. S. (2011). School administrators and the importance of utilising action research. *International Journal of Humanities and Social Science, 1*(14), 78–84.

Kemmis, S., & McTaggart, R. (2005). Participatory action research: Communicative action and the public sphere. In N. K. Denzin & Y. S. Lincoln (Eds.), *The SAGE Handbook of Qualitative Research* (3rd ed., pp. 271–330). London, England: SAGE.

King, R. (2002). Violence and schools in Jamaica: Historical and comparative perspectives. *Institute of Education Annual*, 1–15.

Koshy, E., Koshy, V., & Waterman, H. (2011). *Action research in healthcare*. London, England: SAGE.

Kourkoutas, E., Eleftherakis, T. G., Vitalaki, E., & Hart, A. (2015). Family-school-professionals partnerships: An action research program to enhance the social, emotional, and academic resilience of children at risk. *Journal of Education and Learning, 4*(3), 112–122.

Lee, N. M. (2008). A recycling and resource centre for mathematics: Recycle for maths today—preserve the environment for tomorrow. *Caribbean Journal of Education, 30*(1), 136–159.

Lee, N. M. (2009). Recycling, an alternative source for mathematics resources: Action research experiences of a teacher-trainer. *Journal of Education and Development in the Caribbean, 11*(1), 109–129.

Lewis-Smikle, J. (2006). Literacy and learning through literature in the junior years: A prototype project. *Caribbean Journal of Education, 28*(1), 85–110.

McNiff, J. (2014). *Writing and doing action research*. Los Angeles, CA: SAGE.

Mertens, D. M., & Cram, F. (2016). Integration tensions and possibilities: Indigenous research and social transformation. *International Review of Qualitative Research, 9*(2), 185–191.

Ministry of Education. (2012). *National education strategic plan: 2011–2020*. Kingston: Ministry of Education.

Noffke, S. E. (1997). Professional, personal, and political dimensions of action research. *Review of Research in Education, 22*, 305–343.

Planning Institute of Jamaica (PIOJ). (2009). *Vision 2030 Jamaica: National development plan.* Retrieved from http://www.vision2030.gov.jm/National-Development-Plan

Pottinger, A. (2012). Children's exposure to violence in Jamaica: Over a decade of research and interventions. *West Indian Medical Journal, 61*(4), 369–371.

Senge, P. (2006). *The fifth discipline: The art and practice of the learning organization.* New York, NY: Doubleday.

Sewell, T., Chevannes, B., & Morgan, S. (2003). *Models for transformation of Jamaican schools—A study of masculinities, education and civil society.* Unpublished report.

Stolp, S., & Smith, S. C. (1995). *Transforming school culture: Stories, symbols, values and the leader's role.* Eugene: University of Oregon.

Swantz, M. (1975). The role of participant research in development. *Geografiska Annaler. Series B, Human Geography, 57*(2), 119–127.

Swantz, M. (1996). A personal position paper on participatory research: Personal quest for living knowledge. *Qualitative Inquiry, 2*(1), 120–136.

Tandon, R. (2002). *Linking citizenship, participation and accountability: A perspective from PRIA.* Retrieved from https://assets.publishing.service.gov.uk/media/57a08d3fed915d3cfd0018f0/1052734379-tandon.2002-linking.pdf

Tilbury, D. (2011). *Education for sustainable development: An expert review on processes and learning.* Paris, France: UNESCO. Retrieved from unesdoc.unesco.org/images/0019/001914/191442e.pdf

Wals, A. (2009). *Review of contexts and structures for education for sustainable development 2009.* Paris, France: UNESCO. Retrieved from unesdoc.unesco.org/images/0018/001849/184944e.pdf

Ward, E., Gordon-Strachan, G., Carr, P., & Ashley, D. (2006). Prioritising violence in national public health programmes: Experiences from Jamaica. *African Safety Promotion: A Journal of Injury and Violence Prevention, 4*, 137–145.

Wood, L., & Govender, B. (2013). "You learn from going through the process": The perceptions of South African school leaders about action research. *Action Research, 11*(2), 176–193.

PART III

LESSONS LEARNED AND BEST PRACTICES FOR FUTURE RESEARCH

CHAPTER 8

THINKING THROUGH FIELDWORK ENCOUNTERS IN BRAZIL

Critical Reflections and Future Pathways

Doreen Gordon

A group of progressive scholars in the social sciences has offered sound critiques of the colonizing and neoliberal agendas shaping qualitative research, arguing that traditional approaches are frequently framed within the cultural practices and preferences of the Western world (Bishop, 2005; Tillman, 2002; Rains, Archibald, & Deyhle, 2000; Smith, 1999; Zavala, 2013). These authors have pointed to the need for a critical analysis of the power relationships between researchers and research participants, especially when working with marginalized groups. They also argue against positivistic concepts in qualitative research, such as the neutrality, objectivity, and distance of researchers as well as notions of authority, representation, and accountability in the research process.

New methods of research that challenge traditional approaches have been proposed, such as the inclusion of the voices of native or indigenous

Decolonizing Qualitative Approaches for and by the Caribbean, pages 161–182
Copyright © 2019 by Information Age Publishing

scholars, the use of indigenous epistemologies as frameworks guiding the research process, and methodologies that promote self-determination by participants in different stages of the research process. Scholars such as Jacobs-Huey (2002) and Smith (1999) have argued that indigenous scholars can adopt a technique called critical reflexivity to counteract their "insider" status—this would involve critically thinking about their processes, relationships, and the quality of their data and analysis. However, Narayan (1993) and Griffiths (1998) explain that it is no longer useful to think of researchers as "insiders" or "outsiders"; instead, researchers might be positioned "in terms of shifting identifications amid a field of interpenetrating communities and power relations" (Narayan, 1993, p. 671).

Scholarly reflection on research methods has also been enlivened by fresh and controversial perspectives—such as the postmodern, dialogical, and performative turn in the human sciences, theories of decolonization and critical postcolonial approaches, Third World feminisms, and other critical standpoints (Denzin, 1997, 2005; Freire, 1970; Hall, 1992; hooks, 1981, 1990; Andalzúa, 1983, 1990; Madison, 2005; Conquergood, 1991,1998; Diversi and Moreira, 2009). In varied ways, these approaches have led to broader renewal and critique in the human sciences, specifically in the conduct of qualitative research. While these developments are exciting and important, I argue that decolonizing research strategies is less concerned with the struggle over method and more about creating the spaces that might make decolonizing research possible. The qualitative methods that I will reflect on in this chapter are traditional. I carried out doctoral research on Afro-Brazilian elites in Salvador, Brazil, between 2005–2007, with subsequent follow up visits in the summer of 2013 and 2017.[1] In the following sections of this chapter, I will use the tools of auto-ethnography and interpretative paradigms—particularly critical race theory (CRT), postcolonial perspectives, and feminist theory—to engage with my research and contribute to the conversation about the decolonization of qualitative research in the social sciences.

Auto-ethnography has been described as "a self-narrative that critiques the situatedness of self with others in social contexts" (Spry, 2001, p. 710). It challenges the idea of the objective, distant, and authoritative researcher and creates spaces for self-discovery and learning about others (Chang, 2008, p. 14). In adopting a critically reflexive approach to my ethnography, I will consider what Gornick (2001) has referred to as "self-implication"— that is, seeing one's own part in the situation. I will reflect on the "multiple positionalities" which I occupied as a researcher carrying out fieldwork in Brazil—positionalities that were at times in opposition to each other and which had varying consequences for the research process. Following Evans (2009), I will consider how my way of "seeing" is informed by my sociopolitical and historical epistemology as a Caribbean researcher with an interest in the African diaspora and issues of social justice. Finally, I will explore ways in which our work as researchers can make a difference in terms of decolonizing research methods, by writing the social imaginary in revolutionary ways and by opening spaces for dialogue and social action. I will begin with a story describing my initiation into fieldwork in Brazil.

A JAMAICAN GOING TO BRAZIL

In July 2005, I visited the Brazilian Embassy in Kingston, Jamaica to procure a visa to carry out ethnographic research in the third largest city of Brazil—Salvador de Bahia. I was informed that I needed to submit certain official documents as well as a description of the research I was going to undertake in Brazil. I had already contacted academics at the Federal University of Bahia and received a letter of my official attachment to the Centre for African and Oriental Studies. I dutifully gathered these documents, including proof of my registration in the Anthropology doctoral programme at the University of Manchester, my Jamaican passport, and a few paragraphs about my proposed topic to study upwardly mobile Afro-Brazilians in Salvador.

My goal in carrying out research in Salvador was to explore ethnographically the everyday lives, experiences, and social networks of Afro-Brazilians who had become upwardly mobile in a country with persistent racial and economic inequality. Indeed, although 53% of Brazil's population claim to be Afro-Brazilian (black or brown Brazilians), they comprise a disproportionate number of the poor, are significantly under-represented in national politics, and are socially and economically marginalized in their own country (Dixon, 2016; Mitchell-Walthour, 2017; Telles, 2004).[2] Since the 1990s, however, researchers have noted the growing participation of Afro-Brazilians in middle income occupations such as teaching, engineering, public service, small business and white-collar work (Figueiredo, 2002, 2003; De Santana, 2009). There has also been a shift in the educational achievements of Afro-Brazilians in recent decades, opening the job market at more qualified and higher levels (Hasenbalg & Do Valle Silva, 1999; Sansone, 2003; Telles, 2004). However, new quantitative studies have identified an "elitist profile" for racial inequality in Brazil, the sense that it is more strongly felt by those in higher positions, especially educated Afro-Brazilian women (Campante, Crespo, & Leite, 2004; Lovell, 1999; Mitchell-Walthour, 2017). Focusing on the Afro-Brazilian elite could provide another angle from which to examine how Brazilians coped with, negotiated, or resisted structures of race and class in their society.

A few weeks later, I was asked to attend a meeting with the Consul of Brazil. On the day of the meeting, the secretary ushered me into the Consul's office with an anxious expression on her face. The office had a large glass window offering a panoramic view of Jamaica's commercial capital, New Kingston, with the famous blue-green mountains in the background. However, the expression on the Consul's face was not as pleasant. Presiding behind a broad, mahogany desk was a stern looking man. He let out a heavy sigh, "Are you studying at an American university?" he asked. I explained that I was studying at a university in the United Kingdom and that I would be affiliated with a university in Salvador. Looking like he was about to burst a blood vessel, he declared that, "We do not have black people in Brazil. Brazilians are a mixed-race people." With a dismissive wave of his hand in the direction of the blue-green mountains behind him, he continued, "Here in Jamaica, you have blacks, your country is full of them. But in Brazil people mix. Everybody is mixed, we are a mixture of European, Indian and African."

Keeping quiet proved to be an effective strategy throughout the Consul's telling of the history of Brazil, which was of a country uplifting itself through race mixing. Bahia seemed to be an especially problematic location in the Brazilian landscape for him, upsetting cherished notions of nationhood grounded in ideas of racial blending. Stereotypes of the state of Bahia and its residents, such as their ability to dance and their avoidance of hard work, were expressed in his speech. He warned that,

> Those people in Bahia emphasize and exaggerate the importance of the black contribution to Brazilian people and culture. It is not like that. It is more like what Freyre, our great Sociologist, said about Brazil. He was the first Sociologist to eschew racism and give all the races their proper place. Of course, different parts of Brazil are made up of different people. In the South there are more Europeans. In the North there are more Indigenous people. People from Bahia . . . ah! They love to dance and sing. But don't trust the quality of their work or what those activists say about race at the Federal University of Bahia. Instead, please go to São Paulo and Rio de Janeiro, there you will find the best scholars. They are more objective and rigorous.

Suddenly, he smiled broadly and said that although he was not in agreement with my topic, he wasn't a dictator and that he would issue the visa.

The above description of my encounter with the Consul is reflective of the powerful influence of the Brazilian ideology of racial democracy, popularized at the national level through classic works such as Gilberto Freyre's *The Masters and the Slaves* (1946) and well documented in the vast literature on race in Brazil (Sheriff, 2001; Skidmore, 1999; Telles, 2004; Twine, 1998). This idea of Brazil as a harmonious racial paradise was so popular that in 1949, UNESCO commissioned a study of Brazil's exemplary model of race relations, seen then as an antidote to segregation in the United States, apartheid in South Africa, and particularly the horrors of Nazi Germany. Much to UNESCO's surprise, the scholars who carried out studies in various locations in Brazil revealed that racial prejudice was very much alive and well (Telles, 2004, p. 7). Since this study was completed, social researchers have continued to challenge the central tenets of the idea of a racial paradise with hard data; and a small black movement began to denounce the idea of racial democracy as nothing more than a smokescreen, covering the deep-seated and pernicious racism present in Brazilian society (Mitchell-Walthour, 2017, Telles, 2004).

As a Caribbean scholar, I felt an affinity with the perspective of Afro-Brazilian activists, being part of a tradition of research, writing, and activism from the region that challenges racism and discrimination, critically analyses colonial and postcolonial conditions, and promotes Pan-Africanist thought. My research interests emerged from reading a diverse collection of research on African descendant communities in Latin America, the Caribbean, the United States, the United Kingdom, and South Africa—readings that systematically analysed themes such as race, ethnicity, blackness, class, gender, nationality, colonialism and postcolonialism. These readings shaped the type of questions I asked and the substance of my analysis on race relations in Brazil. However, my experience with the Brazilian Consul caused me to think more critically about my research. For example, I came to appreciate that there are real aspects of peoples' lives in Brazil that underwrite their belief in racial democracy—such as the existence of interracial marriages, friendships between different ethnic groups, and residential integration in some areas. Therefore, Brazil's racial and socio-cultural situation needed to be understood on its own terms. I read Brazilian studies on race relations, engaged with Brazilian academics, and kept a dairy that detailed my personal experiences and observations of social interactions in Brazil. I used these personal reflections in conjunction with my formal notes and interview materials throughout the research process. In addition, I adopted a flexible approach to ethnographic fieldwork, living and socializing in different neighborhoods and talking to people of different ages, genders, and socio-economic backgrounds. This gave me insight into residents' social-cognitive maps of their city and the nuanced and varied ways that they negotiated unequal society in Salvador.

AFRO-BRAZILIAN MOBILITY IN PERSPECTIVE

As a scholar interested in studying African diaspora communities, Brazil was an obvious country to consider because of its large population of African descent, its history of slavery, its persistent racial and economic inequality, and its regional influence and power. Salvador, often referred to as the "Black Rome of Brazil," has long been associated with a strong black identity and culture due to its history as one of the New World's major slave and commercial ports. Indeed, African descendants have maintained strong ties to

West African culture through cuisine, religion, and language in a way that is rivalled by no other diasporic community in the Americas. In recent decades, this representation of the city has taken on magnified proportions with the growth of tourism and black cultural organizations (Dos Santos, 2005). While Salvador appears to be more favourable than most places in the country toward African descendants, social inequalities have long been described as extreme and entrenched (McCallum, 2005). Afro-Brazilian residents confront considerable structural disadvantages in comparison to the Euro-Brazilian elite—such as income disparity, police brutality, high levels of violence in the city, and substandard and underfunded public schools that make it difficult for them to achieve mobility. Nevertheless, past studies have documented the presence of a wealthier segment of the Afro-Brazilian population in the city. Traditionally, these "coloured elites" utilized "whitening" strategies to achieve mobility (De Azevedo, 1996), including being adopted by a white family to become socially white, having white patrons, or pursuing higher education credentials. Alternatively, one could become "whiter" through marriage to lighter skinned spouses, thereby producing lighter skinned children who would have more advantages in the society. This has changed in recent decades, however, as shifting racial politics have influenced a more positive valorization of blackness. In addition, Afro-Brazilians have found opportunities for self-improvement through historical ruptures occurring in the society and the opening of new avenues for social mobility.

To understand the social processes and dynamics of contemporary Afro-Brazilian mobility, I focused on ethnographic observations of the members of seven core families who self-identified as black middle class, their extended kin, and family friends. I carried out semi-formal and unstructured interviews, collecting 115 life histories and genealogies of differently positioned family members. I also participated as much as I could in their daily lives. I met respondents through an initial network of friends in Brazil, employing snowball or chain sampling techniques to recruit other respondents. I also used purposive sampling to identify and conduct interviews and focus groups with black movement leaders and members. In addition, I gathered information from local newspapers, research archives, television programmes, and attended popular events.

During fieldwork, I employed different interview techniques—life histories, genealogies, reflexive dyadic interviews, and interactive interviews. Life histories and genealogies were typically longer sessions conducted either with one or more than one family member, frequently with the aid of memorabilia such as photographs, family albums, and objects or gifts from childhood. These types of interviews revealed rich and detailed information on the experiences, meanings, perspectives, feelings, emotions, and respondents' reactions to events—thereby making space for their voices to be heard. "Reflexive dyadic interviews" are typically one-on-one interviews in which the researcher selects the questions and avoids interfering with or changing the story that is told. (Ellis, 2004, p. 61). I often double checked my information or shared transcriptions of interviews with respondents in a subsequent, private interview. This allowed for more accuracy in understanding, respectful dialogue, and self-determination by respondents.

As Ellis (2004) has argued, these traditional interview situations are useful, but not inherently superior to stories told in other situations. I utilized the "interactive interview," which has been described as a more self-conscious, collaborative process than reflexive, one-on-one interviews (Ellis, 2004, p. 64). These involved three or four people, and sometimes a mix of researchers and participants. For example, when I first began fieldwork, I went to the homes of participants along with another researcher based in Salvador. We had small group discussions with family members about topics such as their perception of their quality of life in the city, challenges or opportunities in access to education, jobs, housing, and health services, and their views on race and racial discrimination in Salvador. These were topics to which we could all relate, and I shared personal experiences from Jamaica. These types of interviews were followed up by a combination of informal discussions and one-on-one interviews.

Research participants lived in varied neighborhoods. Exploring the social networks in which they were embedded revealed the heterogeneity of their lives: they came from a spectrum of social backgrounds—rural and urban—and had varied career trajectories in the civil service, the professions, education, business, the music industry, black movement organizations, banking, food industries, and transportation. Some continued to identify strongly with the working-class neighborhoods where they were raised. However, most people move out of these neighborhoods as soon as they have the chance, living in heavily guarded, modern apartment buildings or gated communities, and socializing in upscale parts of the city where their offices and recreational activities are located. This research dynamic challenged the traditional western assumption in research of the unequal power relations between interviewer (the person assumed to have more power) and interviewee. Access had to be negotiated and credentials checked: this required that I present official letters, documents and IDs, and answer some initial questions. Some of the people I interviewed were not comfortable with being taped or included in photographs. However, I described my research to all interviewees, what I intended to do with the information collected, and the precautions I would take to protect their privacy.[3]

Studies of the black middle classes in the United States, though not directly comparable to black middle classes in Brazil, offer some relevant insights and ways to challenge the focus on western elites.[4] Black middle classes in the United States have been described as economically better off than poorer blacks, yet marginalized when compared to the white middle class.

Furthermore, they are vulnerable to discriminatory practices in both public and personal life (Bowser, 2007; Du Bois, 1999, 1903; Landry, 1987; Patillo-McCoy, 1999). These scholars have also analysed the relationship between middle and lower middle-class blacks. Issues surrounding black mobility were often described as being highly contentious, frequently involving delicate negotiations, practices of differentiation and solidarity, possible accusations of abandoning poorer relatives, and of taking on the values and lifestyles of the whites. These issues are not entirely different in Brazil.

As middle class Afro-Brazilians negotiate the racial hierarchies of their society and the practicalities of everyday life, they must often be selective about social networks and decide on the familial obligations they are willing to fulfil. These social manoeuvrings open them up to criticism from others and sometimes result in a kind of Janus-faced predicament, where individuals display sharply contrasting characteristics in varied contexts.[5] For example, after a few months of living in Salvador, I moved into a working-class neighborhood, living with a family and socializing with their extended kin, some of whom had become upwardly mobile. I met Tarcis, the brother of Pedro, with whom I was living. Tarcis was a lawyer in his 50s who had just acquired a house in a *bairro fino* (fine neighborhood). When I first interviewed Tarcis in his legal office in the city centre, I spoke with him about racism in Salvador and Pedro's claim to have been discriminated against when he applied to the Medical Faculty at the Federal University of Bahia. Tarcis scoffed at Pedro's explanation: "He did not study, that's all! Here in Bahia, black people love to party, go out with their friends, drink and have lots of women. Years later when they are still in the same place, they regret the time they did not spend studying hard to achieve something. At that point, it is really ridiculous to blame your situation on racism" (Interview: October 16, 2005). Unlike most of his siblings, Tarcis had received a good public education and his academic interests were encouraged by his mother. He entered the Law Faculty at the Federal University of Bahia, a traditional bastion of the Euro-Brazilian elite, while working full time and studying at night. He insisted that racism had not hampered his wish to improve himself and that Brazil was a racial democracy. However, others in his family rejected this view, saying that Tarcis had been excluded from university social circles based on white privilege.

Writing ethnography in the context outlined above meant learning to negotiate potentially tense relationships within families and being sensitive to the contradictions and opportunities that social mobility creates for African-descended families. As Jones (2005, p. 767) has argued in relation to working with marginalized ethnic groups, researchers should think about how knowledge, experience, meaning, and resistance are expressed in embodied, tacit, intonational, co-experiential, and covert means. For example, some participants engage with traditional hierarchies of race and class through a personal politics of the body that involves managing their physical appearance with a view to re-styling their self-presentation. For example, the Teixeira family had been part of the higher social classes for generations through kin relations to members of the Euro-Brazilian elite. The immediate family lived in an upscale area of the city and included three sisters, their mother, and an uncle. They were often described by friends as a particularly beautiful and educated family. What was thought to be striking about them was how they presented themselves – their dress, appearance, body language and speech. Bruno, the mother's brother, explained that, "My mother always made sure that we were well dressed, our clothes ironed, our hair looking good before we went anywhere. We were never to go to a party uninvited, standing in a corner in shame. We were always well put together, always in good clothes" (Interview: 22 September 2006). Being well dressed, elegant and demonstrating *boa educação* (well-educated, culturally aware, having a good upbringing) could be used as markers of distinction, setting one apart from the poor, as well as offsetting the risks of racial discrimination within middle class society. In the case of the Teixeiras, education, cultural knowledge, social networks and bodily features are intimately connected and recognized as forms of symbolic capital in the negotiation of their social position. These practices have been neglected in the literature on race relations in Brazil, not least because they do not fit the current research focus on radical processes of social change. In the following sections, I will direct the readers' attention to my positionality and politics, as I locate myself in relation to the subjects of my research.[6] The aim is to develop an engaged, critical perspective on the research process.

ENCOUNTERS IN THE FIELD

In recent years, scholars in the social sciences have paid increasing attention to how gender, race, class, and national origin position researchers and shape the research encounter. These developments have largely occurred due to the increasing number of women, people of colour, and Third World scholars working in fields such as Anthropology, Cultural Studies, African Diaspora Studies, and Queer Studies. Their presence has raised new existential and epistemological questions about the fieldwork encounter, leading to scholarship addressing issues of positionality and power (Anzaldúa 1983, 1990; Caldwell, 2007; Diversi & Moreira, 2009; Freire, 1970; hooks, 1981, 1990, 1992; Hordge-Freeman, 2015; Narayan, 1993; Twine & Warren, 2000). Some of these scholars are searching for new ways to engage with the subjects of their research that challenge and resist ideologies of domination, oppression, and deterministic categories. For example, two Brazilian anthropologists have written an interesting, co-constructed narrative about their fieldwork encounters in Brazil (Diversi and Moreira, 2009). They write about their engagement with marginalized populations in Brazil as white, male, Brazilian academics (albeit with different social backgrounds), using the concept of "betweenness" as decolonizing resistance (Diversi and Moreira, 2009, p. 13–27). They argue that this term has the potential to break down binary oppositions and ideological systems—such as an us/them, either/or view of the world—thereby creating possibilities for finding common ground and dialogue across differences.

The concept of "betweenness" closely captures the sense of socially constructed, fluid spaces and identities that characterized my movements between Jamaica where I live, the United Kingdom where I was studying, and Brazil where I conducted research. In Jamaica, I may be referred to as white, pink, or brown—terms that align me with a light skinned, colonial elite. In the United States or Europe, I become distinctly non-white and Third World. In Brazil and South Africa—countries where I lived for several months—I have been described as "*morena*" (brown/mixed race) or "coloured," respectively.[7] This experience of occupying an in-between identity occurred on different levels. For example, while conducting fieldwork in Brazil, some persons saw me either as coming from a poor, black country or as privileged, especially because I attended a European university and was able to travel. As I spoke English and "refused" to speak Portuguese properly, my status as a foreigner was often reinforced. I was also a single woman in Brazil without a family—a status that could be interpreted as being sexually available to men but potentially threatening to women. My "betweener" status in Brazil was reflected in the reality that I never occupied any single identification uniquely. These nested identities definitely shaped my access to information, as I will explain in the following section.

There were also issues concerning closeness to my research participants. I lived with Brazilian families at different points during my research and sometimes witnessed emotionally upsetting incidents, such as watching a child being insulted or punished, or listening to blatantly sexist or racist comments. I found that creating some distance was necessary. For most of my time in Salvador, I lived in an apartment in a socially mixed neighbourhood near to the city centre. In retrospect, I think this was a good decision that had positive consequences—for example, it was conveniently located, and families would fill me in on occurrences that I had missed. The time away from fieldwork provided me with opportunities to write, recuperate, and process information.

POSITIONALITY IN THE FIELD

My experiences as a researcher on African diaspora communities have influenced my thinking and writing about racialization processes and the centrality of racial negotiations for African descendants in various national contexts. After conducting doctoral research in Brazil, I carried out postdoctoral research in South Africa (2011–2012) and to a lesser extent, at different times in Jamaica. As a scholar of the African diaspora and as a mixed-race woman from the Third World, I produce knowledge that is situated (Haraway, 1988). My understanding of the term "African diaspora" is that it is "a space of mutual recognition of a solidary consciousness across fragmented geographies" (Rahier et al., p. xviii). Despite historical and cultural specificities across national contexts, the African diaspora has become a fundamental term used to conceptualize the experience of African descendant communities, as well as a significant form of academic and political praxis. While studies from other contexts may not directly translate into the Brazilian context, there are still ways in which concepts can be used to deepen scholarly understandings of the similarities and differences among African diaspora communities.[8] One of these concepts is "double consciousness," a term put forward by American sociologist W. E. B. Du Bois that refers to the way black people are forced to not only view themselves from their own perspective, but to see themselves through the eyes of the outside (white) world. According to Du Bois, Black Americans are always struggling to reconcile their "two warring souls," yet this can also be a source of tremendous insight—which he labels "second sight" (Du Bois 1999). This refers to the capacity of African Americans to see incomparably further into race relations when compared to White Americans, and to speak about American society with heightened moral validity. Du Bois's notion of "double consciousness" and "second sight" applied not only to African Americans but to all people who are constructed outside of a dominant, white paradigm.

I hoped to use my positionality as a Caribbean scholar raised in a creole society to develop this "second sight." Indeed, Brazil and the Caribbean have long been described as part of a larger "Plantation-America culture sphere," in view of the importance of this institution upon the history and society of the area, resulting in many common problems and similar contemporary traits throughout the region (Wagley, 1957, p. 5). I thought that this similar context would provide me with unique opportunities for understanding racial negotiations in Brazil. While this was sometimes the case, I was also to discover that my subjectivity in the field was more like managing multiple warring identifications and different layers of ambiguity and power. I found it useful to read the writings of scholars who have critically examined the intersection of racialized, gendered, and national identities as they carried out research in Brazil (Caldwell, 2007; Diversi and Moreira, 2009; Hordge-Freeman, 2015; Twine, 1998). Their reflections on the embodied reflexivity of lived experience resonated with me. How my body and other signifiers were given meaning and interpreted confirmed for me the centrality of race, gender, and body politics in Salvador. For example, my clothes and hair were constantly scrutinized by some Brazilians. In one incident, I visited a black movement organization and was berated by a woman with a short Afro for wearing my hair blow-dried straight—to her this was a sign that I did not accept my blackness. Relating these experiences gives insight into the embodied dilemmas of transnational or diasporic research.

During my fieldwork in Brazil, I lived and socialized in different neighbourhoods, crossing the boundaries of a socially and spatially divided city. For example, I lived in a luxury apartment in a wealthy neighbourhood for a few weeks. This gave me a sense of the lifestyle of the wealthy, many of whom hired support staff such as maids, gardeners, butlers, and nannies, and had access to exclusive services such as ocean piers and boats, restaurants, and clubs. After a few weeks, I moved in with a family in a working-class neighbourhood where I hoped to understand mobility from below. I followed my growing network of Brazilian friends to Candomblé temples[9] and evangelical churches in working class districts, restaurants and bars in popular spots around the city, children's birthday parties in luxury apartment buildings, family vacations in their beach homes, and street parties and festivals, among other activities. Each of these contexts offered different spaces for socialization and required a different *habitus* and way of relating to persons within the specific situation.

Although I was a "betweener," hovering in the uncertainty of shifting positions, I also actively guided these transitions at times, for example, by manipulating my personal style and appearance and by throwing house parties to which I invited my Brazilian friends. They also helped me to become less of a foreigner, by doing things such as encouraging me to buy Brazilian clothes. However, I also had some unexpected experiences. While living in a self-contained apartment in the house of an Italian-Brazilian, I was invited to meals he prepared along with his white Brazilian friends. On one of these occasions, one of his friends seemed perfectly at ease telling me about "dirty black people who smell and do not bathe." To her, I was not *negra* (black) in the Brazilian sense. I was perhaps an honorary white, a foreigner living in the house of her friend. I learned not to react in shock or anger to such comments, but to make key inferences about racial discourse and white habitus in Brazil.

As in most research contexts, the dynamic between myself and my research participants influenced the information they chose to reveal. For example, my skin colour in some contexts was associated with whiteness and privilege, affecting how people in turn described themselves or others to me. However, as they got to know more about my interests in issues of blackness and race, they affectionately referred to me as *nega* or *negona* (black woman). I also found that as a Jamaican, lines of communication quickly opened with most people. Jamaica holds a special symbolic place in Salvador as a country associated with the articulation of a strong black identity and consciousness. Many people wore "Jamaica" T-shirts, and identified strongly with reggae music, especially that of the Marley family, Jimmy Cliff, Gregory Isaacs, and Burning Spear. During my fieldwork, Pelourinho (the historic centre of the city) had a reggae bar, a Jamaican restaurant and shop, and a carnival *bloco* (band) called Olodum that identified with and used the colours of the Rastafari religion. I was certainly able to use this symbolic capital in a variety of social settings in Salvador. I also found that my position as an English speaker from a culture Brazilians considered to be "*legal*" (cool), often placed me among a privileged minority who travelled, studied and worked in global settings. We shared pictures from trips or vacations abroad on social media—as global travellers we were equal.

CRITICAL PERSPECTIVES AND THE STRUGGLE FOR LIBERATION

The Afro-Trinidadian historian C. L. R. James wrote *The Black Jacobins* in 1938 because he believed that the history of the most successful slave revolt in the New World, the Haitian Revolution of 1791–1804, was as significant as the American and French Revolutions. James' writing was not simply an exercise in black pride, *The Black Jacobins* ended with reflections on the relevance of the Haitian Revolution for the struggle for African independence from colonial rule. James understood that what happens to black populations in Africa and around the world poses a potentially revolutionary challenge to structures of inequality in the world at large. C. L. R. James studied revolutions in history because he wanted to help create them and to be part of *the* major project of human liberation—when the oppressed overthrow capitalist exploitation and racial oppression.

In the spirit of C. L. R. James, I understand that race as a social principle tends to put people into boxes that do not accurately reflect reality. The people I interviewed in Salvador were not simply victims of racism and inequality, but actively negotiated this system using a mixture of social, cultural, political, and economic strategies. Not all strategies would be regarded as "revolutionary" from the perspective of black activists or scholars invested in the idea that the black middle classes should be instrumental in changing the conditions of poorer blacks and fighting racial oppression; but there is a desire among many respondents to be considered citizens; with the right to participate and engage in their society just as any other Brazilian person. Other respondents were involved in grassroots community work and actively sought to engage with unequal society, to change the terms of their positioning in Brazilian society and by extension, the world. I turned to feminist perspectives and CRT as I interpreted my ethnographic material, which I found to be flexible and dynamic—a way to deliberately reject "white methods." Feminist theory and CRT both consider "intersectionality," a perspective that emphasizes how social divisions are intermeshed with one another to produce multiple oppressions (Crenshaw, 1989, pp. 139–167). Intersectionality examines race, sex, class, national origin, and sexual orientation, and how their combination is actualized in various settings.

To illustrate the intersectionality approach, I drew from my ethnographic data on everyday life in Brazil, particularly black women living and working in upscale areas of the city for whom beauty and physical appearance emerged as central concerns. For these women, practices and discourses surrounding beauty and body presentation were particularly significant and underscored deeper, politicized issues about race, visibility, social mobility, and citizenship in Brazil. These struggles are racialized and gendered in ways that position the black female body as particularly problematic. In Brazil, a dominant discourse on race has valued physical features associated with whiteness, such as having lighter skin, a narrow nose, thin lips, and straight hair. On the other hand, having dark skin, full lips, and a wide nose are associated with African physical features and assigned a low aesthetic value (Edmonds, 2010; Caldwell, 2007; Gordon, 2013; Hordge-Freeman, 2015). This highlights special issues for black women, because as they climb the social ladder, there is the expectation that their physical appearance will be transformed into socially acceptable feminine ideals that emphasize the submersion of African characteristics, although this is changing both at the societal level and at the level of women's individual perceptions of their beauty (see Gordon, 2013).

Feminist scholars have deepened critical thinking and research on beauty, which I found useful for my research. Researchers such as Cahill (2003) and Gimlin (2002) have argued that beauty is a potentially pleasurable instrument of female agency. These writers emphasize women's subjective experiences of beauty and how they might derive personal satisfaction from styling the body. Indeed, beauty practices and discourses represented an important means through which respondents could have a constructive impact on everyday experiences, defining a space for individual action and for circumventing traditional inequalities. Historically, feminist writings on beauty have tended to emphasize the dominance of Euro-American beauty standards. However, newer approaches have increasingly challenged this Western thinking by exploring cultural logics in specific locales, and creating spaces for decolonizing research on beauty. For example, although whiteness is valued in Brazil, a competing discourse of race exists that promotes the desirability and attractiveness of the brown or mixed-race woman, who typically embodies the national ideal of race mixture (Gordon, 2013; Moreno, Figueroa, and Rivers-Moore, 2013).

Beginning as a theoretical movement within American law schools in the mid- to late 1980s, CRT focused on a critical examination of society and culture and how racial structures, specifically white supremacy, are maintained over time. Although it aims to achieve racial emancipation and promotes anti-subordination, I argue that it is also important to consider what we can learn as scholars from the ordinary work of community organizing and the efforts being made within the black community to struggle against racial oppression. In other words, seeing your research participants as active agents in changing the condition of their lives is also part of decolonizing research. For example, Livio, a research participant who works with the Brazilian government as an economist, runs a community organization that prepares poor, dark-skinned students attending underfunded public schools for success in the competitive entrance examinations for free public universities in Brazil. Livio is in touch with powerful figures in local and national government, as well as intellectuals and activists in Latin America and the United States. His organization is partly funded through a programme at Harvard University. In this environment, social activism across the African diaspora is an effective force. The ideas of black activists from the Caribbean (Marcus Garvey, Walter Rodney), the United States (Martin Luther King, Malcolm X), South Africa (Steve Biko, Nelson Mandela) and key leaders in Brazil (Zumbi dos Palmares, Dandara dos Palmares, Abdias do Nascimento) have been mobilized in Brazilian black movement organizations. Afro-Brazilian scholars and activists are therefore engaged in learning about the history of resistance across the African diaspora and studying and changing the relationship between race, racism, and power. Their activities are key to understanding and challenging processes of racialization and racial discrimination on a wider scale.

Another area of community organizing includes work with Afro-Brazilian women to counteract the psychological effects of dominant racial discourses that give value to having a more European appearance. These organizations promote blackness as a source of pride and focus strongly on the body. Since the 1970s, Afro-Brazilian feminists have brought attention to issues of women's sexual and reproductive health as well as sexual, racial, and domestic violence (Caldwell, 2007; Dos Santos, 2008). Black women's organizations are involved in efforts to build self-esteem among black women through workshops, self-help groups, and community outreach. Workshops on hair braiding underscore efforts to challenge dominant prejudices regarding the hair texture of Afro-Brazilian women (Caldwell, 2007, p. 159). These efforts have had varying effects. In subsequent visits that I made to Salvador in the summers of 2013 and 2017, the organizations involved in this kind of work were developing networks with the state, universities, psychologists, and non-governmental organizations across Brazil and elsewhere to work more deeply on issues of body image, appearance, and psychological health among Afro-Brazilian women and girls. I saw the potential for some of this work to be shared across the African diaspora, perhaps through the medium of photography, video and film.[10]

Researchers have offered innovative techniques for thinking about and engaging with marginalized groups and communities. For example, Diversi and Moreira (2009) experiment with co-narration and what they refer to as "performative auto-ethnography," whereby they include fragments of their conversations and discussions with respondents, snippets of poetry, story-telling, and social action as it unfolds. In the Caribbean, innovative collaborations between scholars and communities are not new. For example, Honor Ford-Smith—a Jamaican actress, scholar, playwright, and poet—has used theatre, performance, the arts, and story-telling to engage in a more satisfying way with communities since the 1970s. She is co-founder and artistic director of Sistren, a theatre collective of working-class women established in 1977. Sistren created its own plays collaboratively, and edited a book of short stories with Ford Smith (Ford Smith, 2005). There are other inspiring and innovative examples like these across Africa, Asia, and the Americas which have long been marginalized from mainstream academic discourse, but are now being considered due to the increased presence of academics from diverse backgrounds.

CONCLUDING COMMENTS

The material presented in this chapter underscores the importance of racialized discourses in postcolonial research and theorizing, and forces us to confront our ideas about difference. Drawing on ethnographic examples from Brazil, I presented a critical reflection on decolonizing the research process. Although this chapter has highlighted ethnography in Salvador, Brazil, the material throws light on the general issue of how African descendants across the diaspora negotiate racialized structures in their societies. Decolonizing research methods such as critical theoretical approaches, performative auto-ethnography, respectful use of audio-visual material, community theatre and popular education, co-narratives, and story-telling can empower scholars to initiate a more sustained dialogue with research participants, communities, and their academic peers about how racialized social systems and hierarchies can be challenged and resisted, thereby offering avenues for dialogue and possible liberation. There is much to be learned from Brazilian and Caribbean anti-racist movements, especially in the present era of Brexit in Europe and the election of Donald Trump in the USA—events which have once again put race and racism in the global spotlight.[11] Brazilian and Caribbean anti-racist movements are instructive for us all, as they challenge our ideas about the way people look, how we perceive blackness, and the cultural meanings we give to physical appearance. Indeed, Miss Jamaica Universe 2017 received worldwide attention recently for confidently stepping onto the global stage with an Afro hairstyle.[12]

Researchers interested in decolonizing the research process frequently engage in critical ethnography—the basic tenet being that of self-reflexivity about issues of power, positionality, race, class, gender, and nationality. Critical ethnography is informed by critical theory and interpretive paradigms, such as CRT, post-colonial perspectives, and feminist approaches. I have shown how these perspectives can help us create spaces in our research for decolonizing work, or for developing research designs that challenge established systems of domination and evoke our common humanity. Self-reflection gives us insight into the factors that shape our perspectives and the situated production of knowledge. In my view, however, it is not meant to stand alone.

Auto-ethnography is most useful when done in combination with other qualitative research techniques (such as interviews, life histories, genealogies, and journaling), and the incorporation of theoretical perspectives to interpret one's material. The goal should be analysis and cultural interpretation, to connect the researcher's perspectives to the wider socio-cultural context. It is my hope that the material presented in this chapter will inspire readers to re-imagine research design—continuing the deconstruction of power and privilege for the benefit of Caribbean knowledge, communities, and participants.

NOTES

1. Respondents self-identified and/or were identified by others as being black middle class. I included income as a defining characteristic of middle class status (Neri, 2008) by asking questions on respondents' range of income. However, income is not always a reliable measure of class. Respondents also discussed education, neighborhood residence, type of house, and access to health insurance as defining features of class status. For a more detailed discussion of the trajectories, origins, identities, and lifestyles of the contemporary black middle classes in Salvador, please see Figueiredo (2002, 2003), De Santana (2009) and Gordon (2015).

2. The Brazilian national census collects date on race, using the categories Black, Brown, Yellow, White, and Indigenous. In this article, I am most interested in the category Black (Pretos) and Brown (Pardos)—the latter being a racially mixed category. When I refer to them together, I use the term Afro-Brazilian or African descendant.

3. Researchers studying elites have written about similar methodological issues concerning access, trust, privacy, and conducting interviews (Dexter 2006; McDowell 1998; Smith 2006; Zuckerman 1972).

4. For example, business, political, and bureaucratic elites of capitalist societies that are the focus of a small but growing literature on elites (Dexter, 2006; Marcus, 1983; McDowell, 1998; Nader, 1969; Smith, 2006; Zuckerman, 1972).

5. I borrow the term "janus-faced" from discussions of ethnic consciousness and identity in Wade's (2001) work on racial identity and nationalism in Latin America and Comaroff's (1987) work on the nature of ethnicity and its diverse experiential forms.

6. By "subjects," I mean both the topics and themes of my research as well as my research participants.

7. In South Africa, I carried out post-doctoral research between 2011–2012 at the University of Pretoria.

8. African Diaspora Studies was developed in the 1990s in the United States, with an increased amount of scholarly work exploring issues of race, culture, and politics in black diaspora communities. Paul Gilroy's work has had a particularly important impact on the development of this field of study (Gilroy, 1987, 1993a, 1993b).

9. Candomblé temples, which are led by a priest or priestess, are often called "terreiros" or "casas" (houses). Temples are often the homes of Candomblé followers and are used for religious purposes. Candomblé is an Afro-American religious tradition, practiced mainly in Brazil, often combining elements from African religion and Catholicism.

10. The growing popularity of technology and the user friendliness of cameras and videos have led to an increased use of visual tools in the research process. However, critical reflection by researchers is needed when collecting and using visual images in educational research. Ethical issues of trust within the research relationship and the rights of those who are depicted in visual material should be seriously considered. Respectful use of visual materials should involve community participants in filming their own realities—for example, see Turner (1992).

11. After World War II, there was a massive rejection of "race" on a global level and a repudiation of Nazism and Nazi racial theories. Race was rejected as a biological fact, followed by desegregation in the USA and the rise of multiculturalist perspectives and policies in many countries. Indeed, many people thought that the world had entered a post-racial era—only to be faced with the current wave of nationalism, ultra-conservative politics, and intolerance now sweeping across many nations.

12. See Kristina Rodulfo's article in POPSUGAR, "Miss Jamaica wore an Afro at Miss Universe 2017, and we are so here for it" (December 17, 2017). Retrieved online from https://www.yahoo.com/lifestyle/m/9ca3264e-0668-3adb-aa42-c57d2d5efea4/ss_miss-jamaica-wore-an-afro-at.html

REFERENCES

Anzaldúa, G. E. (1983). La Prieta. In C. Moraga and G. E. Anzaldúa (Eds.), *This bridge called my back: Writings by radical women of colour* (pp. 198–209). New York, NY: Kitchen Table, Women of Colour Press.

Anzaldúa, G. E. (1990). *Making face, making soul/ Haciendo Caras: Creative and critical perspectives by women of colour.* San Francisco, CA: Aunt Lute Foundation Books.

Bishop, R. (2005). Freeing ourselves from neocolonial domination in research: A Kaupapa Maori approach to creating knowledge. In N. Denzin and Y. Lincoln (Eds.), *The SAGE handbook of qualitative research* (pp. 109–138). Los Angeles, CA: SAGE.

Bowser, B. P. (2007). *The black middle class: Social mobility – and vulnerability.* Boulder, CO: Lynne Rienner.

Cahill, A. J. (2003). Feminist pleasure and feminist beautification. *Hypatia, 18*(4), 42–64.

Caldwell, K. L.. (2007). *Negras in Brazil: Re-envisioning black women, citizenship, and the politics of identity.* New Brunswick, NJ: Rutgers University Press.

Campante, F., Crespo, A., and Leite, P. (2004). Desigualdade salorial entre raças no mercado do trabalho urbano Brasileiro: Aspectos regionais. *Revista Brasileira de Economia, 58*(2), 185–210.

Chang, H. (2008). *Autoethnography as method.* Walnut Creek, CA: Left Coast Press.

Comaroff, J. (1987). Of totemism and ethnicity: Consciousness, practice, and the signs of inequality. *Ethnos: Journal of Anthropology, 52*, 301–323.

Conquergood, D. (1991). Rethinking ethnography: Towards a critical cultural politics. *Communications Monographs, 58*, 178–194.

Conquergood, D. (1998). Beyond the Text: Toward a performative cultural politics. In S. J. Dailey (Ed.), *The future of performative studies: Visions and revisions* (pp. 25–36). Annandale, VA: National Communication Association.

Crenshaw, K. (1989). Demarginalizing the intersection of race and sex: A black feminist critique of anti-discrimination doctrine, feminist theory, and antiracist politics. *University of Chicago Legal Forum.* Chicago IL: University of Chicago Law School.

De Azevedo, T. (1996). *As elites de cor numa cidade Brasileira.* Salvador: Editoria da Universidade Federal da Bahia.

De Santana, I. (2009). À margem do centro: Ascensão social e processos identitários entre negros de alto escalão—O caso de Salvador. PhD Dissertation, Universidade Federal de Bahia, Salvador, Brazil.

Denzin, N. (1997). *Interpretive ethnography: Ethnographic practices for the 21st century.* Thousand Oaks, CA: SAGE.

Denzin, N. (2005). *Performance ethnography: Critical pedagogy and the politics of culture.* Thousand Oaks, CA: SAGE.

Dexter, L. A. (2006). *Elite and specialized interviewing.* Colchester, England: ECPR Press.

Diversi, M. and Moreira, C. (2009). *Betweener talk: Decolonizing knowledge production, pedagogy, and praxis.* New York, NY: Routledge.

Dixon, K. (2016). *Afro-politics and civil society in Salvador da Bahia, Brazil.* Gainesville: University Press of Florida.

Dos Santos, J. T. (2005). *O poder da cultura e a cultura no poder.* Salvador, Bahia: Edufba.

Dos Santos, S. B. (2008). Brazilian black women's NGOs and their struggles in the areas of sexual and reproductive health: Experiences, resistance, and politics. PhD Thesis. Austin: The University of Texas at Austin.

Du Bois, W. E. B. (1899). *The Philadelphia negro: A social study.* Philadephia, PA: University of Philadelphia Press.

Du Bois, W. E. B. (1999). *The souls of black folk.* 1903. New York, NY: Vintage Books.

Edmonds, A. (2010). *Pretty Modern: Beauty, sex, and plastic surgery in Brazil.* Durham, NC: Duke University Press.

Ellis, C. (2004). *The ethnograhic eye: A methodological novel about autoethnography.* New York and Oxford: Altamira Press.

Evans, H. (2009). The origins of qualitative inquiry in the Caribbean. *Journal of Education and Development in the Caribbean, 11*(1), 14–22.

Figueiredo, A. (2002). *Novas elites de cor: Estudo sobre os profissionais liberais negros de Salvador.* São Paulo: Annablume.

Figueiredo, A. (2003). *A classe média negra não vai ao paraíso: Trajetórias, perfis e negritude entre os empresários negros* [The black middle class does not go to paradise: Trajectories, profiles and blackness among black entrepreneurs]. PhD Dissertation. Rio de Janeiro: Universidade do Rio de Janeiro.

Ford Smith, H. (2005). *Lionheart gal: Life stories of Jamaican women.* Kingston, Jamaica: The University of the West Indies Press.

Freire, P. (1970). *Pedagogy of the oppressed.* (20th anniversary ed.). M. Bergman Ramos (Trans). New York, NY: Continuum.

Freyre, G. (1946). *The masters and the slaves* (S. Putnam, Trans.). New York, NY: Knopf.

Gilroy, P. (1987). *There ain't no black in the Union Jack: The cultural politics of race and nation.* Chicago: University of Chicago Press.

Gilroy, P. (1993a). *The black atlantic: Modernity and double-consciousness.* Cambridge, MA: Cambridge University Press.

Gilroy, P. (1993b). *Small acts: Thoughts on the politics of black cultures.* London, England: Serpent's Tail.

Gimlin, D. (2002). *Body work: Beauty and self-image in American culture.* Berkeley: University of California Press.

Gordon, D. (2013). A beleza abre portas: Beauty and the racialized body among black middle class women in Salvador, Brazil. *Feminist Theory 14*(2), 203–218.

Gordon, D. (2015). Negotiating inequality: The contemporary black middle classes in Salvador, Brazil. In K. Hart and J. Sharp (Eds.), *People, money and power in the economic crisis* (pp. 106- 128). New York, NY: Berghahn Press.

Gornick, V. (2001). *The situation and the story: The art of personal narrative.* New York, NY: Farrar, Straus & Giroux.

Griffiths, M. (1998). *Educational research for social justice: Getting off the fence.* Buckingham, England: Open University Press.

Hall, S. (1992). Cultural studies and its theoretical legacies. In L. Grossberg, C. Nelson and P. Treicher (Eds.), *Cultural Studies* (pp. 277–294). New York, NY: Routledge.

Haraway, D. J. (1988). Situated knowledges: The science question in feminism and the privilege of partial perspective. *Feminist Studies 14*(3), 575–599.

Hasenbalg, C. A. and Do Valle Silva, N. (1999). Race and educational opportunity in Brazil. In R. Reichmann (Eds.), *Race in contemporary Brazil: From indifference to inequality* (pp. 53–66). State College: Pennsylvania State University.

hooks, b. (1981). *Ain't I a woman: Black women and feminism.* Boston, MA: South End.

hooks, b. (1990). *Yearning: Race, gender, and cultural politics.* Boston, MA: South End.

hooks, b. (1992). *Black looks: Race and representation.* Boston, MA: South End Press.

Hordge-Freeman, E. (2015). *The colour of love: Racial features, stigma and socialization in Black Brazilian families.* Austin: University of Texas Press.

Jacobs-Huey, L. (2002). The natives are gazing and talking back: Review of the problematics of positionality, voice and accountability among "native" anthropologists. *American Anthropologist, 104*(3), 791–804.

James, C. L. R. (1963). *The Black Jacobins.* 1938. New York, NY: Vintage Press.

Jones, S. H. (2005). Autoethnography: Making the personal political. In N. Denzin and Y. Lincoln, *The SAGE handbook of qualitative research* (pp. 763–792). Thousand Oaks, CA: SAGE.

Landry, B. (1987). *The new black middle class.* Berkeley: University of California Press.

Lovell, P. (1999). Women and racial inequality at work in Brazil. In M. Hanchard (Ed.), *Racial politics in contemporary Brazil* (pp. 138–153). Durham, NC: Duke University Press.

Madison, D. S. (2005). *Critical ethnography: Method, ethics, and performance.* Thousand Oaks, CA: SAGE.

Marcus, G. E. (1983). *Elites: Ethnographic issues.* Albuquerque: University of New Mexico Press.

McCallum, C. (2005). Racialized bodies, naturalized classes: Moving through the city of Salvador da Bahia. *American Ethnologist 32*(1), 100–117.

McDowell, L. (1998). Elites in the City of London: Some methodological considerations. *Environment and Planning A, 30*(12), 2133–2146.

Menchú, R. (2010). *I, Rigoberta Menchu: An Indian woman in Guatemala.* London and New York, NY: Verso.

Mitchell-Walthour, G. (2017). Economic pessimism and racial discrimination in Brazil. *Journal of Black Studies, 48*(7), 675–697.

Moreno Figueroa, M. G. and Rivers-Moore, M. (Eds.) (2013). Beauty, race and feminist theory in Latin America and the Caribbean. *Feminist Theory 14*(2), 131–136.

Nader, L. (1969). Up the anthropologist: Perspectives gained from studying up. In D. Hymes (Ed.), *Reinventing Anthropology* (pp. 284–311). New York, NY: Random House.

Narayan, K. (1993). How native is a "native" anthropologist? *American Anthropologist, 95,* 671–686.

Neri, M. C. (2008). *The new middle class.* Rio de Janeiro: Fundação Getúlio Vargas/ Centro de de Politicas Socias. Retrieved on 23 November, 2017 from http://www.cps.fgv.br/ibrecps/M3/M3_MidClassBrazil_FGV_eng.pdf

Pattillo-McCoy, M. (1999). *Black picket fences: Privilege and peril among the black middle class.* Chicago: University of Chicago Press.

Rahier, J. M., Hintzen, P. C. and Smith, F. (2010). *Global circuits of blackness: Interrogating the African diaspora.* Urbana-Champaign: University of Illinois Press.

Rains, F. V., Archibald, J-A., & Deyhle, D. (2000). Introduction: Through our eyes and in our own words. *International Journal of Qualitative Studies in Education, 13*(4), 337–342.

Sansone, L. (2003). *Blackness without ethnicity: Constructing race in Brazil.* New York, NY: Palgrave Macmillan.

Sheriff, R. E. (2001). *Dreaming equality: Colour, race, and racism in urban Brazil.* New Brunswick, NJ: Rutgers University Press.

Skidmore, T. E. (1999). *Brazil: Five centuries of change.* Oxford, England: Oxford University Press.

Smith, K. E. (2006). Problematizing power relations in elite interviews. *Geoforum, 37,* 643–653.

Smith, L. T. (1999). *Decolonizing methodologies: Research and indigenous peoples.* London, England: Zed Books.

Spry, T. (2001). Performing autoethnography: An embodied methodological praxis. *Qualitative Inquiry, 7,* 706–732.

Telles, E. E. (2004). *Race in another America: The significance of skin colour in Brazil.* Princeton, NJ: Princeton University Press.

Tillman, L. C. (2002). Culturally sensitive research approaches: An African-American perspective. *Educational Researcher, 31*(9), 3–12.

Turner, T. (1992). Defiant images: The Kayapo appropriation of video. *Anthropology Today 8*(6), 5–16.

Twine, F. W. (1998). *Racism in a racial democracy.* New Brunswick, NJ: Rutgers University Press.

Twine, F.W. and Warren, J. W. (2000). *Racing research, researching race: Methodological dilemmas in critical race studies.* New York, NY: New York University Press.

Wagley, Charles. (1957). Plantation America: A culture sphere. In V. Rubin (Ed.), *Caribbean Studies: A Symposium* (pp. 3–13). Seattle: University of Washington Press.

Wade, P. (2001). Racial identity and nationalism: A theoretical view from Latin America. *Ethnic and Racial Studies, 24*(5), 845–865.

Zavala, M. (2013). What do we mean by decolonizing research strategies? Lessons from decolonizing, indigenous research projects in New Zealand and Latin America. *Decolonization: Indigeneity, Education, and Society 2*(1), 55–71.

Zuckerman, H. A. (1972). Interviewing an ultra-elite. *The Public Opinion Quarterly, 36,* 159–175.

CHAPTER 9

DECOLONIZING CARIBBEAN HERITAGE

Lessons Learned and Best Practices for Future Research

Anne Pajard

By the end of the 20th century, Caribbean heritage was institutionally defined by an inherited European conception, which developed hand in hand with the formation of national identities. It represented the greatness of nations and was founded on the value of rare, ancient, precious objects and monuments as historic proof of the value of cultures and people. Those definitions excluded its construction of colonized people at different levels and all who were not part of the elite, delegitimizing their culture, visions of the past and transmissions. Those who were in the shadows of this Modernity, were those who felt oppressed by the past and its continuities and they began to demystify the positive value of Modernity, showing its hidden face and extreme violence deployed out of Europe. This violence affected Europe in a boomerang effect "Choc en retour" with the advent of World War II (Césaire, 2004, p. 13). Furthermore, the Holocaust shook the making

Decolonizing Qualitative Approaches for and by the Caribbean, pages 183–203
Copyright © 2019 by Information Age Publishing
183

of history and knowledge, showing that oppressors could voluntarily erase traces of the past as to deny humanity. Struggles for freedom and equality as anticolonial, underground and feminists' movements converged with larger questionings of the idea of the truth after World War II, in complex intertwined dynamics.

Poets and intellectuals from the Caribbean, such as Aimé Césaire and Frantz Fanon (Fanon, 1971), made a significant contribution to the transnational struggles against imperialism and colonial systems, grounded on connections of local experiences, multiple world junctions facilitated by their travelling, encounters and commitments. This first Caribbean generation hardly criticized and deconstructed evidences that had inferiorized people. From the 1960s the Caribbean had seen the development of the second generation of discourses, illustrated by many intellectual movements from Creoleness (Bernabé, Chamoiseau, & Confiant, 1989) to the thought of Archipelago (Benítez-Rojo, 2008). The movements were inspired by these predecessors but also by cultural practices that were delegitimized long ago. These discourses can be seen as an effort to employ a decolonized project for Caribbean people and societies so as to reveal their own creativity, strength and abilities. Poets such as Derek Walcott and Edouard Glissant, have undertaken a rehabilitation of Caribbean people and inhabited spaces as territories with resources and agencies. In their work, the Caribbean is seen as both a real and utopic space. It is a space that allows the understanding of fragmentation and abilities to perform differently in the common space as well as a fertile ground to rebuild each other and to design a horizon to renew the sight of the past and the vision of a territory, breaking with erected borders.

> There is a territory wider than this—wider than the limits made by the map of an island—which is the illimitable sea and what it remembers. (Walcott, 1992, para. 45)

They have shared within a worldness of connexity opposite to globalization, new perspectives to imagine how the "ordinary" could rise from different patterns based on the "relation" instead of intrinsic essentialized elements; on "diversality" instead of sameness, on creation and movement instead of fixity. Their work underpinned pathways to review the idea and processes of heritage from its social and living functions. Nevertheless, in the 21st century, the issue of heritage still stigmatizes many conflicts, distrusts and uncomfortable feelings in the Caribbean. Actors have to contend with the lack of thorough analyses as well as more explicit frameworks in dealing with Caribbean heritage in its diversity (monuments, material, natural and intangible), its connectedness, and complexity; all of which constitute challenges for social well-being and sustainable development.

Accordingly, this chapter presents data from a *multidirectional approach* study which emerged at the end of a doctoral study to highlight the role of what is termed *territorialities* within the context of heritage. The chapter further investigates underlying aspects of concurrent perceptions of the definition of heritage. It aims to design new pathways to understand heritage in its social functions, as a process that can reveal and contribute to the reappropriation of resources, a social linkage between time and spaces for shared benefits. First I present the idea of heritage, its legacy and perspectives in a Caribbean context linked to the world. Second, I provide examples of difficulties, challenges, or problematic attitudes toward heritage that appears as symptoms of problems. Lastly, I illustrate an identification of paradigmatic obstacles and present some perspectives for future research and social actors.

DECOLONIZING THE LEGACY OF HERITAGE: GLOBAL CONTEXT AND CARIBBEAN SPECIFICITIES

The problematics of Caribbean heritage intertwines specific aspects and challenges in a global world. Heritage is linked to the human social condition but it also became an international institutionalized concept that originated from the formation of European national identity and with the beginning of colonization. People, individually and collectively, inherited a world, objects, processes, norms and legal systems they did not choose, but they are also actors of a transmission process that can act on the present and the future. The goal is then to identify the constraints and seek the freedom we have vis-à-vis the past and its prefiguration. It engages in a long and complex process.

Caribbean societies inherited many remnants such as books and monuments from the slavery and colonial period. These "materialities" have an ambiguous status. As witnesses of the past, they obviously embed information. They can be considered as heritage because of their antique appearance and rare features, but at the same time as a non-heritage because of their negative symbolic value that recalls the way this past was institutionalized, the legitimacies and/or delegitimizations that limited the subject's places and their possibilities to act. These troubled feelings toward the past are reinforced by new impossibilities to easily share elements largely considered as a positive value. Interviews with librarians, for example, highlighted the impossibility of digitizing works from anticolonialists and from authors of the postcolonial period (even when they are no longer published), although they represent an important legacy for recent nations. Caribbean nations adopted the Berne Convention, an international agreement goverening copyright that prevents full public sharing of knowledge and content before at least 50 years after the author's death (WIPO, 2017). This legal international framework inherited from the period of Modernity helps to reproduce the representation of an unbalanced heritage in favour of the colonial vision in internet space, which constitutes the main media for representation and circulation of information in the contemporary world.

The changing status of Caribbean popular cultural practices such as storytelling, music and dance becoming heritage objects and tourism products also raise many questions. It can encourage new spectacularizations, the renewal of cultural essentialism myths, denying the diversity of connections and the creativity of living Caribbean societies. The diversification of what is defined as heritage in the 21st century does not seem to have gone hand in hand with a reformed way of reimagining connections between people. Changing objects considered as heritage or changing technologies that support its circulation, doesn't mean that minds, normalized values, legal systems and tools are sincerely changed. Heritage processes implicitly define many "we," whose conceptions are impacted by the idea of cultural identity as sameness developed within Modernity. Contemporary conceptions unconsciously embed many aspects of those normalized visions of the common space inherited from precedent constructions that limits the renewing of the idea of heritage. Many Internet algorithms also favor new "enclosures," homophily, and polarization (groups sharing the same view) by accounting for users' preferences (Bessi et. al., 2016).

Heritage can be seen as a barometer of the way societies are imagining, acting, publicizing and normalizing the relationships that characterize the social condition. Decolonizing heritage does not mean to erase or deny what comes from the colonial order (ideas, materialities, possessions and meanings) but to develop a conscious and active relation toward the past in specific contexts. It can be seen as a necessity to build unrestricted postures, to be vigilant of new forms of dominations and inequalities and to engage in an ongoing process centered on the research of shared benefits for the populace.

Caribbean Historical Context: Understanding the Building of a Non-Heritage Space Linked to the Building of a Non-Territory

The Caribbean was one of the first places of globalization, politically wrought from the 16th century to serve the benefits of Modernity of European territories, who were experiencing the first world globalization that came with the industrialization of a slavery system based on racial theorization. The paroxysmic violence embedded within slavery and colonialism, its intensity and duration, shaped Caribbean societies. The native people have been largely exterminated and the majority of the contemporary Caribbean population consists of descendants who have been displaced due to the economic profits of colonial nations. This construction breaks the possibility of adopting an atavistic myth of origin (Glissant, 2006) which founded on the myth of the superposition-fusion of a cultural, geographical and political space built upon the European national identities. It places the Caribbean in a favoured position to rethink paradigms of the postmodern world marked by displacements, circulations, and localness (Apadurai, 1996) as well as worldness connections.

The *ante* colonial cultures of Caribbean people and places, have been willingly amputated to dehumanize people, to erase their past and at the same time to demonstrate their lack of humanity. Slavery represents the paroxysmic illustration of this strategy. The willingness to hinder communication and limit the leaving traces of realities was omnipresent: separating people sharing the same languages on different plantations, prohibiting the learning of reading and writing and limiting the registration of voices in legal systems (Rogers, 2015) constitute some examples. The Caribbean, its inhabitants and living territories were made for other territories, written by others, dispossessed, created and seen as objects unable to act. It "was there to be written about, not to write itself" (Walcott, 1992 para. 30). This structural process still impacts the Caribbean and the way the self can be taught.

Nevertheless, despite this political and economical oppressive framework, Caribbean people used their agencies to create underground imaginative systems, (Bonniol, 2013), with their abilities, memories, imagination, contacts, contexts and capacity to develop communication and transmission processes in their everyday lives. Thus, the natural environment and the configuration of each space in an archipelago are fully embodied within different, but connected, cultural dynamic practices and symbolic orders.

The coexistence of two interacting orders, one institutionalized and legitimate, valued and created from, by and for the colonial order and the other one illegitimate for social daily life, created a specific dislocation that impacted the "communicative action" (Habermas, 1981). Not only did this affect the meaning of language but also in a specific communicative capacity embodied in social activities. After the abolition of slavery, the diversity of the populace was growing, workers came from different places of the world such as India, Africa, China, Syria and Lebanon. They were faced with new forms of inferiorization in unwholesome competitions fostered by the colonial order.

As a result of the conception of a non-existing place as a full living territory, heritage had very little political attention from the colonial metropoles. It was mainly linked to the promotion of the colonial vision and economy (Cummins, 2004), and largely restricted to white elites. By the end of the 20th century, despite the political decolonization, the Caribbean was mainly seen as a non-heritage space. The Caribbean heritage didn't fit within the internationalized institutional conception of heritage promoted by the UNESCO 1972 Convention (Van Hoof, 2000).

The region was perceived without any exceptional value for the world, except the *exotic* landscapes of beaches, attractive for mass tourism that replaced the plantation economy from the latter half of the 20th century. Some researchers consider this touristic economy as an historical *continuum*, a neocolonialist system (Wong, 2015). The reappropriation of an inclusive heritage encountered the challenge of the reappropriation of spaces as living territories for independant as well as non independant countries. This required taking care of specific contexts, effective social transmissions processes and abilities to build balanced links with the world.

Framework to Renew Posture Toward Heritage

Caribbean intellectual and poetic discourse went beyond the dichotomies of the *Western/rest of the world* or *self/others* to identify the process of alienation and its actors. Alienation is defined by a reverse process while that which denies ones humanity, agency and, makes one a stranger, is himself the stranger (Fanon, 1971, p. 71). Notably, one who is unable to get involved in a relationship, unable to take part in an environment and wants to possess the world instead of living in it and sharing it, is the stranger. The alienation process also has effects such as driving people to perceive themselves in the sight of the other, as objects.

Foucault's archaeology method applies to the knowledge of the past and is useful to search the conditions of what is considered as valid (Foucault, 2008). It can be applied to heritage and by reverse questioning, helps to identify what is disqualified. It requires cross-examination of *heritageness* or *patrimoniality* of things and also relations to the past that are disqualified, out of a legitimate sphere. If the past itself is unattainable, we can face the transmission process.

Trouillot (2015) invites us to question events and narrations that linked the present to the past, their conditions of productions, frameworks that shape the stories, transmission processes and all elements that intervene with their status. Investigating heritage draws attention on the way heritage has been and is predicted, anticipated or silenced. Glissant's (2006) arguments with "art of traces" and "thought of traces" opens to a *consciousness of the trace* that invites one to think of the past as paths. The poet coins two meanings to the term trace. In the French West Indies, "trace" also refers to a small path that was used and recognized by Maroons to attain freedom but disguised for their *trackers*. Glissant draws attention to the intention of the quest of traces, which can also be fully considered as a crucial question with contemporary uses of internet traces. Glissant designs another type of genealogy, where ancestrality and heirs are predecessors and successors, sharing intentions, senses and directions.

In his Nobel Prize lecture, Derek Walcott (Walcott, 1992) also originally enlightens towards the past that can help to renew perspectives. Performance is an essential aspect of the described local social scenes. Theses performances are characterized by a social capacity to create where participants contribute with their own memories, heritage and knowledge to enrich the ongoing collective performance. This displaces the approach towards heritage, from objects with naturalized values to living and dynamic processes that constitute the center of new questionings.

METHODOLOGY AND DATA:
A MULTIDIRECTIONAL APPROACH

The starting point of this research was to understand the conceptual and actual problems that heritage raises in the Caribbean and to consider new paths. As the problem is not a fact but a complex phenomenon, I utilized a multidirectional approach methodology to investigate interacting aspects that intertwines at different scales. This expression has been inspired by Rothberg (2009) who has used the term "multidirectional" to describe interactions between Jewish and colonial memory in the public space. Our use implies a broader meaning that involves the exploration of a network of traces of different natures and their underlying interactions. As a result, the data collected and the type of analysis applied during four years of a doctoral research were adapted to each element.

The corpus built for the research investigated opposite referents and disruption about the two subjects (heritage/Caribbean) in a wide range of documents and data from different places and languages such as thesaurus, encyclopedias, dictionaries, scientific and professional literature, media, websites and social networks analysis. Additional data was gathered through observations and interviews with heritage actors, from organizations, networks and heritage projects, texts and data from institutions, law, lists and conventions. Cross-analysis was built iteratively to identify problematic nodes and transverse active spheres. The expression *multidirectional approach* emerged at the end of the research to purport this complex methodology and to highlight the role of what we called *territorialities*.

Cross-Analysis: Understanding the Importance of "Territorialities" in Heritage Issues

While some cross-cutting issues emerged as ubiquitous such as the political, economic framework and the techniques of inscription and circulation;

the geographical features and relationship to space is a fertile starting point to capture the complexity of the sayings about the Caribbean. The analysis of *territorialities* and production of the *territory* constituted a transversal line of investigation applied to all the aspects of the subject. It allows analyzing cultural aspects at distinct levels, their sedimentation and flux, while avoiding the risk of essentialization of *identity*. Physical places are also linked to heritage issues. As physical and mental spatializations could be an interesting starting point for other social phenomenon analysis, I will describe briefly the methodology designed. The term *territorialities* embed the recognition of different kinds of relationship to geographical referents and their role in contemporary human interactions. We distinguished two types of territorialities that condition human conceptions and actions:

Type 1: Physical Space of the Experience
- "Inhabited" space, lived in the long term
- "Temporary" space, living space considered as a transit
- "Visited" space

Type 2: Imagined Space
- Space "horizon," space in which one considers its future
- "Inherited" space, ancestry, transmission relation
- Space of "connivance," space associated to friends, subject of a work...
- Mediatized space, represented space (texts, pictures, sounds, multimedia)

Diverse territorialities intervene at diverses densities in social action. I paid attention to the importance of effective and symbolic links with personal and collective destinies–negative/positive charges of territorialities)–historicities/contemporary issues. The goal was to better identify how territorialities act in the common space, in stated and/or hidden ways, from heritage dynamics. The research questions that guided the study were:

- How territorialities are qualified, disqualified, intervene in organizations, projects, production of discourse and intellectual circulation, generate and/or influence the equilibrium/imbalance between various forms of territorialialities and territorial production?
- What is the role of stated and underlying territorialities in heritage conflicts?
- How territorialities conditions positioning, perspectives, enunciation and the information environment?

Qualitative Analytical Procedures

Qualitative approaches were privileged. Automated or modelable approach wouldn't have been relevant. Corpuses are not entirely digitized and further; it would have limited the analysis to toponyms or geographical names and masked the complexity of cultural elements that symbolically refer to places and their individual and collective interacting meanings.

Territorialities in the Media Space

This typology refers to the following questions: What are the statements and territoriality underlying, implicit in the "we" and "you" and/or indices (cultural references to territories)? How are they staged? How do they interact in the statements of the past in the public space? Do they have an impact in the manifestation of conflicts in the public space?

Types of Analysis: textual analysis of geographic data such as place of publication, distribution and language. Elements analyzed included territorialities in the organization of knowledge, the structuring of "norms," and in "binarisations" for/against in heritage conflicts. Places of enunciation, places and area of imagined audience and real audiences (spaces of experience, imagined spaces).

Territorialities in Organizations, Associations, Infrastructures, Events

Corpus: websites and social networks of organizations, documentation of organizations and projects (digital and printed), field observations, speeches, interviews and discussions with stakeholders in different categories (founders, members, participants).

Type of Analysis: collection of factual and balanced information on the consideration (qualification/disqualification, balance/imbalance) territorialities and territories (factual and feelings of the actors). Elements analyzed: territorialities governance models establishment and representation places, territorialities participants according to the statutes, effective meeting places, territoriality and territories statements and references.

Biographies: Impact of Territorialities in Action/Social Commitment

Questioning territorialities and their impact in the intellectual circulation, in the commitment: Where were the individuals born? Where did they live? What are the geographical occurrences that appear directly and indi-rectly in their work, in their sayings, in their actions?

Corpus: collection of factual material from biographies, interviews and observation.

Type of Analysis: correlation between trajectories, action and discourse.

This multidirectional approach has made it possible not to be limited to the visible elements in the analysis of the problems related to the heritage of the Caribbean. We will briefly expose some examples of events or pos-tures which can be considered as symptoms of the heritage communication dysfunctions before identifying underlying central questions and opening perspectives to rethink heritage as a factor of social link.

FINDINGS

Discord, Conflicts, and Obliteration: Symptoms of Problems Toward the Idea of Heritage in the Caribbean

Starting from conflicts and contestation, this section also shows that the absence of questioning the awkwardness towards the idea of heritage brings about unconscious evasion, obliteration and distortion strategies, which are observed particularly in the treatment of objects representing the colonial past. These can also impact the way cultural practices are treated as heri-tage. Even if some new Caribbean nations often change what is declared as heritage, they did not necessarily modify the professional, legislative tools and framework of heritage and its consequences.

The point made with examples below does not consist of formulating judgements on the validity of claims or accusations towards actors but, re-veal a worrisome absence of communication. The coexistence of separated spheres of communications, disqualifying each other from a vision of the common space, creates frustrations, social rupture and reinforces poten-tial violence.

Examples in the French Caribbean

In 1991, in the island of Martinique, the head of the statue of Joséphine (the empress of the settler group and wife of the emperor Napoléon who restored slavery) -erected in Fort-de-France in the 19th century and already displaced in 1974 by Aimé Césaire-, was cut off and stolen by anonymous individuals. This action, qualified in the database of the French Ministry of Culture as an "act of vandalism" (1992), illustrates a contestation of the of-ficial representation of the past. This action marks a rupture that still deeply modifies the initial symbolism order of this material heritage in the pub-lic space, conferring a double meaning. A symbol of colonial power, the amputated statue, has since been regularly defaced by anonymous individuals to reinforce this contestation. It became an unusual symbol of contested heritage and an original way to introduce tourists to the Caribbean's complex history. However, there are still some who recurrently ask that the statue be removed, denying unconsciously its popular symbolic significance as heritage of contestation and resistance.

Colonial heritage is far from being the only starting point of conflicts. Contemporary public art that echoes or claims a relation to the past are also elements which create contestation. An illustration of this is the installation of totems as a part of a project led by the famous author Patrick Chamoiseau employed by the local governance, hailed by art critics and many amateurs, but surprisingly experienced popular criticism. The Martinican daily local newspaper *France-Antilles* titled the affair, "Saint-Pierre–The Totems of Discord." The most intense criticisms were around the totems made by the artist François Piquet. According to the Mayor, some inhabitants asked for the displacement of the totem, considering that the work "would not correspond to their culture or their devotion, because according to them, the totem seemed too mystical." Popular criticism was also focused on the amount of expenditure on the project whereas other social priorities could have been considered. These contestations did not open a dialogue between the contestants and the one that ordered and/or realized the totem.

In Guadeloupe, the destruction of a stela, also called "stela of discord"[1] by the local media illustrates this phenomenon. The project of implanting a stele in memory of the first French settlers began in Guadeloupe by a cultural circle composed of some "békés" (descendants of white slave masters). It aroused strong opposition, in a context of socio-ethnic tensions revived by an altercation between a "béké" and an "Afro-Guadeloupean" client of a restaurant. Seven local associations filed legal claims against the implantation of the stele, considering it as an apologia for slavery and the slave trade. The claim was subsequently rejected by the court. The stela, later erected in 2015 was destroyed a few weeks later on the call of associations and local popular figures of activism. Actors of the discord never communicated directly, creating even more separation between their respective referents around the question of heritage. Moreover, political leaders were once more silent in this conflict. Nonetheless, tensions in Guadeloupe not only revolve around colonial heritage or socio-ethnic issues.

Despite the very wide-ranging success of the initiative and the originality of its architecture and mediations, the Memorial ACTe (MACTE), the first large-scale heritage institution in the Caribbean dedicated to slavery and its memories, carried out by local institutions, faces strong local criticism from its genesis to its current state. While it is difficult to determine whether they are relatively isolated or not without more investigations, these criticisms

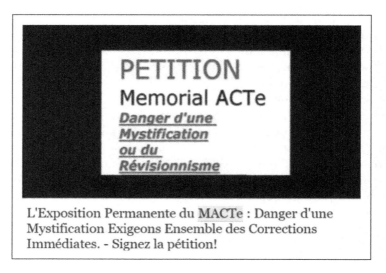

Figure 9.1 Internet petition against MACTe *Source*: A. Pajard, 2017. Screen capture from facebook. Petition available on change.org

are very present in social Internet networks,[2] websites as well as in local or national media[3] (see Figure 9.1).

Recurring criticisms, whether justified or unjustified, are concerns about the narration, place where the institution was erected,[4] the financial costs of the project, the cost of entry considered excessive for the Guadeloupeans and the low integration of local actors in the initiatives. In the Caribbean, those conflicts are not limited to non-independent territories.

Examples in the English-Speaking Caribbean

In Trinidad and Tobago, conflicts are frequently stigmatizing opposition between the group considered[5] as Afro-descendants and Indo-descendants. In 2005 a complaint was lodged by representatives of Hindus and Muslims to declare the Trinity Cross, a national order of merit erected shortly after independence, unconstitutional. This event evoked many tensions and debates on the colonial Catholic heritage of the country which went as far as questioning the name of the country (Brereton, 2012). The question of colonial heritage brings into play tensions and competitions between groups that seem to reinforce oppositions and imagined homogeneous genealogies. To maintain itself, the colonial power, was rooted in negative competition and mistrust between ethnic groups and social groups, which left traces at multiple levels reactivated by new contexts. New forms of race essentialization in the 21st century foster a return to the colonial imagination of homogeneous and separated communities which are evacuating the complexity of real societies. It limits the possibility to build a connected heritage that would fully consider the stigmata that affected different individuals, groups and shaped memories.

Jamaica also seems to deal with difficulties in sharing the diversity of its heritage perceptions and claims. The Bob Marley museum as well as rastas touristic tours sold by travel agencies erased some fundamental aspects of Rastafari culture and religion. The Rasta component of Jamaican national identity seems to be grounded on the world fascination which offers a watered-down version that keeps some consensual elements and discards the rest (Henry, 2015). Similarly the tension surrounding Pinnacle, the emblematic site of the birth of the Rastafari movement in Jamaica, demonstrates the lack of a deep communication between opposite actors.

In 2015, members of the Rastafari community declared land and property claims and launched the "reoccupy Pinnacle campaign" initiating marches, physical occupations, as well as internet activism on websites and social networks. Pinnacle, claimed by the Rastafari community, is considered by others as a part of the national heritage of Jamaica. Articles of the *Jamaica Observer*,[6] were partisan against the campaign, reinforcing a dual perspective that impedes a shared vision of different experiences and interpretation of the location and its multidirectional historical, symbolic and social values. The government's position seemed articulated on the external tourism potential (attractiveness of rastas symbols for tourism). The difficulty to focus on internal social challenges echoes colonial processes that provoked a *dispossession of self*.

Contestation and conflicts appear as the only possibility to express heritage claims for the Caribbean populace in public spaces. At least, it demonstrates that the relationship to the past is considered as something important for Caribbean people and that it is no longer possible to dispossess the populations of its representations in the public space.

From Institutional Problems to Larger Problematic Attitudes

Despite political efforts of decolonization and national mottos such as "out of many, one people," the building of independent Caribbean nations and nationalisms largely, unconsciously, used the model of the European national identity, a "kit" (Thiesse, 1999, p. 14) to build a national official story of the history. This process, excluding different visions, is still active in the Caribbean. It conjugates with traces of alienation, a vision of the self for others and it constitutes a barrier to dialogue based on the sharing of multidirectional perspectives.

The difficulty of facing this complexity drives Caribbean institutions and political actors—at all levels: local, national, transnational- to avoid heritage questions or challenges: law implication, lack of legislation (Siegel et al., 2013), precarious financial, structural and human resources allocated to the authorities in charge of heritage and weakness in the provision of training (Siegel et al., 2013). Some countries such as Saint Lucia do not even have National museum. This lack of involvement is also reflected by the mainly inexistant or non-updated internet websites and social network pages observed in our research.

The CARICOM strategic plan 2015–2019[7] illustrates on a wider scale, the non-recognition of Caribbean heritage and its social value. On a 189-page document, the term "heritage" appears only three times referring to symbolic values of Caribbean unity without any concrete program contrary to other branches. More so, with the exception of the reference to the Caribbean Festival of Arts (Carifesta) event organized by the Caribbean Community (CARICOM), occurrences to "cultural" are always linked to tourism and economic benefits. The only reference to popular practices appears in a negative aspect referring to the SWOT (i.e., Strength, weaknesses, opportunities and threat) table of the "youth" sector (p. 185), associated with negative social behaviors linked to globalization.

Furthermore, problematic attitudes toward heritage are not limited to public institutions. Some private places, especially present day plantations, present a schizophrenic discourse: one type of narration for those identified as "local" visitors -articulated on slavery and resistance- and another for those identified as "tourist" -articulated on the nobility of the objects, the history of the settler's family who founded the place. Some narration also reproduces unconsciously or consciously parts of Eurocentric narrations minimizing the role of enslaved people in the building of societies which had been noticed by researchers (Cornwell & Stoddard, 2007). Others narrations that may want to radically remove colonial narratives are using similar processes, by just replacing actors (Cornwell & Stoddard, 2007) or reversing perspectives. Many of the Caribbean's national identity stories have been built from ground zero which would have started with independence and which obliterated all elements that are not aligned with the national myths. Traces of alienation processes, model of the sameness in national identity formation, the maintaining of some privileges of social groups, as well as international economic profit systems such as mass tourism organizations, constitute the main factors of these negative reproductive processes. In some instances, these attitudes mainly resulted from the gap between different dimensions of Caribbean heritage that do not adjust to an inherited conception of the institutional treatment of heritage. It is therefore necessary to examine the elements in tension with the traditional conception of heritage and to design solutions instead of attempting perverted adjustments.

MODIFYING THE PARADIGMS OF HERITAGE TO IMAGINE NEW MODELS AND CONCRETE SOLUTIONS

The goal of this section is to sketch a framework to change paradigms as well as concretise approaches to better perform and reorganize the way to deal with the heritage question in Caribbean public space. The prior work allowed us to identify obstructing elements. These problematic aspects will be confronted with other models of action. Designed perspectives will be grounded on a reinterpretation of the ideas developed by the Caribbean poets, but also on the analysis of the concrete experiences of Caribbean projects.

Collaborative Projects in the Caribbean

Our research not only paid attention to conflicts and problems but also to interesting models that would build innovative organizations. We observed a variety of original initiatives in the private sector, from individuals to associations and small heritage businesses. We noticed that many of them expressed the determination in filling the vacuum of public institutions, so as to represent and share some aspects of Caribbean heritage. Some examples, handmade pathway to honor Eugene Mona, a popular heritage singer of cultural resistance in Martinique, museum, as in *The Indian Caribbean Museum of Trinidad and Tobago*[8] inaugurated in 2006, or cultural places as in, *La savane des esclaves*,[9] dedicated to popular cultural practices of the descendants of slaves; seem to have more approbation than some public initiatives. We observed that these kinds of initiatives are largely based on participative approaches. They associate with the public, not only by visiting and watching, but by sharing a concrete experience in the form of workshops or events. Many associations are also recording popular knowledge about music, dances, tales or others specific subjects considered as heritage. However, those initiatives also raise important questions especially concerning large visibility on the internet and long term preservation which is not insured because this demands specific skills and expensive equipment.

The second type of initiative that caught our attention is based on large collaborative participation and shared benefits. I noticed that pan-Caribbean projects created very specific models that can be considered as original and innovative. The TRAMIL[10] network, a collaborative initiative born in the 1980's is one of our privileged examples of an inclusive model (Pajard

& Gavillán Suárez, 2017) legitimizing popular heritage. TRAMIL is a program of applied research to popular medicine in the Caribbean. It actually implicates 25 Caribbean territories and is a trilingual project (Spanish, English, and French).

The project built a specific inclusive organization around a strong methodology that aims to validate therapeutic traditional popular uses for the benefit of the Caribbean population. From ethnopharmacological survey to scientific validation and public restitutions (diffusion, workshop, print publications, and internet open access database), different kinds of actors are involved: the public, health professionals (nurses, doctors, and pharmacists), chemists, biologists, and private small micro business (agriculture and laboratory that produce and sells product), programmers and librarians. If TRAMIL is largely animated by activists, it also relies on public institutions (universities, botanical gardens, etc.) that support different aspects of the projects.

In a different branch, we also analyzed collaborative initiatives grounded on digital open access and long term preservation challenges. The two Caribbean collaborative digital libraries we observed (http://www.manioc.org and http://www.dloc.com) are building innovative approaches (Pajard, 2017). Held by diverse institutions, mainly universities libraries,[11] they implicate many individual and collective actors that join their efforts to renew the making of heritage with a large conception. They work on a performing model that evolves with involved actors working to find original solutions to get around obstacles.

Observations, surveys and analysis conducted during these four years were very useful to understand some concrete obstacles and solutions actors imagined and implemented. This transversal and multidirectional approach largely helps to build the following perspectives.

SOME PARADIGMATIC PROBLEMS
AND THE OPENING OF PERSPECTIVES

Displacing the Positive Value of Heritage

The positive value is intimately linked to the idea of heritage. As the Caribbean populace experienced the reverse effects that delegitimized culture and abilities, the question of the positive value of heritage is the first problematic element to address. The lack of questioning impedes in caring and taking care of individual and collective pains associated with the past and to engage a rehabilitation process. Denying part of the past that contributed to each other's constructions also fosters the intergenerational transmission of traumas.

The positive value of heritage must be rethought; from a positive value associated with the truth that the intrinsic nature of objects, things or events should prove, to a positive value centered on the "relation," the act of sharing that defines balanced transmission and communication processes. Suffering can for example have a positive value, not in itself and its causes but by the expression that transform it in energy. It is not only a way to prevent the repetition of disasters, but also constitute a source of inspiration and creativity that relates to others. The displacement of the positive value also seems necessary in order to allow diverse voices and to deploy interconnected relations without reproducing new delegitimation processes.

Objects, situations, events can be understood as a point of junction of multiple expressions and feelings, with negative associations for some and positive for others. It allows the integration and opens a reappropriation of different aspects of heritage, from "materialities" possessions that came from the colonial period to cultural practices and art work that claim a relation to the past. The main goal is to be attentive to the participatory process and to the openness of articulations of diverse senses of positivity. In this way, Heritage can constitute a bridge and rehabilitate fertile links between still largely separated branches of social activities, recognizing the role of each mindset and actors: individuals and their memories, artists and their creative voices, historians and researchers. They gather information and put in original forms so as to enlighten masked aspects that constitute a diversity of multidirectional resources.

Facing the Invisibility, Make it Tangible

As invisibility was a tool for dehumanization, the Caribbean actors may think from the invisibility standpoint, to engage a process of investigating traces of the past following the invitation of the writer and philosopher Edouard Glissant in *the consciousness of the trace.* This can start by asking some simple questions for each project. What don't we present and represent? Why? What could we do to rebalance representations? For example, why do people talk about intangible heritage in our contemporary world? Aren't there material heritage? How can we make things and practices tangible and what does it imply?

Thinking that there are no tangible elements linked to cultural practices may be one of distorted ideas internationally normalized that has to be deconstructed in a decolonized approach. Popular cultural practices use and make objects that come from transmission and recreate them to adapt to the contemporary needs. These objects in and out of themselves drive an idea of authenticity which is drastically different to the one of "sameness" which has to take place in a legitimate order.

Therefore, there is a deconstructed idea that only objects originally coming from the past can give information about the past and contribute to transmission acts. This breaks a presupposed unilateral "truth" of the past to enhance the transmission of effective and symbolic resources. Changing the way we look at elements can foster a point of view which rehabilitates connections and a sharing process of multiple individual stories, human lives and environmental links. Objects, as others elements of the world such as plants andlandscapes, are tangible elements. They are also potential points of mediation, of junctions between mankind; places and time in a living world humans are part of. Pharmacist and writer Emmanuel Nossin, involved in TRAMIL, considers in his book (Nossin, 2010) that plants are mediating elements, interfaces of communication between human and different dimension of their world (social, spiritual, etc.) and as such, intervene in remediation processes. Nevertheless, making this tangible is questioning the process or transforming tangible elements of life in documents that make them sharable.

FURTHER RETHINKING THE TANGIBLE QUESTION: THE MAKING OF MATERIALITIES AND THE CONSENT OF "THE SEPARATION OF SELF"

Masking the importance of materiality with globally successful expressions such as intangible heritage encourages unconscious attitudes. The act of recording or engraving is essential and aligns with heritage legitimation in a globalized world. Nevertheless, it changes when the materiality is made not only *a priori* but *a posteriori* (Pajard & Ollivier, 2017). Tangible heritage changes the status of the elements in fixed documents that are going to have their own lives differently, out of their original context. The context also has to be thought of in this process but with the consciousness that it will always be partial. The making of heritage is the making of the "tangible." It impacts the nature of the transmission and the way to share.

Therefore heritage projects should pay close attention to the way people and cultural practices are transformed into tangible things that are circulated infinitely. Hence, it is not possible to imagine a fair heritage without the plain consciousness of the "separation of the self" from participating actors. Derrida (2014) chose this expression to talk about a documentary film made about his own life. Participating subjects (films, photographs, etc.) have to be cognizant that their self will be shared with the world and will be out of their control. Individuals also have to be implicated as subjects, to be full participants of this separation process, to adhere to the goals, bring willingly their part, to trust participants of the organization and to have all elements giving their approval and trust.

CONCLUSIONARY THOUGHTS: THE PERFORMANCE
MODEL APPLIED TO HERITAGE

Nature and culture as well as linear visions of times or mathematical perception of spaces, territories and their political boundaries have to be positioned as perceptions of the world. The point is not to reject all that came with Modernity but to understand them as intellectual constructions and to open up to diverse possibilities of perceiving and activating connections between humankinds and the living world they are part of. The model of "sameness" is fundamentally incompatible to the idea of a balanced world but still reproduces and creates tensions and misunderstanding between individuals and groups.

The performing allegories used by Walcott can inspire models of organizing heritage projects that captures each component of the society and evolve within their context. Imagining heritage as a common space that belongs to everybody because it doesn't belong exclusively to anyone is nevertheless challenging because it is still completely illegitimate in our contemporary world structure based on a private and marketable vision of benefits. Actors involved in decolonizing heritage will have to pursue innovative resistance paths that make social performances possible. They will have to engage in a constant quest for autonomy that is equivalent with the consciousness of contemporary underlying systems that constitute barriers to a fully integrative heritage. They will also have to invent solutions to overcome obstacles and design adaptive solutions in an ongoing process to truly become decolonial.

NOTES

1. *Stèle de la discorde, 97* [website], s.d., consulted on 04/05/2017, retrieved from http://97land.com/guadeloupe-la-stele-de-la-discorde
   Nicolas Ledain, *La stèle en hommage aux premiers colons ne sera finalement pas érigée, Guadeloupe 1ere* [local TV], 23/01/2015, consulted on 04/05/2017, retrieved from http://la1ere.francetvinfo.fr/guadeloupe/2015/01/23/la-stele
   -en-hommage-aux-premiers-colons-ne-sera-finalement-pas-erigee-224115.html
2. See for example Richard-Viktor Sainsily Cayol letter, « J'ai dit non au MACTe », [facebook content], https://www.facebook.com/notes/richard-viktor-sainsily-cayol/jai-dit-non-au-macte/10154714739389687/
3. Natalie Levisalles. Esclavage: en Guadeloupe, une mémoire troublée. *Libération* [daily national newspaper], 08/05/2015, consulted on 04/05/2017, retrieved from http://www.liberation.fr/societe/2015/05/08/esclavage-en-guadeloupe
   -une-memoire-troublee_1299781
4. a factory that was considered by some as a symbolic place of social memories, lives and struggles.

5. Our research ovoid to naturalized groups. In its starting point, the methodology considered a group as a "set" enunciated as such. It allows to investigate on how enunciations are built, and how they can change in times, connecting to local or transnational discourses, events and/or specific contexts and challenges.

6. Louis Moyston, "Pinnacle: the truth about the matter." *Jamaica Observer,* Tuesday, February 4, 2014, consulted on 05/03/2017, retrieved from http://www.jamaicaobserver.com/columns/Pinnacle–the-truth-about-the-matter_15943398#disqus_thread
   Pinnacle—satisfying the demands of history, *Jamaica Observer,* Sunday, February 9, 2014, consulted on 05/03/2017, retrieved from http://www.jamaicaobserver.com/editorial/Pinnacle—satisfying-the-demands-of-history_15991071

7. CARICOM (2014), Strategic plan for the Caribbean Community 2015–2019, Guyana, 2014. Retrieved from http://cms2.caricom.org/documents/11853-the_strategic_plan_vol2-final.pdf

8. The Indian Caribbean Museum [internet website], retrieved from http://www.icmtt.org/

9. La savane des esclaves [internet website], retrieve from http://www.lasavanedesesclaves.fr/

10. TRAMIL [internet website], retrieve from http://www.tramil.net/en/

11. A list of institutions involved in collaborative digital libraries can be found on each digital library website.
    Manioc's partners: http://www.manioc.org/partenaires.html
    Dloc partners : http://www.dloc.com/info/partners?l=en

REFERENCES

Appadurai, A. (1996). *Modernity at large: cultural dimensions of globalization.* Minneapolis: University of Minnesota Press.

Benítez-Rojo, A. (2008). The new Atlantis: The ultimate Caribbean archipelago. In L. Paravisini-Gebert, & I. Romero-Cesareo (Eds.), *Displacements and transformations in Caribbean cultures* (pp. 214–224). Gainesville: University Press of Florida.

Bernabé, J., Chamoiseau, P., & Confiant, R. (1989). *Eloge de la créolité.* Paris, France: Gallimard.

Bessi, A., et al. "Users polarization on Facebook and YouTube." *PloS one,* 11.8 (2016): e0159641.

Bonniol, J. (2013). "Un miracle créole"? *L'Homme, 3,* 7–15. Retrieved from https://lhomme.revues.org/24682

Brereton, B. (2012). Our cross to bear: The Trinity cross, heritage and identity in Trinidad and Tobago. In B. A. Reid (Ed.), *Caribbean heritage* (pp. 46–57). Jamaica: University of the West Indies Press.

Césaire, A. (2004. *Discours sur le colonialisme* (4th ed.). Paris, France: Présence Africaine.

Cornwell, G. H., & Stoddard, E. W. (2007). From sugar to heritage tourism in the Caribbean: Economic strategies and national identities. In C. Jayawardena

(Ed.), *Caribbean tourism: More than sun, sand and sea* (pp. 223–239). Kingston, Jamaica: Ian Randle.

Cummins, A. (2004). Caribbean museums and national identity. *History Workshop Journal, 58*(1), 224–245. Retrieved from http://www.jstor.org/stable/25472762

Derrida, J. (2014). In Bougnoux D., Stiegler B. (Eds.), *Trace et archive*. Paris, France: INA.

Fanon, F. (1971). *Peau noire masques blancs*. Paris, France: Seuil.

French Ministry of Culture. (1992). Monuments historiques: Statue de l'Impératrice Joséphine, située sur la savane. Record of the *Mérimée*. Retrieved from http://www.culture.gouv.fr/public/mistral/merimee_fr?ACTION=CHERCHER&FIELD_1=REF&VALUE_1=PA00105984

Foucault, M. (2008). *Les mots et les choses*. Paris, France: Gallimard.

Glissant, E. (2006). *Une nouvelle région du monde: Esthétique I*. Paris, France: Gallimard.

Habermas, J. (1981). *Theory of communicative action, volume one: Reason and the rationalization of society* (T. McCarthy, trans.) Boston, MA: Beacon Press.

Henry, A. (2015). *Cultural heritage and representation in Jamaica: Broaching the digital age* [Master]. Retrieved from http://hdl.handle.net/10315/30733

Jeudy, H. (Ed.). (1990). *Patrimoines en folie*. Paris: Ministère de la culture et de la communication; Edition des sciences de l'homme.

Nossin, E. (2010). *Les plantes médiatrices à fonction apotropaïque*. Martinique: Exbrayat.

Pajard, A. (2017). L'héritage malgré soi ? Le couple patrimoine-territoire à l'épreuve de la Caraïbe. Doctoral thesis. Martinique: Université des Antilles.

Pajard, A., & Ollivier, B. (2017). Traces et légitimation du passé: Des objets aux corps. In B. Galinon-Mélénec (Ed.), *Traces du corps*. Paris, France: CNRS éditions.

Pajard, A., & Gavillán Suárez, J. (2017). TRAMIL: a partir el uso medicinal de las plantas, un modelo único de colaboración en el Caribe. In ACURIL congress. San Juan: ACURIL.

Rogers, D. (Ed.). (2015). *Voix d'esclaves*. Paris, France: Karthala.

Rothberg, M. (2009). *Multidirectional memory: Remembering the holocaust in the age of decolonization*. Redwood City, CA: Stanford University Press.

Siegel, P. E., Hofman, C. L., Bérard, B., Murphy, R., Hung, J. U., Rojas, R. V., & White, C. (2013). Confronting Caribbean heritage in an archipelago of diversity: Politics, stakeholders, climate change, natural disasters, tourism, and development. *Journal of Field Archaeology, 38*(4), 376–390.

Thiesse, A. (1999). *La création des identités nationales: Europe XVIIIe–XXe siècle*. Paris, France: Seuil.

Trouillot, M. (2015). *Silencing the past: Power and the production of history*. Boston, MA: Beacon Press.

Van Hoof, H. (2000). Etat de la mise en œuvre de la convention du patrimoine mondial dans les Caraïbes. In H. Van Hoof (Ed.), *Le patrimoine culturel des Caraïbes et la convention du patrimoine mondial* (pp. 13–23). Paris, France: CHTS.

Walcott, D. (1992). *The Antilles: Fragments of epic memory* [Nobel Prize lecture]. Retrieved from https://www.nobelprize.org/nobel_prizes/literature/laureates/1992/walcott-lecture.html

WIPO (2017). *Contracting parties, Berne convention*. Retrieved from http://www.wipo.int/treaties/en/ShowResults.jsp?lang=en&treaty_id=15

Wong, A. (2015). Caribbean island tourism: Pathway to continued colonial servitude. *Études Caribéennes*, (31–32). doi:10.4000/etudescaribeennes.7524

CHAPTER 10

DISRUPTING THE COLONIAL GAZE

Emancipatory Imaginings of a Caribbean Centered Research Praxis

Frank Tuitt

I have visited Antigua many times throughout my life. What started out as an initial visit at the age of 9, when my parents first took my siblings and I to meet our grandparents and my father's homeland, has become a regular occurrence over the years. The initial visits at a young age were my first encounters with a tropical island where ripe mangoes, sugar cane, rum and raisin ice cream, and sweet fried bananas (later known as plantains) were plentiful. As I matured into my young adulthood, I began to appreciate Antigua even more with the realization that I could visit a different beach every day of the year; and for the first time see musicians live and in person playing SOCA music that I heard as a child as I introduced my friends to carnival. As a full grown man, it took the passing of my grandmother to appreciate the massive nature of my extended family. Having eleven aunts and uncles, dozens of cousins, and numerous friends of the family who we also referred to as uncles and aunties or with titles such as Mister and Miss, it was evident that family—along with the food, music and land—was a central part of my Caribbean identity.

Now more than 40 years after my first visit when I landed in Antigua and made it to the counter to hand the immigration officer my American passport, being greeted with "welcome home" feels normal. Today, being in Antigua feels natural. So natural that, in recent years, I have been thinking about conducting qualitative research on how Antigua prepares its students to be successful in college. Recognizing that good intentions do not always produce positive outcomes, this volume comes along at a perfect time. Having been born in England, raised in a West Indian household to a Guyanese mother and Montserratian/Antiguan father, my connection to the Caribbean was cemented at an early age. Nevertheless, it would be foolish of me to think I could engage in authentic research on the basis of annual trips to the island without doing the work necessary to disrupt the colonizer-within that my academic training has embedded in me. Fortunately for me, and many other academics who are seeking to utilize decolonizing research methods, this volume provides some insight into best practices for disrupting the colonial gaze.

THE COLONIAL ACADEMIC GAZE WITHIN US

George Yancy (2008), in his article, "Colonial Gazing: The Production of the Body as Other," describes the dynamics of colonialism "as a means of socially producing reality, shapes colonized bodies through powerful processes of inscription" (p. 2). Yancy argues that there is a violent aspect of colonialism that requires a way of thinking that defines all that is good in European terms. Moreover, not only did the colonizer impose this Eurocentric way of viewing the world to justify their oppressive actions; they also coerced the colonized to adopt Eurocentric ways of being in the world—what Yancy refers to as "White ideological discursive formations" (p. 2). Thus, if we follow Yancy's premise, anyone desiring to conduct research in a Caribbean context (myself included) has already been contaminated by way of socialization (education/training) to engage in colonial gazing where we begin to betray our authentic selves and adopt colonial ways of viewing the world (Yancy, 2008). Accordingly, what follows is a brief description of how we become colonial gazers and what can be done to disrupt the colonial gaze within us.

The Training of Colonized Scholars

As a Professor of Higher Education, I have the privilege of training future scholar practitioners who are equity-minded, socially conscious, and committed to education as the practice of freedom (hooks, 1994). However, recently I have been reminded that in spite of my greatest desire to produce radical researchers who are prepared to use their scholarship as a weapon for social change, the colonial and hegemonic training regimes that are prevalent in traditional academic institutions are difficult to overcome. Two recent encounters exemplified this unfortunate reality for me. First, I had the opportunity to collaborate with two former students and one current student to produce a special issue of a Caribbean Journal focused on educational development in the region. My three colleagues have all spent significant time in the Caribbean as two were born in Jamaica and the other in Trinidad. What stood out to me as we reviewed the articles submitted for consideration in this special issue was the extent to which, in the name of "rigor," my colleagues were so committed to reviewing the submissions through the hegemonic lens of what constitutes quality academic writing. Having reviewed my three colleagues' own personal writings, I am completely clear that they are committed to disrupting colonial and hegemonic practices in their own work. However, somehow the process of moving from writer to reviewer allowed for the colonial gaze within them to surface.

In Alan Chun's (2008) article, "The Postcolonial Alien in Us All: Identity in the Global Division of Labor," he argues that "the institutional system in which we are embedded ultimately defines who 'we' are subjectively and regardless of what we happen to be ethnically" (p. 692). While I am reluctant to wholeheartedly reject the importance of our racial and ethnic identities on our professional sense of self, Chun's position that we are a byproduct of the institutional regime of academic practices and discourses that shape our authorial subjectivities merits consideration. Sofia Villenas (1996) in her article, the "Colonizer/Colonized Chicana Ethnographer: Identity, Marginalization, and Co-optation," highlights this point further where she examines what happens when marginalized individuals and groups become university-sanctioned researchers of their own communities. Villenas would argue that in my example we became the professional and intellectual gatekeeping structure as journal publication referees that sought to reinforce our legitimacy and privilege potentially at the expense of communities we claim to closely identify with. Villenas' (1996) warning is a concrete reminder that the internalization of oppressive discourses, "especially as a product of institutionalized education and university training" (p. 71), can lead to a disempowerment of the very communities we are trying to uplift.

Apparently, the colonial gaze within us all can emerge when we find ourselves in the position of having to make decisions about what constitutes quality research in a Caribbean context. Disrupting the colonial gaze within us requires that we ignore the seductive sirens that lure us to reinforce hegemonic dispositions that further marginalize the communities we claim to be trying to liberate.

NAVIGATING THE COLONIZED/COLONIZER–
INSIDER/OUTSIDER DILEMMA

The second example of the importance of disrupting the colonial gaze involves a recent conversation I had with one of my advisees, a very talented PhD student, who spent the past year in Ethiopia on a Fulbright fellowship conducting her dissertation research. This student, who identifies as Ethiopian and Black, is well on her way to becoming a successful scholar of gender equality in STEM higher education. In our discussion about her experience collecting data for her dissertation, we were both struck by how challenging it was for her to conduct research in the country where she was born. Understanding the importance of researcher positionality as an insider and outsider, Okoye was well aware that being an Ethiopian naturalized citizen of the United States would matter in terms of her engagement with study participants. Specifically, in the most recent draft of her dissertation she writes:

> As a doctoral student examining the experiences of Ethiopian women in undergraduate science and technology programs, I recognize the convergence of my personal experiences and academic goals. Like many women of color in academia, I completed research within my own community with the hope of empowering and fortifying that community.

Like Chandra Mohanty (2003), Okoye was determined to return to a place viewed as home "in order to create a location for Third World immigrants and other marginalized scholars like [herself] who saw themselves erased or misrepresented within the dominant Euro-American feminist scholarship and their communities" (p. 503). However, what we did not anticipate is the extent to which Okoye would feel displaced—homeless (my emphasis)—in a place to which she was so closely tied. While I am encouraging Okoye to continue to reflect on and try to make meaning of the discomfort she experienced, part of me feels like I did not adequately prepare her to navigate the colonizer/colonized—insider/outsider dilemma.

In his article, "Border Crossing Subjectivities and Research: Through the Prism of Feminists of Color," Roland Sintos Coloma (2008) explores "the dilemma of belonging as an insider/outside researcher in communities that one affiliates with vis-à-vis ethnic/national, linguistics, educational, gender, sexual, and other axes of difference" (p. 12). Coloma would argue that Okoye's dilemma emerged as a result of her experiencing "the simultaneous position of becoming an insider and outsider" (p. 12) which gave rise to her feelings of homelessness. Coloma reminds us that once we leave our homelands in pursuit of education we further subject ourselves to the potential of embracing the colonizer within us all. I am not sure if Okoye would agree with my assessment here, but I believe that her sustained time in Ethiopia forced her to come face to face with the double consciousness that was embedded within her. As a first generation Black middle class immigrant woman who now prioritizes English as her first language, Okoye's Americanized consciousness was in constant conflict with her Ethiopian cultural self. Accordingly, it became harder to disrupt the colonial gaze that resulted in Okoye viewing her homeland in ways that potentially rendered it inferior.

Another example of this tension between colonized/colonizer—insider/outsider was the decision to collect data using English as the exclusive language of choice for both qualitative (interviews) and quantitative (survey) aspects of the data collection. At face value the decision to use English made sense. Okoye's dissertation will be written in English. Her oral defense will be in English. Overall, when she writes articles from her dissertation it is likely that they will be in English as well. In our last meeting, I asked her to briefly reflect on what impact her decision to prioritize English might have on the data collection process for this research, considering that for all of the participants English would be their secondary language. I suspect that a participant's decision to participate in an English only research process was influenced by their comfort with using English. Alternatively, some participants may potentially embrace a colonial mentality where they view the opportunity to practice speaking English as a positive one.

Coloma (2008) references Fanon's (1965) technique of colonial mentality, stating that this reminds us that the legacy of imperialism encourages indigenous folks "to internalize a view of themselves as intellectually, culturally, and physically inferior in comparison to those in the west" (p. 16). In theory, Coloma suggests that Okoye's Americanness, which carries with it the embodiment of cultural Whiteness by way of citizenship, education, appearance and language, may differentiate and elevate to a higher status and potentially play into the neo-colonial dynamics between the researcher (university-sanctioned colonizer) and local Ethiopian participants (colonized).

To her credit Okoye recognized and made sense of this tension. In the final draft of her dissertation she stated:

> In trying to superimpose my own frustrations on the women I interviewed and surveyed, I often centered the very oppression that I was trying so hard to resist. Colonialism is dizzying that way; it gives rise to itself and reinforces itself. To this present day, this is an area I have struggled with in research. More pointedly, I gradually came to understand that I am an extension of the colonial enterprise. Many of the methodological and analytic decisions I made in this process privileged my own comfort and ease as a researcher from the West, even at the expense of creating a more authentic narrative about the women I was studying.

Okoye's growth in the research process reminds us that the positionality of both the researcher and researched can shift their collective locations on the continuum of insider/outsider and colonizer/colonized even in situations where careful attention is paid to decolonizing frameworks and approaches.

In both examples above, the importance of decolonizing approaches to research are clear. Scholars seeking to disrupt the colonial gaze must be aware of the potential challenges related to: (a) overcoming our hegemonic education and training; (b) exposing the colonial mentality embedded in our Eurocentric and Western ways of viewing the world; and (c) navigating the insider/outsider—colonizer/colonized dilemma. As I contemplate my own possible exploration of a qualitative research project in my second homeland Antigua, my approach would be to pay particular attention to the best practices that have emerged out of the chapters in this volume and activate my emancipatory imagination in an effort to design a decolonized approach to research that deconstructs power and privilege to benefit knowledge, communities and participants.

LESSONS LEARNED: FUTURE DIRECTIONS
FOR QUALITATIVE RESEARCH IN THE CARIBBEAN

In regards to the best practices conceptualizing a decolonized approach to conducting qualitative research in the Caribbean, three themes emerged from the chapters in this volume. They are: (a) the importance of the researcher truly being acquainted with their authentic self from an intersectional perspective; (b) leveraging the power of critical, community centered, and decolonizing frameworks and methodologies that prioritize local/indigenous epistemologies; and (c) activating the imagination to uncover the hidden traces of emancipation. Collectively, these three areas provide insight as to how researchers can disrupt the colonial gaze within and increase the likelihood of unleashing their emancipatory imagination to actualize a Caribbean centered research and praxis.

Developing an Intersectional Consciousness

Several of the authors in this volume espouse the importance of individuals hoping to conduct research in the Caribbean context truly getting to know their authentic self from an intersectional perspective. For example, in Chapter 8, Gordon identified the need for self-reflexivity about issues of power, positionality, race, class, gender, and nationality. During her fieldwork in Brazil, Gordon came to understand that her "multiple positionalities" were at times in conflict with each other, which had varying consequences for her research process. With an awareness of how social divisions are intermeshed with one another to produce multiple oppressions (Crenshaw, 1989), Gordon recognized that engaging in the hard work of getting to know her authentic self *from* and *through* an intersectional analysis would give her insight into the factors that shaped her perspectives in and regarding the research process.

According to Coloma (2008), an intersectional understanding of one's multiple interlocking dispositions empowers the researcher to ruminate on the multi-dimensionality of their positionalities that could positively or negatively impact the overall study. Coloma argues that the concept of intersectionality recognizes that subject positions are connected, rather than being compartmentalized or distinct; as such, researchers' engagement in the research process should begin from within the often neglected sites of converging. In doing so, researchers with a deep understanding of their authentic selves through an intersectional lens have a greater likelihood of discerning their research subjects' multidimensional experiences.

Anne Pajard, in Chapter 9, "Decolonizing Caribbean Heritage: Lessons Learned and Best Practices for Future Research," described what could be seen as the benefit of having an intersectional consciousness. She noted that a multidimensional approach allowed her to analyze cultural aspects at distinct levels, their sedimentation and flux, while avoiding the risk of the essentialization of identity. Similarly, in Chapter 8, Gordon found that negotiating researcher subjectivity in the field was similar to managing multiple warring identifications and different layers of ambiguity and power. As she tried to understand these experiences, she found it useful to read the work of scholars who have critically examined the intersection of racialized, gendered and national identities as they carried out research in Brazil.

According to Gordon, their reflections on the embodied reflexivity of lived experiences confirmed for her the centrality of race, gender, and body politics and allowed her to better understand how her body and other signifiers might be given meaning and interpreted. In citing Hurtado (2003), Coloma (2008) refers to this type of embodied reflexivity as "theory in flesh" that empowers minoritized researchers to move from the margin to the center as "they forge intellectual and political spaces that highlight multidimensional subject positions and foreground the ontology, epistemology and methodology of the oppressed" (p. 17).

Utilizing Critical, Community-Centered, Decolonizing Frameworks and Methodologies

According to Adams (2014), one way to illuminate and possibly counteract the coloniality of research is to engage the methodological practice of accompaniment. Specifically, Adams argues that decolonizing methodologies value local "ways of knowing in which researchers immerse themselves in the flow of community life and experience events alongside people in the context of everyday activity" (p. 469) so that they can understand reality from local perspectives. Elder and Odoyo (2018) extend this notion by noting that decolonizing methods include: conducting research in the local language, embracing local ways of knowing, and empowering local participants to direct the research. Not surprisingly, many of the chapters in this volume provide insight as to how researchers seeking to disrupt the colonial gaze can utilize critical, community-centered, and decolonizing frameworks in a Caribbean context.

Engaging Native Tongues

In her examination of three decades of qualitative educational research produced by the Schools of Education (SOE) across the three campuses of the University of the West Indies 1990–2016, Amanda Thomas (Chapter 4) reported that Caribbean Creole was often viewed as an impediment to learning—more often than not identified as deficit rather than supportive of student's ability to succeed. This trend in Caribbean educational research is not surprising as Lewis-Fokum (Chapter 5) highlighted that there was a de facto language policy in which English was superior to all languages, including the other European languages in the colony because of the assumption that English was morally and intellectually superior to Creole. Accordingly, researchers who prioritize the use of standard English (like Okoye) in their data collection run the risk of potentially alienating participants who share sentiments similar to what Spencer describes in Chapter 3 as being the language of superiority, associated with whiteness and wealth. For example, Spencer observed that attempts to motivate students to learn standard English were challenging due to the language's association with elitism, corporate and political spaces of access to wealth and symbolic associations with "whiteness."

Arguably, the more mastery one has of any Western language the greater his/her chances are likely to embody Whiteness (Sardar, 2008). Notably, researchers choosing to prioritize indigenous languages in the data collection process will be advised to not assume that using Creole or Patois in the Caribbean will work for all participants involved in the research. For example, Spencer (Chapter 3) notes that Creole has been stereotypically associated with Western notions of blackness as connected to individuals who are uncivilized and uneducated. The unfortunate reality is that some participants are likely to re-inscribe colonial perspectives that privilege some languages over others. What is important to consider is how the form of speaking you prioritize will assist in the decolonizing of knowledge. Gordon (Chapter 8) was intentional about using her positionality as a Caribbean scholar who had grown up in a creole society to develop a more authentic understanding. Likewise, Spencer (Chapter 3) found that having a Jamaican researcher who was competent in both the use of Jamaican Creole and the institutionalized English language was a benefit because students were empowered through the act of hearing their own voices as they detail their own experiences. As one might expect there are important decisions to be made regarding what language(s) are prioritized in the research process.

According to Lincoln and González y González (2008), interviewing in a local language can give the researcher "grammatical liberty, access to colloquialisms, and idiomatic freedom, so that deeper meanings in other languages may be exposed" (p. 792). They suggest that providing access via native languages can expose linguistic subtleties that may be lost in translation (Lincoln & González y González, 2008). Conversely, on the back end of the research process investigators may experience tension regarding how the data will be represented as they traverse the terrain between their decolonizing aspirations and professional responsibilities to their academic discipline (Lincoln & González y González, 2008). In general, engaging local native tongues like Creole can ensure that individuals committed to a decolonizing approach to research in a Caribbean context will ensure that localized ways of knowing via indigenous epistemologies, ideologies, and discourse are at the center of the knowledge construction process.

Embracing Indigenous Ways of Knowing

According to Porsanger (2004), one way to break free from Western academic thought is for scholars to decolonize theories through the use of indigenous epistemology and "make visible what is special and needed, what is meaningful and logical in respect of indigenous peoples' own understanding of themselves and the world" (p. 107). Porsanger posits that "epistemology, which deals with ways of knowing especially with reference to the limits and validity of knowledge is indeed one of the most essential basic elements of indigenous [decolonizing] methodologies" (p. 111). Not surprisingly, several of the chapters in this edited volume affirm the importance of embracing indigenous ways of knowing. For example, in Chapter 2, Haynes and Stewart contend that researchers using grounded theory method in a Caribbean context should first familiarize themselves with the practices of the Caribbean people and develop an understanding of the indigenous ways of life. "It is through capturing the true cultural traditions, customs and practices of the people or participants that new knowledge deviating from Western standards of conducting research will be created" (Haynes & Stewart, Chapter 2).

Additionally, in Chapter 7, Ferguson noted that we avoid relying on our training to interpret facts, but instead seek to recover local values, traits, beliefs, and arts to inform our decisions during the research process. She found that you can decolonize the research process by engaging voices that might previously have been marginalized, gone unnoticed, or simply not prioritized. By legitimizing local and indigenous knowledge—knowledge that historically has not been viewed as valid—Ferguson allowed her participants to share their perspectives, which in turn allowed her research to be responsive to the particular contexts within which the schools she was studying were situated and operating.

Spencer (Chapter 3) argues that in decolonizing research we need to create research practices which give credibility to our own ways of being and demonstrate what works well and what is no longer suited to fit local realities. Thomas (Chapter 4) concurs. She strives for de-colonial shifts in intellectual focus to recognize the importance and equality of knowledge produced within diverse geographical contexts. Likewise, for Thomas, local theory building begins through the localized epistemological construction of knowledge found within a local setting. Gordon (Chapter 8) provided another example of grounding her research in local epistemologies where she drew from her ethnographic data on everyday life for black women whose practices and discourses surrounding beauty and body presentation were particularly significant and underscored deeper, politicized issues about race, visibility, social mobility, and citizenship in Brazil.

By leveraging local and indigenous ways of knowing scholars hoping to decolonize their research in a Caribbean context can increase the likelihood that the results of their study are communicated in a manner that is culturally appropriate and understandable (Ferguson, Chapter 7). In support of such efforts, Chinn (2007) identifies six decolonizing methods (storytelling, indigenizing, connecting, writing, representing, and naming) as critical "strategies that engage participants in examining lives, society, and institutions in ways that challenge dominant perspectives" (p. 1253). Utilizing these decolonizing strategies can empower research participants to play a greater role in determining the direction the study takes.

Empowering Local Participants

In Chapter 7, Ferguson advises future scholars who are interested in conducting decolonizing research within a Caribbean context to avoid the imposition of their arrogant techniques, but respect and combine their skills with the knowledge of the researched or grassroots communities, accepting them as full partners and co-researchers. Likewise, in Chapter 2, Haynes and Stewart contend that it is important to reposition the power not only in the hands of researchers but in that of the participants as equal co-researchers. Unfortunately, all too often research in indigenous communities tends to extract knowledge about rather than co-construct knowledge with the researched. Alternatively, Vasquez-Fernandez, Hajjar, Sangama, Lizardo, Pinedo, Innes, and Kozak (2017), in an effort to avoid the extractive tendency of Euro-Western science, were intentional about "advancing approaches and methods that aspired to be decolonizing, respectful and culturally sensitive" (p. 9). To accomplish this goal, they sought to establish relational accountability where they fostered meaningful dialogue with their collaborators in order to co-construct new knowledge (Vasquez-Fernandez et al., 2017). This type of research prioritizes collaboration "whereby participants' voices are considered expert and the engagement between researchers and participants is understood to be transformative for both parties within their shared cultural contexts" (Samaroo, Dahya, & Alidina, 2013, p. 441). By valuing indigenous communities as true partners in the co-construction of knowledge, there is a greater likelihood that the research process will be sensitive to both the local participants and the local context (Tilley, 1997).

Many of the chapters in this volume echoed a true desire for developing authentic partnerships by using critical methods and frameworks that empower local participants to be active contributors to the research process. For example, George (Chapter 6) learned that when she demonstrated through words and actions her commitment to relinquishing and sharing traditionally held power, the microgenetic approach she used served a decolonizing role by placing her in a position to observe and listen closely to children's problem-solving approaches, thereby privileging their understanding above her own. Similarly, Ferguson (Chapter 7) used a participatory action research (PAR) methodology that was designed to be social, involved, practical and collaborative, emancipatory, critical, reflexive, and dialogic. She observed that PAR allowed for more frequent interactions with the local participants and provided a greater level of collaboration, which facilitated a deeper understanding of the meanings and reasons behind their beliefs and practices. Finally, Gordon (Chapter 8) used an indigenous epistemology as a conceptual framework and methodology to promote self-determination by participants in different stages of the research process. Specifically, life histories and genealogies were conducted either with one or more than one family member to explore cultural logics in specific locales, thereby creating spaces for decolonizing research on beauty. By utilizing these tools, Gordon was able to initiate a more sustained dialogue with research participants about how racialized social systems and hierarchies could be challenged and resisted, offering avenues for dialogue and possible liberation.

Overall, the chapters in this volume remind us that a decolonized approach to conducting research in a Caribbean context necessitates that researchers engage local languages, embrace local ways of knowing, and empower local participants so that they may become authentic true partners in the research process. Vasquez-Fernandez et al., (2017) view this process as an iterative one where, prior to the co-construction of new knowledge, relationships are cultivated among allies by way of extensive engagement that allows for a research design that is culture, place and context sensitive. In the next section of this concluding chapter, I draw upon the wisdom and insights of the authors in this important edited volume to address the benefit of utilizing a decolonizing qualitative approach to activate the imagination to uncover the hidden traces of emancipation.

Unleashing our Emancipatory Imagination Through Decolonizing Qualitative Approaches

According to Kamara and Van Der Meer (2005), one of the important elements in designing a decolonizing [qualitative] methodology is the intentional process of transforming perspectives. They argue that "decolonization doesn't assume the rejection of all Western knowledge. Rather, it suggests that there must be a recentering of the theoretical debates and applied research based upon the perspectives of all people" (pp. 5–6). By advocating for the colonized to create models in which they are the subject not the object of the research, the co-construction of knowledge can be used as a weapon to empower and facilitate human liberation (Kamara & Van Der Meer, 2005). Thus, another goal of designing decolonizing methods is to create opportunities for colonized people to reframe, redefine, and rename one's current and future realities based on their individual and collective liberatory interests (Kamara & Van Der Meer, 2005). For example, for Smith (1999) reframing is about assuming control over the ways in which indigenous issues are conceptualized and approached. "The framing of an issue is about making decisions about its parameters, about what is in the foreground, what is in the background, and what shadings or complexities exist within the frame" (Smith, 1999, p. 153). Ultimately, these decolonizing practices contribute to reclamation of his-tory, from an indigenous perspective which is necessary for transformative restoration (Kamara & Van Der Meer, 2005).

Many of the chapters in this edited volume affirm that an overarching goal of decolonizing qualitative approaches for both the researcher and researched is to disrupt the colonial gaze by activating the emancipatory imagination to uncover the hidden traces to freedom (Pajard, Chapter 9). For example, Pajard (Chapter 9) noted that changing the manner in which we frame elements can lead to the development of intellectual constructions that open up to diverse possibilities of perceiving and activating connections between humankinds and the living world we are part of. Pajard argued that with the right methodological approach Caribbean people could use their agency to design "traces"—underground imaginative systems that can serve as a path to freedom.[1] Similarly, Lewis-Fokum (Chapter 5) posited that by combining critical and positive discourse analysis within a decolonizing framework, we can begin to design emancipatory possibilities that are indigenous, participatory, sustainable and liberatory. Correspondingly, Gordon (Chapter 8) recognized that through sustained engagement with indigenous participants and communities about how racialized social systems and hierarchies can be challenged and resisted, opportunities for transformative dialogue and potential liberation were possible. Finally, Spencer (Chapter 3) found it extremely helpful to empower the teachers in her study through observation, reflexivity, and other approaches that were designed to facilitate a more self-conscious theorizing and practical demonstration of new kinds of engagement that promote an emancipatory and unconventional approach to understanding and responding to a problem.

In their article "What Part of Me Do I Leave Out?: In Pursuit of Decolonizing Practice," Lavia and Sikes (2010) caution that because the colonial gaze is within us, those seeking to decolonize their approach to qualitative research in a Caribbean context must always deconstruct their methodologies. They state:

> Whilst we have sympathy with Audre Lorde's (1984, p. 112) much quoted injunction to use the "master's tools to dismantle the master's house," we take the view that, where appropriate, the tools (in this specific case, research methodologies and methods) must also be turned upon themselves, as well as the house, in order to "rupture the scientific shackles that chain us to the broken promises of Enlightenment/modernist discourse" (Demas & Saavedra, 2004, p. 216). (Lavia & Sikes, 2010, p. 92)

Recognizing that even in the greatest desire to disrupt the colonial gaze within us, we can fall short, Lavia and Sikes (2010) suggest that we must commit to both deconstructing and reconstructing our research practices "as part of a sociological imagination, treating any reinforcement of colonial ideals as scandalous and immoral" (p. 92). Ultimately, we must keep in mind that attempts to unleash emancipatory imagination can reinforce the very practices we are seeking to decolonize. One of Lavia and Sikes students from St Lucia captured this very statement when he stated:

> We must be careful not to create through research, institutionally, subtly loose or oppressive systems in the name of decolonization. While there appears to be a move to reject Western ways of doing things, we must beware of potentially new colonists, locals or other foreigners who, because of their positions of power, can influence practice and use of research. (p. 93)

CONCLUSION

Overall, the chapters in this volume provide a nice blueprint for those seeking to design a decolonized approach to research in a Caribbean context that deconstructs power and privilege to the benefit of knowledge, communities and participants. Collectively, these authors suggest that those of us aspiring to conduct decolonizing research in Caribbean context must commit to: (a) the development of an intersectional consciousness; (b) utilizing critical and community-centered frameworks that facilitate engaging local languages, embracing indigenous ways of knowing, and empowering local participants; and (c) unleashing the emancipatory imagination. As someone belonging to the Caribbean diaspora, who is hoping to conduct research in Antigua in the near future, these best practices offer some guidance for the work that is needed to disrupt the colonial gaze within me that was developed at an early age during my first encounters with my second homeland.

In the introduction to this chapter, I reflected on some of my earlier impressions and fascinations with Antigua. In discussing the early connections that evolved into a deep intimate sense of belonging, I neglected to share some of my negative reactions from my first encounter with Antigua. I neglected to share that I could not understand why I had to use the bathroom in a wooden outhouse. I neglected to share that I did not understand why my grandmother's home lacked an abundance of running water or why rain was a welcomed visitor for the containers at the side of the house. I neglected to share that I thought I was superior to my cousins because my version of the King's English was more civilized than their Antiguan Creole. Little did I know at the time that the colonizing gaze within me was nurtured as a young lad born in England and raised as an immigrant in the United States, and that the subsequent education/training that I would receive at some of the U.S. elite institutions including Harvard would do little to disrupt my Western socialization.

Fortunately for me, unlearning my hegemonic training and liberating the decolonizer in me seems possible thanks to the combination of being raised by Caribbean parents; being re-educated and reconnected to my Caribbean roots by an amazing group of cousins, aunts, uncles, friends, colleagues, and students; and being introduced to decolonizing scholars like Freire and Fanon, as well as the numerous authors from this edited volume. While the work ahead is daunting, the wisdom emanating out of this edited volume has significantly increased the odds that I will be able to overcome hegemonic education and training; exorcise the colonial mentality embedded in my Eurocentric and Western ways of viewing the world; and navigate the insider/outsider dilemma. Overall, this edited volume provides the next generation of Caribbean activist scholars with a set of considerations that will empower them to discern "the academic traditions of West as contemptuous of—and estranged from—the realities of their peoples... and affirm their right to reclaim their heritage from alien hands" (Institute of the Black World, 1974, pp. 31–32).

NOTE

1. According to Pajard (Chapter 9, this volume) in the French West Indies, "trace" also refers to a small path that was used and recognized by Maroons to reach freedom but disguised for their trackers.

REFERENCES

Adams, G. (2014). Decolonizing methods: African studies and qualitative research. *Journal of Social and Personal Relationships, 31*(4), 467–474.

Chinn, P. W. (2007). Decolonizing methodologies and indigenous knowledge: The role of culture, place and personal experience in professional development. *Journal of Research in Science Teaching, 44*(9), 1247–1268.

Chun, A. (2008). The postcolonial alien in us all: Identity in the global division of intellectual labor. *Positions, 16*(3), 689–710.

Coloma, R. S. (2008). Border crossing subjectivities and research: Through the prism of feminists of color. *Race Ethnicity and Education, 11*(1), 11–27.

Crenshaw, K. (1989). Demarginalizing the intersection of race and sex: A Black feminist critique of antidiscrimination doctrine, feminist theory, and antiracist politics. *University of Chicago Legal Forum,* 139–167.

Elder, B. C., & Odoyo, K. O. (2018). Multiple methodologies: Using community-based participatory research and decolonizing methodologies in Kenya. *International Journal of Qualitative Studies in Education, 31*(4), 293–311.

hooks, b. (1994). *Teaching to transgress: Education as the practice of freedom.* New York, NY: Routledge.

Hurtado, A. (2003). Theory in the flesh: Toward an endarkened epistemology. *International Journal of Qualitative Studies in Education, 16*(2), 215–225.

Institute of the Black World. (1974). Education and Black struggle: Notes from the colonized world. *Harvard Educational Review.* Cambridge, MA: Harvard University Press.

Kamara, J., & Van Der Meer, T. (2005). Constructing decolonizing methodologies: Theories and praxes of differences. *The Discourse of Sociological Practice, 7*(1), 2.

Lavia, J., & Sikes, P. (2010). 'What part of me do I leave out?': In pursuit of decolonising practice. *Power and Education, 2*(1), 85–96.

Lincoln, Y. S., & González y González, E. M. (2008). The search for emerging decolonizing methodologies in qualitative research: Further strategies for liberatory and democratic inquiry. *Qualitative Inquiry, 14*(5), 784–805.

Lorde, A. (1984). *Sister outsider: Essays and speeches.* The Crossing Press: Feminist Series.

Mohanty, C. T. (2003). "Under Western eyes" revisited: Feminist solidarity through anticapitalist struggles. *Signs: Journal of Women in Culture and Society, 28*(2), 499–535.

Porsanger, J. (2004). An essay about indigenous methodology. *Nordlit, 8*(1), 105–120.

Samaroo, J., Dahya, N., & Alidina, S. (2013). Exploring the challenges of conducting respectful research: Seen and unforeseen factors within urban school research. *Canadian Journal of Education, 36*(3), 438.

Sardar, Z. (2008). Foreword to the 2008 edition. In *Black skin, white masks* (pp. vi–xx). New York, NY: Grove Press.

Smith, L. T. 1999. *Decolonizing methodologies: Research and Indigenous peoples*. Dunedin, New Zealand: University of Otago Press.

Tilley, V. Q. (1997). *Indigenous people and the state: Ethnic meta-conflict in El Salvador* (Doctoral dissertation). University of Wisconsin, Madison.

Vasquez-Fernandez, A. M., Hajjar, R., Sangama, M. I. S., Lizardo, R. S., Pinedo, M. P., Innes, J. L., & Kozak, R. A. (2017). Co-creating and decolonizing a methodology using indigenist approaches: Alliance with the Asheninka and Yine-Yami peoples of the Peruvian Amazon. *ACME: An International Journal for Critical Geographies*.

Villenas, S. (1996). The colonizer/colonized Chicana ethnographer: Identity, marginalization, and co-optation in the field. *Harvard Educational Review, 66*(4), 711–732.

Yancy, G. (2008). Colonial gazing: The production of the body as "Other." *Western Journal of Black Studies, 32*(1), 1–15.

ABOUT THE EDITOR

Saran Stewart, PhD is a senior lecturer of Comparative Higher Education and Deputy Dean for the Faculty of Humanities and Education at the University of the West Indies, Mona Campus. She was selected as a 2018 African Diaspora Emerging Scholar by the Comparative and International Education Society. She is a Salzburg Global Fellow and recipient of the 2017 and 2018 Principal's Awards for Most Outstanding Researcher and Best Research Publication from The UWI, respectively. At the core of her research, Dr. Stewart's research examines issues in comparative education, decolonizing methodologies, postcolonial theories, critical/inclusive pedagogy and access and equity issues in higher education. She is co-editor of the book, *Race, Equity and the Learning Environment: The Global Relevance of Critical and Inclusive Pedagogies in Higher Education* (Stylus). Her research has been published in the *Journal of Diversity in Higher Education, Journal of Student Affairs, Postcolonial Directions in Education Journal* and the *Journal of Negro Education,* to name a few. She is also the Coordinator for the MA in Higher Educational Management and MA in Student Personnel Administration programmes as well as the Chief Editor of the *Journal of Education and Development in the Caribbean.*
Email: saran.stewart@uwimona.edu.jm

More impressive than her scholarship, Dr. Stewart is also a transformative pedagogue. She is reflective, woke, and thoughtful in the execution of her teaching.

—Dr. Nicole Joseph (Vanderbilt University)

Decolonizing Qualitative Approaches for and by the Caribbean, page 221
Copyright © 2019 by Information Age Publishing
All rights of reproduction in any form reserved.

ABOUT THE CONTRIBUTORS

Shenhaye Ferguson is a PhD student in Higher Education at the Morgridge College of Education, University of Denver. With a background in higher education administration she holds a Masters of Arts in Higher Educational Management (distinction) and a BA in History (first class honours). She received the awards for Most Outstanding Graduate and Excellence in Academic Performance in her Masters of Arts Programme in 2017. She is also a Teaching and Research Assistant. Driven by a passion for growth and development, she also tutors students at the primary and secondary level in Mathematics and the Arts. Her primary scholarly interests include education leadership, literacy, and access to higher education for students from inner-city communities as well as diversity and inclusion. She has presented at academic conferences and has co-authored her first publication which explores access and persistence in higher education in the Caribbean.

Email: Shenhaye.Ferguson@du.edu

Therese Ferguson is a Lecturer of Education for Sustainable Development at the School of Education, the University of the West Indies, Jamaica. She is also the Programme Leader for Change from Within, a school-based initiative in Jamaica which addresses violence and indiscipline as well as Coordinator of the Education for Sustainable Development Working Group within the School of Education. With a PhD in Environmental Management Dr. Ferguson's teaching and research interests lie in education for

Decolonizing Qualitative Approaches for and by the Caribbean, pages 223–226
Copyright © 2019 by Information Age Publishing
All rights of reproduction in any form reserved.

sustainable development, environmental education, and children and the environment. Her work has been published in journals such as *Environmental Education Research, Journal of Geography in Higher Education, Geography Compass, Caribbean Journal of Education,* and the *Journal of Education and Development in the Caribbean.* She also has co-authored chapters in two edited book volumes.

Email: therese.ferguson02@uwimona.edu.jm

Chayla Haynes Davison received her PhD in Higher Education from the University of Denver in 2013. Prior the professoriate, Dr. Haynes Davison served the higher education and student affairs profession for 15 years as a scholar practitioner. She joined the Educational Administration and Human Resource Department at Texas A&M University in 2016. Dr. Haynes Davison is a critical qualitative researcher who explores issues of power and powerlessness through the scholarship of teaching. In addition to having her research featured in the Journal of Critical Scholarship in Higher Education and Student Affairs, the National Association of Student Affairs Professionals Journal, and the Journal of Negro Education, her scholarly contributions also includes two co-edited books, Interrogating Whiteness and Relinquishing Power: White Faculty's Commitment to Racial Consciousness in the Classroom (Peter Lang Publishing) and Race, Equity, and the Learning Environment: The Global Relevance of Critical and Inclusive Pedagogies (Stylus Publishing). The impact of her research thus far was recently recognized by the American College Personnel Association, which named Dr. Haynes Davison a 2016 Emerging Scholar Designee.

Email: chayla.haynes@tamu.edu

Lois George is a passionate, early career academic who has graduate degrees in Mathematics Education from the University of Southampton and Measurement, Testing and Evaluation from University of the West Indies, Cavehill Campus, Barbados. She is currently a Lecturer in Mathematics Education at the University of the West Indies, Mona Campus in Jamaica, but her career as an educator began in the Commonwealth of Dominica as first a Mathematics teacher at the secondary school level and then later as an administrator. Among her research interests include Mathematical cognitive development and interventions with children who have mild to moderate difficulties with Mathematics. Dr. George has served as assistant examiner for Mathematics for the Caribbean Examination Council for 10 years and a reviewer for the British Journal of Educational Psychology. She is also member of the British Society for Research into Learning Mathematics and National Council for Teachers of Mathematics.

Email: lois.george@open.uwi.edu

Doreen J. Gordon is a Lecturer in Anthropology at the University of the West Indies, Mona Campus, Jamaica. She received her doctorate in Anthropology from the University of Manchester for ethnographic work on the contemporary black middle classes in Brazil. She was formerly a Research Fellow in the Human Economy Programme at the University of Pretoria, South Africa. Her fieldwork in Brazil, South Africa, and Jamaica is ongoing and she also has considerable experience teaching in cross-cultural settings.
Email: doreen.gordon03@uwimona.edu.jm

Yewande Lewis-Fokum is a Lecturer of Communication and Arts Education at the School of Education, the University of the West Indies, Mona Campus, Jamaica. She received her undergraduate degree and Diploma in Education from the University of the West Indies in 1997 and 1999 respectively. Thereafter, she completed a master's degree in Education from Harvard University in 2002. She completed her doctorate in Education from the University of Iowa in 2010, and then taught at the Mico University College, Jamaica, in the Language, Literacy and Literature department from 2010 to 2012. Since 2012, she has been teaching at the School of Education, University of the West Indies, Mona campus. Her research interests include the teaching of English literacy in a Creole-speaking environment, teacher training, and issues of language and power in society using Critical Discourse Analysis as both a theory and a methodology.
Email: yewande.lewis@uwimona.edu.jm

Anne Pajard has a background in library and publishing, with a BA in Literature and a Master's degree in Information and Communication Sciences. She is an expert in digital humanities and manages the Caribbean collaborative digital library Manioc.org at Université des Antilles since 2009. Following over a decade of publications and conference presentations in France and several Caribbean countries, she commenced her doctoral studies in Information and Communication Sciences. Dr. Pajard completed her PhD in 2017. Her works at the Laboratoire Caribéen de Sciences Sociales (Social Sciences Caribbean Laboratory) focuses on heritage, cultural memories, identities conflicts, representations, discourses and circulations in a decolonial perspective. Interested in transnational connections, Dr Pajard develops a multidirectional approach to go further locally/globally as well as individually/collectively dichotomies in the understanding of social phenomena. She's also a member of the E-laboratory on Human-Trace-Complex (System Digital Campus UNESCO) and an executive member of the Association of Caribbean University, Research and Institutional Libraries (ACURIL).
Email: anne.pajard@univ-antilles.fr

Aisha Spencer is a lecturer in Language and Literature Education at the University of the West Indies, Mona Campus, Jamaica. She has been teaching language and literature for over twenty years and is especially passionate about finding innovative forms of pedagogy to help children and young people better connect with and enjoy all genres of literature. She is the founder and director of Talk the Poem, the island's first national poetry recitation competition for secondary schools and is the co-editor of an anthology of Caribbean poetry, entitled '*Give the Ball to the Poet': A New Anthology of Caribbean Poetry*. She has published scholarly articles on Poetry Pedagogy and Caribbean. Her areas of research interest are in Literature Education, Children's Literature, gender and nationalism and postcolonial literatures. She is associate editor for the *Journal of Education and Development in the Caribbean* (JEDIC), an editor of Children's books and poetry and acts as Cultural Adviser & Editor (Caribbean) for Lantana Publishing, which is based in the United Kingdom.

Email: aisha.spencer02@uwimona.edu.jm

Amanda K. Thomas is a doctoral student in Research Methods and Statistics at the University of Denver. Most of her teaching experience has been in introductory research methods, Caribbean social problems and development studies. Her research interests include culturally responsive and transformatory educational praxis, postcolonial research paradigms and mixed methods research. She also holds a Master of Science in Sociology with Distinction, from the University of the West Indies, St. Augustine Campus, Trinidad.

Email: Amanda.K.Thomas@du.edu

Frank Tuitt is the Senior Advisor to the Chancellor and Provost on Diversity and Inclusion at the University of Denver and Professor of Higher Education in the Morgridge College of Education. His research explores topics related to access and equity in higher education; teaching and learning in racially diverse college classrooms; and diversity and organizational transformation. Dr. Tuitt is a co-editor and contributing author of the books: *Race and Higher Education: Rethinking Pedagogy in Diverse College Classrooms; Black Faculty in the Academy: Narratives for Negotiating Identity and Achieving Career Success; Contesting the Myth of a Post-Racial Era: The Continued Significance of Race in U.S. Education; and Race, equity, and the learning environment: The Global Relevance of Critical and Inclusive Pedagogies in Higher Education.* Dr. Tuitt received his doctorate from the Harvard Graduate School of Education and his BA in Human Relations from Connecticut College.

Email: frank.tuitt@du.edu

Made in United States
North Haven, CT
10 June 2022